Puppets and "Popular" Culture

Puppets and "Popular" Culture

Scott Cutler Shershow

Cornell University Press   *Ithaca and London*

First published 1995 by Cornell University Press.

Library of Congress Cataloging-in-Publication Data

Shershow, Scott Cutler, 1953–
    Puppets and "popular" culture / Scott Cutler Shershow.
        p.   cm.
    Includes bibliographical references and index.
    ISBN 0-8014-3094-1
    1. Puppet theater.   2. Popular culture.   3. Representation
(Philosophy)   I. Title.
PN1972.S45   1995
791.5′3—dc20   94-39911

Contents

Illustrations

Acknowledgments

Portions of Chapter 2 and Chapter 3 of this book were published as " 'The Mouth of 'hem All': Ben Jonson, Authorship, and the Performing Object," *Theatre Journal* 46.2 (May 1994); and "Punch and Judy and Cultural Appropriation," *Cultural Studies* 8.5 (1994). I thank the editors of the respective journals for their comments during the publication process, and for their permission to reprint this material. I would also like to thank the organizers or moderators of various conference panels and seminars before whom I presented portions of the book: Herbert Coursen, Alexander Leggatt, Katharine Eisaman Maus, Ellen M. Pollak, and Gary Taylor. The staff at the Folger Shakespeare Library, the Houghton Library and Theater Collection at Harvard, and the Huntington Library gave me valuable assistance with tracking down references and illustrations. I also thank the Boston University Humanities Foundation, whose award of a Junior Fellowship in 1992 allowed me the time to complete the research for the book.

Over the course of this project many friends and colleagues have assisted me by reading drafts, offering comments and suggestions, sharing unpublished work, or directing me to sources. They include Lynda E. Boose, Lawrence Breiner, Julia Prewitt Brown, William C. Carroll, Huston Diehl, Frances E. Dolan, Daria Donnelly, Keir Elam, Suzanne Gossett, Eugene A. Green, Charles L. Griswold, Jr., Jayme Koszyn, Lynne Layton, Josephine Lee, Sarah Lyons, Scott Michaelsen, John Paul Riquelme, Charles J. Rzepka, Stephen Scully, James R. Siemon, Roger Shattuck, and David Wagenknecht.

In addition, Stanton B. Garner, Jr., and William B. Worthen have my particular gratitude for their detailed and trenchant reviews of the final draft. I also thank Amanda Heller for her superb copyediting of the manuscript, and Bernhard Kendler, Carol Betsch, and their colleagues at Cornell University Press for their many labors on behalf of the book.

Finally, I want to address a few additional words to three of the people already named. For many years now one of the great joys of my life has been the knowledge that Scott Michaelsen's stern yet playful intelligence could be found at the other end of a phone line. In our regular conversations as well as in his careful readings of my work, Scott has profoundly influenced my understanding of literary theory and culture, while also sharing with me what Tony Kushner calls "the difficult education of the heart."

A professor visiting Boston University from England who met me in the company of William C. Carroll later expressed to me his mild surprise at Bill's youth since he had met so many people on both sides of the Atlantic who looked back (and up) to him as teacher, scholar, and mentor. I similarly express my gratitude to Bill, who has read and commented on drafts of this book from its earliest all the way to its final stages, and who has also been in every other way the most generous of colleagues and friends.

Fran Dolan has helped me in more ways than I can describe or enumerate. She was the first to encourage me to think that what initially seemed a diminutive subject was worth this much attention. Later, she repeatedly read and commented on drafts of the whole book; directed me to references and primary texts; and, most important, shared bread (and puppets) with me during the joyful summer when most of the pages that follow were written. In a very real sense this is her book as well as mine, and I dedicate it to her accordingly.

S. C. S.

Puppets and "Popular" Culture

Introduction

To Southworke Fair, very dirty, and there saw the Puppet-show of
Whittington, which was pretty to see; and how that idle thing doth
work upon people that see it, and even myself too.
                              —Samuel Pepys, *Diary*, September 21, 1668

An extensive body of literature, beginning in the nineteenth century, documents the astonishing geographic and ethnographic variety of puppet theater
and attempts to recreate the actual puppet performances of various times and
places, such as the one seen by Pepys on a particular day in the mid-seventeenth century.[1] I am more interested, however, in Pepys's reaction to the
show, a reaction that surprises him and that he carefully records. To Pepys the
show is at once trivial and powerful (an "idle thing" that "works"); and what
strikes him most is the incongruity between its conditions ("very dirty")
and its effect ("pretty to see"). In this book I argue that perceptions such as
Pepys's are neither personal nor idiosyncratic but culturally constructed. I

---

[1] Nineteenth- and early twentieth-century discussions of puppet theater, some of which I cite later in
other contexts, include John Payne Collier, ed., *Punch and Judy*, with illustrations by George Cruikshank
(London, 1828); and T. C. H. Hedderwick, *The Old German Puppet Play of Doctor Faust* (London, 1887),
each of which includes lengthy prefaces about the history of European puppetry; Charles Magnin, *Histoire des marionettes en Europe: depuis l'antiquité jusqu'à nos jours* (1861; rpt. Paris: Slatkin, 1981); Richard
Pischel, *The Home of the Puppet-Play*, trans. Mildred C. Tawney (London: Luzac, 1902); and Max von
Boehn, *Dolls and Puppets*, trans. Josephine Nicoll (New York: Cooper Square, 1966).

look at some of the many ways in which an ancient and enduring form of "popular" or "folk" culture, puppet theater, was described, defined, disparaged, celebrated, and exploited by theorists and thinkers, playwrights and performers, in a variety of historical periods. Like Pepys, these writers typically separate themselves from the object of their discursive attentions and yet in so doing appropriate it, use it, make it somehow their own. "How that idle thing do work upon *people* that see it," exclaims Pepys, "and even *myself* too!"

This book, therefore, is neither a history of puppetry nor a survey of its conventions and characteristics. Instead, it looks at the historical intersection of representations and material practices, the complex and dynamic interaction between modes of literary, aesthetic, or theatrical distinction and the social conditions of the subjects who construct and employ them. I observe how, in a wide variety of discourse from an extended historical period, the puppet was envisioned and re-visioned—as metaphor, metadramatic device, or marker of cultural subordination—for as I assume throughout, the specific process by which any mode of cultural production is defined as "folk" or "literary," "high" or "low," "popular" or "elite," is inseparable from a process of appropriating and using the products thus categorized. The puppet theater is a particularly illuminating example of this process. Even its literal conditions—in which a material icon or figure serves as the vehicle or mouthpiece for some absent and invisible "author"—are a virtually inevitable metaphor for the entwined processes of cultural definition and appropriation. What Susan Stewart has observed of "the miniature" applies perhaps even more intensely to the puppet, which has often seemed to possess an inescapable theatricality not only on the diminutive stages where it literally performs, but also as an imagined object in a discursive space "on which we project, by means of association or textuality," the anxieties and constructions that shape our social lives.[2]

I make no attempt to be precise in my definition of the puppet or "performing object." Although I am content with Frank Proschan's semiotic definition of performing objects as "material images of humans, animals, or spirits that are created, displayed, or manipulated in narrative or dramatic performances,"[3] I do not concern myself with the technical differences between forms—between, say, glove puppets and marionettes, or even between

[2] Susan Stewart, *On Longing: Narratives of the Miniature, the Gigantic, the Souvenir, the Collection* (Baltimore: Johns Hopkins University Press, 1984), 54.
[3] Frank Proschan, "The Semiotic Study of Puppets, Masks, and Performing Objects," *Semiotica* 47.1–4 (1983): 4.

such histrionic objects and dolls, automata, or other movable figures. Although I may occasionally observe the different social and cultural values ascribed to puppetry of varying levels of technical sophistication, I do not construct taxonomies among such differences or speculate on their aesthetic or semiotic effect.[4] As I suggest later in this account, the cultural similarity of dolls, puppets, and automata is embodied in the etymological genealogies of the words that refer to performing objects in English and other European languages. By extension, anything that has been defined or envisioned as a "performing object" is appropriate to my analysis. I have, however, made the methodological decision to refrain from discussing the various traditions of Asian puppetry, primarily because my expertise is with Western (and specifically English and American) culture, but also because I am unwilling to essentialize the performing object in terms of any intrinsic or universal histrionic effects, preferring to view puppetry as a socially determined practice within a particular cultural context.

Some of the other terms that I am obliged to employ and that remain central to this project are considerably more difficult. I have already referred to puppetry as an instance of popular culture, thus linking two terms each of which is elusive and which join to raise what Stuart Hall calls "horrendous" definitional and theoretical questions.[5] In practical terms, I have assumed that most of the actual puppet theater observed by the writers discussed in this book was popular in that it was oral, ephemeral, and itinerant, functioning at the margins of the economic market and accessible to the broadest possible range of spectators—not only in terms of social class but even in terms of age. Indeed, across an extended historical period, puppet theater has gradually moved toward its present status as a mode of performance primarily for children as though the diminutive theatrical object recreated its audience in its own image. Nevertheless, in form and subject matter the puppet theater also proves to be a particularly clear example of what Peter Burke calls the "two-way traffic" between popular and elite modes of culture, and also demonstrates what scholars have discovered to be the cultural conservatism of the popular.[6] In the early modern period, for example, puppets were still

---

[4] This is the project, I would suggest, of the work on puppet theater that derives from the semiotic study of folk art by Petr Bogatyrev and other members of the Prague Linguistic Circle, such as the essays of Henryk Jurkowski. See my discussion and citations in Chapter 4.

[5] Stuart Hall, "Notes on Deconstructing 'the Popular,'" in *People's History and Socialist Theory*, ed. Raphael Samuel (London: Routledge & Kegan Paul, 1981), 227.

[6] Peter Burke, *Popular Culture in Early Modern Europe* (New York: New York University Press, 1978), 58; see also Petr Bogatyrev, "Forms and Functions of Folk Theater" [1940], in *Semiotics of Art: Prague*

performing the biblical stories that had been performed by actors in the Middle Ages; similarly, in the eighteenth century puppets were still performing the story of Dick Whittington, Lord Mayor of London, who had been a familiar symbol of "social mobility and accumulation" since the fifteenth century.[7] Actual puppet performers both past and present, as a modern puppeteer puts it, also sometimes lament "their low and ridiculous status in society," and correspondingly attempt "to be part of the respectable legitimate theater establishment."[8] These and other characteristics of the puppet stage suggest the more general conclusion that the popular never exists in pure or unadulterated form, but is instead a cultural category emerging out of a dynamic process of mutual transmission and reception, constituted only in the never-ending process of cultural appropriation and definition.

Thus, my two most difficult and crucial terms—*culture* and *appropriation*—must be held in a kind of suspension, since, as I will suggest in more detail, their meanings become ever more problematic across the trajectory of my project. I begin by arguing, as many other recent students of popular culture have done, that cultural consumption inevitably involves a process of cultural appropriation. From the broad surveys of historical cultural practice by historians such as Michel de Certeau, Roger Chartier, and Natalie Zemon Davis, to the specific readings of contemporary literature, television, and life-styles by John Fiske, Stuart Hall, Dick Hebdige, Janice Radway, and many others, scholars have suggested that cultural consumption always "creates ways of using that cannot be limited to the intentions of those who produce."[9] Without ignoring the significant differences within

---

School Contributions, ed. Ladislav Matejka and Irwin R. Titunik (Cambridge: MIT Press, 1976), 53.

[7] The quoted phrase is from Peter Linebaugh, *The London Hanged: Crime and Civil Society in the Eighteenth Century* (New York: Cambridge University Press, 1992), 29. On the subject of puppet theater in various periods, see George Speaight, *The History of the English Puppet Theatre*, 2d ed. (London: Robert Hale, 1990), an indispensable reference book to which I am thoroughly indebted throughout. A play no longer extant called *The Legend of Wittington* is mentioned as a popular favorite about 1607 in Francis Beaumont's *Knight of the Burning Pestle* (Ind. 20). On the historical Whittington, see Jean Imary, *The Charity of Richard Whittington: A History of the Trust Administered by the Mercers' Company, 1424–1966* (London: Athlone Press, 1968).

[8] Peter Schumann, *The Old Art of Puppetry in the New World Order* (Glover, Vt.: Bread and Puppet Theater, 1993), 7. For confirmation of Schumann's point, see the quotations from other contemporary American puppeteers in Eileen Blumenthal, "Serious Puppets," *American Theatre* (January 1989): 21–24.

[9] The phrase is from Roger Chartier, "Culture as Appropriation: Popular Cultural Uses in Early Modern France," in *Understanding Popular Culture: Europe from the Middle Ages to the Nineteenth Century*, ed. Steven L. Kaplan (Berlin: Mouton, 1984), 234. See also Chartier's *Cultural History: Between Practices and Representations*, trans. Lydia G. Cochrane (Ithaca: Cornell University Press, 1988); Michel de Certeau, *The Practice of Everyday Life* (Berkeley: University of California Press, 1984); and Natalie Zemon Davis, *Society and Culture in Early Modern France* (Stanford: Stanford University Press, 1975), especially "The Reasons

this considerable body of important work, I want to observe how most of it focuses on what De Certeau calls "the ingenious way the weak make use of the strong"[10]—that is, the reappropriation of "elite" or, in some cases, "mass" culture by people on whom such practices had been imposed by the imperatives of social aspiration or the strategies of the market.[11] Chartier, for example, has described how petit bourgeois readers in sixteenth- and seventeenth-century France took various cultural materials—Bibles, chapbooks, *livres d'heures*, and the like—and adapted them for the discursive needs of their own lives and class interests.[12] Radway, similarly, focuses on a cultural practice that is typically popular in its accessibility to vast numbers of consumers, though not in its conditions of production and distribution—the contemporary "romance" novel. She argues that the women who read such books "resist, alter, and reappropriate the materials designed elsewhere for their purchase."[13]

By contrast, I focus on the discursive appropriation of popular culture in and by texts that, in nearly all cases, embody the aspirations of bourgeois culture toward an elite or "literary" cultural status. I consider many texts and practices (Renaissance drama, eighteenth-century journalism, modern avant-garde theatrical theory, and the like) which are located at the frontier between the elite and the popular, and in which, moreover, such categories may be viewed in the process of their discursive construction.[14] Such texts and

---

of Misrule," and "Printing and the People," in which Davis describes how "the sixteenth century populace impose[d] its uses on the books that came to it" (225). For a broad anthropological inquiry into the mechanisms of popular resistance, see James C. Scott, *Weapons of the Weak: Everyday Forms of Peasant Resistance* (New Haven: Yale University Press, 1985), and *Domination and the Arts of Resistance: Hidden Transcripts* (New Haven: Yale University Press, 1990). On the cultural appropriation of contemporary mass culture, see, among others, John Fiske, *Reading the Popular* and *Understanding Popular Culture* (both Boston: Unwin Hyman, 1989); Stuart Hall and Tony Jefferson, eds., *Resistance through Rituals: Youth Subcultures in Post-War Britain* (London: Hutchinson, 1976); Dick Hebdige, *Subculture: The Meaning of Style* (London: Methuen, 1979); and Janice Radway, *Reading the Romance: Women, Patriarchy, and Popular Literature* (Chapel Hill: University of North Carolina Press, 1984).

[10] De Certeau, *The Practice of Everyday Life*, xvii.

[11] I am, of course, sidestepping the vexed problem of mass culture, which in the influential though frequently questioned view of the Frankfurt school, was also "dominant" in that it was constituted by deliberately commodified and widely distributed cultural products contrived in a quasi-popular voice or style. The question of mass culture is not directly relevant to the majority of the historical examples surveyed in this book; I do, however, briefly address this question at the end of the final chapter.

[12] See Chartier, "Culture as Appropriation."

[13] Radway, *Reading the Romance*, 17.

[14] These texts and practices are similar to what Michael Bristol calls "the texts of carnival"—in which "reciprocal pressure, contamination, and the diversity of speech types and discursive genres is greatest." Michael Bristol, *Carnival and Theater: Plebeian Culture and the Structure of Authority in Renaissance England* (New York: Methuen, 1985), 85. Cf. Ronald Paulson's definition of "popular" works as those that

their writers enlist the performing object as it were against itself in a much larger project of cultural subordination, as part of that vast, multihierarchical system of behavioral, cultural, and aesthetic distinction which social theorist Pierre Bourdieu has anatomized in the last few decades.[15] As I show in various ways throughout the chapters that follow, the puppet was repeatedly inscribed in Western culture as a marker or rubric of the "low": as a cultural practice literally situated in the marginal social spheres of carnival, fairground, and marketplace; as a parodic or degraded form of theatrical performance subordinate to "legitimate" or literary drama; as an inanimate object associated with the bodily and the material in their conventional opposition to the spiritual; and even as sign, trope, and metaphor in a hypothetical hierarchy of being and representation, the passive vehicle of a mastering authorial form. This cultural lowness was declared and instantiated in bourgeois texts that also participated in the construction of a particular kind of reader and a particular kind of aesthetic and cultural *perception*. Nevertheless, the same texts typically reveal an inescapable fascination with performing objects; indeed, sometimes they bring the process of cultural definition full circle by reconstruing the puppet as the bearer of an indeterminate theatrical "magic" or of a transcendent, ahistorical cultural power. Thus, the puppet may be seen to figure in that recurring cultural process described by Peter Stallybrass and Allon White, in which "high discourses, with their lofty style, exalted aims and sublime ends, are structured in relation to the debasements and degradations of low discourse," and in which, more generally, the act of cultural appropriation becomes "constitutive of the very formation of middleclass identity."[16]

---

contain "traces of a subculture in which we can infer a mass of people below the level of the classics-reading, property-owning, and voting interests." Ronald Paulson, *Popular and Polite Art in the Age of Hogarth and Fielding* (Notre Dame: University of Notre Dame Press, 1979), ix.

[15] See, especially, Pierre Bourdieu, *Distinction: A Social Critique of the Judgment of Taste*, trans. Richard Nice (Cambridge: Harvard University Press, 1984), and *Language and Symbolic Power*, ed. John B. Thompson, trans. Gino Raymond and Matthew Adamson (Cambridge: Harvard University Press, 1991).

[16] Peter Stallybrass and Allon White, *The Politics and Poetics of Transgression* (Ithaca: Cornell University Press, 1986), 3, 201. The complex interdependence of categories of taste and social class has also been discussed by many other writers. Peter Burke, for example, has remarked how the nineteenth-century scholars who "discovered" popular culture "came from the upper classes, to whom the people were a mysterious Them, described in terms of everything the discoverers were not (or thought they were not)" (*Popular Culture*, 9). Stanley Aronowitz has similarly argued that, in the early modern period, "the key to the historical preservation of the aesthetic hierarchy by which some modes of artistic production are called 'high' lay in its important function with respect to maintaining the hegemony of the new bourgeois class in the wake of the demise of the aristocracy." Stanley Aronowitz, *Roll Over Beethoven: The Return of Cultural Strife* (Hanover: Wesleyan University Press/University Press of New England, 1993), 63. For Bour-

Such an argument, however, finally problematizes the concept of appropriation, and even the larger concept of culture itself, by questioning the autonomy of the latter as in any sense the "property" or "possession" of specific social classes or groups. I thus choose to suspend the word *culture* between and within at least two different levels of meaning. On the one hand, influenced by the scholars who laid the theoretical groundwork for the emerging field of cultural studies, I employ a working definition of culture as (to cite Stuart Hall's useful summary) "*both* the meanings and values which arise amongst distinctive social groups and classes, on the basis of their given historical conditions and relationships, through which they 'handle' and respond to the conditions of existence; *and* as the lived traditions and practices through which those 'understandings' are expressed and in which they are embodied."[17] Thus, I often refer to "popular" or "working-class" or "literary" culture in discussing writers for whom such categories had crucially distinct meanings. On the other hand, as I continue to suggest, elite and popular modes thoroughly interpenetrate each other; even the very *idea* of elite or literary culture has always been a self-constructed and self-proclaimed category, while the term *popular* is, correspondingly, almost always imposed on "practices never designated by their actors as such."[18] Therefore, although *appropriation* seems to denote precisely a dynamic cultural process that, in any case, I consider primarily as described in the discourse of its participants, this term's implied dualism of self and other, the appropriator and the appropriated, is finally inadequate to the complex intermingling, the "ground rending and re-mending," that unfolds over time within the practices and representations of dominant and subordinate groups.[19] As Fredric Jameson

dieu, in perhaps the most sweeping sense, the bourgeoisie as a class is constituted precisely by their sense of propriety toward the distinctive signs and "heritage" of high culture: thus "the enterprise of cultural appropriation . . . is inscribed, as an objective demand, in membership of the bourgeoisie, and in the qualifications giving access to its rights and duties" (*Distinction*, 23).

[17] Stuart Hall, "Cultural Studies: Two Paradigms," in *Media, Culture, and Society: A Critical Reader*, ed. Richard Collins et al. (Beverly Hills: Sage, 1986), 39. Hall is here summarizing a "paradigm" he identifies with the work of Raymond Williams and E. P. Thompson. Williams himself repeatedly defined and redefined this crucial term throughout his career, and his theoretical arguments were inseparable from an intense historical account of how culture as both word and concept emerged *in* culture. See especially Raymond Williams, *Culture and Society, 1780–1950* (1958; rpt. New York: Columbia University Press, 1983), xvi-xvii and passim; *Marxism and Literature* (New York: Oxford University Press, 1977), 75–141; and *Keywords: A Vocabulary of Culture and Society*, 2d ed. (New York: Oxford University Press, 1983), 84–93.

[18] Roger Chartier, keynote address, conference on popular cultures, Massachusetts Institute of Technology, October 1992.

[19] Scott Michaelsen's work in progress on Anglo-Amerindian identity politics, from which I adapt the cited phrase, has powerfully influenced my thinking about cultural difference.

has suggested, culture "is not a 'substance' or a phenomenon in its own right; it is an objective mirage that arises out of the relationship between at least two groups," and "culture must thus always be seen as a vehicle or a medium whereby the relationship between groups is transacted."[20]

But even if my argument finally exhausts its own terms by questioning whether rival groups ever "have" their "own" coherent and autonomous "cultures," I nonetheless insist on an analytic view of discourse and cultural practice as materially constructed and conditioned by systems of domination. Indeed, struggles to define and appropriate certain cultural ideas or practices, even those that take place within discourse, always have stakes not limited to the manifest content of those ideas and practices. I thus continue to employ the idea of cultural appropriation to suggest the violent relationality with which so-called popular and literary modes of theater not only are inextricably linked in a direct process of mutual parody and allusion but also cooperate in the discursive construction of what Bourdieu calls "distinction," the "transfigured, misrecognizable, legitimate forms of social class."[21] In this book I look at an unusual example of these ongoing processes of cultural order and subordination and consider how the "mere" puppet or performing object—by turns disparaged or celebrated for its popular status— was enlisted in the construction of a series of interlocking social and aesthetic hierarchies.[22]

The book as a whole, while not a history, is nevertheless roughly chronological in its organization as a means of acknowledging that the cultural and semiotic valence of the puppet derives from, as it is perpetually saturated with, the social realities of the periods and places where it appears. Through-

---

[20] Fredric Jameson, "On 'Cultural Studies,'" *Social Text* 34 (1992): 33–34.

[21] Bourdieu, *Distinction*, 250.

[22] In so doing I provide additional data toward, but no definitive answer to, what Raymond Williams calls the "central question of the relations between 'material' and 'symbolic' production" (*Keywords*, 91). Bourdieu's "reflexive sociology" may also be understood as an attempt to overcome the division between, in the words of Loïc J. D. Wacquant, "social divisions and mental schemata," which Bourdieu sees as "structurally homologous because they are *genetically linked*." Bourdieu asserts that "cumulative exposure to certain social conditions instills in individuals an ensemble of durable and transposable dispositions that internalize the necessities of the extant social environment, inscribing inside the organism the patterned inertia and constraints of external reality." Pierre Bourdieu and Loïc J. D. Wacquant, *An Invitation to Reflexive Sociology* (Chicago: University of Chicago Press, 1992), 13. Even more broadly, this enormous question, whose roots are in the celebrated if outmoded Marxist distinction between base and superstructure, may be said to underlie current attempts to project a radical new interdisciplinarity (or antidisciplinarity), joining not only the humanities but also the social and natural sciences in a unified project that takes account at once of the cultural and linguistic factors conditioning scientific explanation and the material, economic, and political factors that shape all symbolic practices.

out I argue that the puppet or performing object is figurally implicated in Western discourse about theater, about theatrical and literary authorship, about representation itself; and these concepts, which specifically relate to the actual conventions and conditions of the performing object, participate in the construction of even larger systems of cultural distinction. I employ etymologies, readings of specific texts, and descriptions of social practice in following webs of connection rather than chains of linear argument. Indeed, I work throughout at the level of what must be considered habits of thought, whose ultimate origins are elusive but whose traces can be viewed in the vagaries of influence and cultural transmission and in intricate patterns of association and textuality. Even in the most literal historical sense, puppet theater undoubtedly had no precisely discernible origin, but rather, emerged independently at different times and places amid a variety of other human image-making activities. The obvious similarities that occur in the conceptualization and theatrical manifestations of the puppet across time and space are markers not of archetypes and universals that somehow imprint themselves on mind and matter, but of socially conditioned habits of thought filtered through the same multifarious processes of culture that they also shape.

In the Chapter 1, "Performing Objects in the 'Theological' Theater," I sketch the broad outlines of the discursive landscape covered by this book. I suggest that the idea of a performing *object* figures in hierarchical Western ideas about being and representation since their earliest formal stages, and that these philosophic and theological associations underlie the more specific cultural appropriations I observe in subsequent chapters. In Platonic philosophy one glimpses the conceptual roots of a particular vision of representation that I refer to, following Roland Barthes and Jacques Derrida, as the "theological" theater—a theater in which player-puppets are seen to *embody* the sovereign intentions of an author-creator.[23] Throughout this book I intend this phrase to suggest the philosophical and cultural hierarchies that would later be imposed on the unruly conditions of actual dramatic performance, while also conceding the profound ontological suspicion with which the theater has also been viewed both by Plato himself and in later Christian theology. This hierarchy of authorship and representation, given memorable philo-

---

[23] Roland Barthes refers to classical Western ideas of authorship as "theological" in his celebrated essay "The Death of the Author" (1968), rpt. in *Image, Music, Text* (New York: Farrar, Straus and Giroux, 1974), 146. Jacques Derrida, similarly, refers to the Western vision of theatrical representation as "the theological theater" in his reading of Antonin Artaud, "The Theater of Cruelty and the Closure of Representation," in *Writing and Difference*, trans. Alan Bass (Chicago: University of Chicago Press, 1978), 235–36.

sophical shape in the allegory of the Cave (in which Plato specifically invokes puppet theater), and later manifest in Judaeo-Christian proscriptions of idolatry, both reflects and shapes correspondingly hierarchical ideas of gender, social class, and aesthetic value. Thus, I argue that the construction of a theological theater and a corresponding hierarchy of aesthetic distinction is inseparable from a larger cultural process that continually subordinates, even demonizes, forms of social and sexual difference. Considering ways in which the puppet figures in a variety of discourses and cultural practices, including Christian iconophobia, witchcraft, the Protestant Reformation, and others, I track networks of cultural association that reemerge in different form later in history and in the book.

The three chapters that follow have a broad chronological focus covering, respectively, the Renaissance, the Enlightenment, and the modernist period. In each case I look at ways in which the actual social conditions of playwrights and performers both suggested and contradicted a conventional figural comparison to the puppet, and how the evolving power relations of the theater invested the puppet with cultural associations available for appropriation in other modes of discourse. Chapter 2, "Authorship and Culture in Early Modern England," focuses on the extraordinary half century that produced virtually all of what are now considered the canonical works of English Renaissance drama. As I suggest, the playwrights and pamphleteers of the period frequently reveal their familiarity and fascination with puppets, which performed frequently in the streets and marketplaces of Renaissance London. Accordingly, the puppet became a rubric for popular performance in its opposition to a drama increasingly concerned to declare its own legitimacy, and whose producers were engaged in what we recognize today as the cultural construction of theatrical authorship. I also suggest how, in a related but larger process, the performing object—associated in antiquity with the theological opposition of matter and spirit and thus subordinate on a hypothetical hierarchy of representation—became a discursive site on which social anxieties about class and gender, dress, deportment, and corporeality were projected. Ben Jonson, who is commonly conceded to be pivotal in the Renaissance construction of authorship, and whose works evoke an intricate constellation of social values and animosities, is a recurrent topic of interest throughout the chapter. I consider the references to puppetry that emerge in nearly every one of Jonson's major plays and in the works of many other playwrights of the period, and conclude with a detailed examination and comparison of Shakespeare's *Tempest* (1611) and Jonson's *Bartholomew Faire* (1614)—each of which, in slightly different ways, reinscribes this mode of explicitly popular performance into a legitimate literary context.

In Chapter 3, "The Violence of Appropriation: From the Interregnum to the Nineteenth Century," I suggest how performing objects continued to figure forth concepts of theatrical authorship, political authority, and cultural distinction. I look at how the puppet was appropriated by pamphleteers, satirists, and periodical essayists of the Interregnum and beyond, for whom it served as a metaphoric weapon in specific historical and political conflicts, and by playwrights and performers who transformed the puppets of the popular tradition into fashionable vehicles of quasi-legitimate theater. In both cases the puppet became a highly charged marker of cultural distinction: a discursive anchor for a nascent system of bourgeois taste, and an epitome of that spectrum of paratheatrical entertainment (mime, opera, acrobatics, and the like) often seen as contaminating the properly literary drama. This chapter concludes with a retrospective reading of the most famous of all puppet characters, Punch, who inhabits the margins of eighteenth-century theater and then reemerges as a form of street performance at the end of the century, even while simultaneously being reappropriated in a wide range of discourse about nationalism, popular culture, and the social effect of drama.

Finally, in Chapter 4, "Modern and Postmodern Puppets, in Theory and Practice," I consider the extensive theoretical conversation about puppets and authorship which began around the turn of the twentieth century and continued into the high-modernist era, when playwrights and theorists developed a virtual obsession with puppets and performing objects. Here I move beyond the national boundaries of British drama to reflect the increasing cosmopolitanism of dramatic theory and practice in this period. Surveying the writings and careers of theatrical innovators from Alfred Jarry and Gordon Craig at the turn of the century to the members of the futurist and Bauhaus movements before and after the First World War, I suggest how various avant-garde theaters once again appropriated the puppet out of complex and sometimes contradictory cultural impulses. In each case rhetorics by turns mystical, communal, and utopian mask fantasies of overwhelming authorial control. The "über-marionettes" or kinetic stages called for by various innovators became the vehicles of radically hierarchical and theological theaters whose theoretical structures resemble, and in one case reflect, the political ideology of an emergent fascism. In approximately the same period, as I go on to suggest, early semioticians were also seizing on the performing object as a paradigm of representation in ways that reproduce some of the theoretical strategies of the modernist stage, and reveal the continuing cultural authority of a quasi-Platonic, hierarchical habit of thought. I conclude by placing several recent reappropriations of the puppet by mass culture (film and television) into the larger context sketched in the chapter. The transformation of the puppet into a vehicle of children's theater—in which performing objects become means for transmitting bourgeois American values across both generational and international boundaries—represents a theoretical terminus of the process of cultural appropriation.

I concede that my concentration throughout this book on the appropriation of the so-called popular by relatively more privileged forms of discourse usually denies me the chance to focus, as many other scholars have done, on the popular as a site of "struggle," "resistance," and "evasion" of the dominant culture.[24] In any case, I would argue that some of the scholars whose work has shaped my own are occasionally too quick to privilege a kind of "imaginary" cultural resistance that, notwithstanding its very real significance and effect, is hardly commensurable with the implacable structures of material power and authority. I remain conscious that my argument may seem, at least to some readers, to defuse or to disarm the unmistakable power of the puppet to express for different times and places what Bakhtin calls "the people's unofficial truth." In fact, however, such regrets or apologies finally make sense only within the paradigm I am trying to destabilize. The impulse to celebrate an authentic and truly popular culture finally replicates the cultural logic of domination which it critiques merely through inversion. But to recognize that the puppet, despite its histrionic power and historical endurance, *never* wholly escapes discursive appropriation, and that popular puppetry, despite its apparent moments of carnivalesque subversion, is thoroughly imbued with the cultural and social hierarchies it seems to threaten, is to make the duality of culture and "sub"-culture, and thus the process of distinction, more difficult to maintain. In even larger terms, to observe that this "low," "idle," and literally diminutive practice nevertheless looms large within the cultural struggles in which we are still engaged is to suggest much larger ironies as well, and indeed, to throw into question the concepts of cultural legitimacy and literary value against which the pejoratives, like the puppet itself, have always been defined.

[24] I take these phrases from Fiske, *Reading the Popular*, 2, and Hall, "Notes on Deconstructing 'the Popular,' " 227.

One

Performing Objects in the "Theological" Theater

I argue throughout this book that the historical relationship between puppet theater and the human stage suggests the essential identity of so-called popular or elite practices within a master field of cultural distinction. This cultural field, I assume throughout, is radically contingent on prevailing patterns of social domination and conditioned by recurrent metaphysical and theological habits of thought. Here at the outset I consider how the puppet becomes a topos or conventional image in various discourses from antiquity to the early modern period, including Plato's dialogues, the anti-pagan polemics of the church fathers, and the discourses of witchcraft and religious reformation in the sixteenth century. In these disparate examples the process by which a "performing" object is animated or "in-spired" by some external authority becomes a model not only of theatrical performance but of representation itself; and puppetry as an observed popular practice is judged, defined, invested with particular social meanings, and inscribed in a system of cultural value.

"A Puppet Made by Gods":
Plato and the Hierarchy of Representation

> Do you see that the spectator is the last of the rings I spoke of, which receive their force from one another by virtue of the loadstone? You, the

rhapsodist and actor, are the middle ring, and the first one is the poet himself. But it is the deity who, through all the series, draws the spirits of men wherever he desires, transmitting the attractive force from one into another. And so, as from the loadstone, a mighty chain hangs down.

—Plato, *Ion* 535e-536a

Plato's allegory of the Cave is perhaps the most influential representation of representation in Western culture. In this celebrated passage from the *Republic* Plato figures forth the basic philosophic vision still associated with his name, in which a singular truth descends into multiple images and embodied signs, and in which not only human artifacts but all sensory appearances are mere shadows or reflections of some higher, absolute reality. But Plato's allegory also contains within it, as he makes clear in passing, a secondary metaphor:

> Picture men dwelling in a sort of subterranean cavern with a long entrance open to the light on its entire width. Conceive them as having their legs and necks fettered from childhood, so that they remain in the same spot, able to look forward only, and prevented by the fetters from turning their heads. Picture further the light from a fire burning higher up and at a distance behind them, and between the fire and the prisoners and above them a road along which a low wall has been built, as the exhibitors of puppet shows have partitions before the men themselves, above which they show the puppets. . . . See also, then, men carrying past the wall implements of all kinds that rise above the wall, and human shapes and shapes of animals as well, wrought in stone and wood and every material. (514b–c)[1]

In allegorical terms the "implements" and "shapes" that shadow the light of the fire, and the distant sun of truth outside the cave, seem to represent intelligible concepts or philosophical ideas, some form of intermediate being between mere sensory perceptions (the shadows on the cave wall) and absolute reality. On another level of metaphor, however, they are also figurally equivalent to the objects manipulated by what Plato here calls *thaumatopoios*, "the exhibitors of puppet shows."

[1] All quotations from Plato are from *The Collected Dialogues of Plato*, ed. Edith Hamilton and Huntington Cairns (Princeton: Princeton University Press, 1961). Citations are given parenthetically in the text.

In Plato's text, therefore, a hierarchical *theory* of representation conjoins and cooperates with the discursive appropriation of a particular cultural *practice*—puppet theater. For Plato the puppet serves as a secondary metaphor within a philosophical parable, but that metaphor itself depends on the puppet's material existence as an iconic (and performing) object: an artifact of stone or wood embodied or invested with a particular histrionic identity. Thus, the puppet, a "figure" in both senses, becomes a peculiarly clear paradigm of all representations—which are, in Plato's famous formulation, mere copies of a copy, at "three removes" from truth (597e). I want to suggest, however, that this ontological lowness of the puppet on Plato's hierarchy of representation finally corresponds to the assigned lowness of puppet theater within a hierarchy of cultural and social distinction. In the *Republic* and elsewhere in Plato's writings, one thus glimpses the early stages of the discursive strategy I consider throughout this book—a strategy in which a particular form of low or popular culture is defined as such even while it is being appropriated (as rubric, symbol, or metaphor) within the very discourse that constructs such categories. Both in Plato's text and in the broad Western tradition whose habits of thought he so profoundly influenced, the puppet or performing object would be a discursive site where the metaphysical oppositions of truth and image, presence and representation, intersect with the social and cultural oppositions of high and low, literary and popular, master and servant, male and female, and the like.

Plato's overall critique of representation in the *Republic* is itself both social and metaphysical, proceeding from a relatively specific argument about the moral effect of acting (both on actors and on audiences) to a far more sweeping condemnation of all forms of mimesis. In Book 3, in the process of considering the appropriate education for the guardians of his ideal city, Socrates suggests that any kind of acting or mimicry causes a pernicious loss of selfhood and ethical discipline in the actor. "A man of the right sort," he insists, will be willing to imitate only "the good man when he acts steadfastly and sensibly" (396c)—not just because to imitate bad behavior would be beneath his dignity, but also, more important, because the imitated action tends to realize or re-create itself in the imitator. Therefore, the potential guardians should only "imitate what is appropriate to them—men, that is, who are brave, sober, pious, free and all things of that kind" (395c). Conversely, as Socrates adds emphatically: "We will not then allow our charges, whom we expect to prove good men, being men, to play the parts of women and imitate a woman young or old wrangling with her husband, defying heaven, loudly boasting, fortunate in her own conceit, or involved in misfortune and possessed by grief and lamentation—still less a woman that is sick, in love, or in labor. . . . Nor may they imitate slaves, female and male, doing the offices of slaves" (395d).[2]

Later Socrates makes an analogous argument regarding the theatrical audience. The appeal of theatrical representation is "to the inferior part of the soul," and the actor, "feeding fat the emotion of pity" in his audience, makes it correspondingly more difficult for us "to restrain it in our own sufferings" (606b). This inferior part of the soul corresponds to, as it also predominates in, the same inferior classes of humanity whose imitation Socrates had previously proscribed. In the early section Socrates and his interlocutors agree that "the mob of motley appetites and pleasures and pains one would find chiefly in children and women and slaves and in the base rabble" (431c). And again, as the dialogue nears its end, Socrates contends that "the very best of us, when we hear Homer or some other of the makers of tragedy . . . accompany the representation with sympathy and eagerness. . . . But when in our own lives some affliction comes to us . . . we plume ourselves upon the opposite, on our ability to remain calm and endure, in the belief that this is the conduct of a man, and what we were praising in the theater that of a woman" (605d). In the *Gorgias* Socrates similarly diminishes tragic drama by construing it as merely a form of "rhetorical public address," which is moreover "addressed to a people composed alike of children and women and men, slaves and free" (502c–d). The pernicious emotional effect of representation is thus firmly linked, in Plato's thought, to particular forms of social and cultural subordination. A linked chain of categories—the rabble, the woman, the child, the slave—joins in a collective vision of otherness that Plato associates with both the subject and the object, the actor and the audience, of theater in particular and of representation in general. Thus, Plato's social and metaphysical critiques of representation entwine to suggest an essential identity of the theatrical subject and object. Representation is *of* multiplicity and *for* the

---

[2] Numerous feminist theorists have addressed Plato's strangely divided views on women. In an obvious contradiction he allows women an equal role in the guardianship of the ideal city and mandates equal education for boys and girls, yet he does so in a dialogue that also expresses the inferiority of women to men in nearly every respect. See, for example, in addition to the passages cited in my text, 455c–456e. For useful evaluations of the role of women in Platonic philosophy, see Lynda Lange, "The Function of Equal Education in Plato's *Republic* and *Laws*," in *The Sexism of Social and Political Theory: Women and Reproduction from Plato to Nietzsche*, ed. Lorenne M. G. Clark and Lynda Lange (Toronto: University of Toronto Press, 1979), 3–15; Susan Moller Okin, "Philosopher Queens and Private Wives: Plato on Women and the Family," in *Feminist Interpretations and Political Theory*, ed. Mary Lyndon Shanley and Carole Pateman (University Park: Pennsylvania State University Press, 1991), 11–31; and Elizabeth V. Spelman, "Woman as Body: Ancient and Contemporary Views," *Feminist Studies* 8.1 (1982): 108–31.

multitude: for the "nondescript crowd assembled in the theater" (*Republic* 604e–605a).

That the puppet should also take a central place within the interlocking cultural and representational hierarchies of Plato's thought depends, in part, as I have suggested, on the puppet's material conditions as an object invested with motion, identity, and histrionic "life." The usual Greek word for "puppet" is *thauma*, which could also mean "wonder" or "marvel," and which is probably derived from the verb *theaomai*, "I gaze upon or look at."[3] The word itself thus seems to embody in its etymology the pernicious histrionic unity of spectator and spectacle, subject and object, which I have suggested is a crucial aspect of Plato's critique of representation. In the *Sophist* Plato indicts the contemporary rhetoricians of Greek culture for what he contends, here and elsewhere, was their social and philosophic corruption. "What can be the secret," the Stranger asks Theaetetus, "of this magical power [*thauma*] of sophistry" (233a)? The word, in this passage sometimes translated as "trick," has here folded over onto itself to take the duplicitous or ironic sense of a "pretended wonder"; and this semantic progress from the magical and the wondrous to the merely histrionic and rhetorical is, once again, a descent from the metaphysical to the social. In the allegory of the Cave, Plato's word *thaumatopoios* combines *thauma* and the verb *poieo* ("to make," the root of the English word *poet*), and thus literally means something like "a maker of wonders." In other surviving Greek texts, however, *thauma* seems to mean something like "a juggler's show," and *thaumatopoios* can refer to an acrobat as well as a puppeteer.[4] Thus, the etymology as a whole—marked by this discursive slippage from the magician to the trickster, from veritable wonder to entertainment and legerdemain—conveys a distinct sense of the socially marginal, a smell of the street and the marketplace. Several centuries after Plato, the writer Athenaeus would lament that "the Athenians yielded to Potheinus the marionette player the very stage on which Euripides and his contemporaries performed their inspired plays"[5]—a passage that, like many others I cite, confirms at once the prevalence of puppet theater as cultural practice and the discursive effort to mark such a practice as culturally low.

Correspondingly, Plato's figural use of the puppet may also derive, at least in part, from his familiarity with the ritual automata used in various Near

---

[3] I am grateful to my colleague Stephen Scully for his assistance with these derivations.

[4] See, for example, Theophrastus, *Characters* 27.7.

[5] Athenaeus refers to Potheinus while mentioning a whole variety of popular histrionic performers including jugglers, parodists, magicians, and sleight-of-hand artists. Athenaeus, *The Deipnosophists* (London: William Heinemann, 1927), bk. 1, 19d–20a.

Eastern religious practices and with image magic, which was evidently widespread in the ancient world. Herodotus, in an often-cited passage, mentions how Egyptian women celebrated the Dionysiac festival with "puppets [*thauma*] a cubit long moved by strings, which are carried about the villages by women, the male member moving and near as big as the rest of the body."[6] Such idols might have suggested to Plato precisely the kind of descent from transcendent meaning to vulgar illusion that in the *Republic* seems to draw from Socrates his most vehement attacks on representation. For example, as Socrates exclaims in a moment of apparent exasperation, "Scene painting falls nothing short of witchcraft, and so do jugglery and many other such contrivances" (602d). Elsewhere Plato also reveals his characteristic disapproval of what C. L. Dodds describes as the "method of magical attack by maltreating a wax image of one's enemy," a practice that, Dodds suggests, enjoyed a vogue in fourth-century Athens.[7] In the *Republic* Socrates seems to allude to this practice when he scornfully refers to "soothsayers" who "are masters of spells and enchantments that constrain the gods to serve their end" (364c). In the *Laws* Plato also condemns and legislates against the practice of doing harm to someone with "a manikin of wax set up in the doorway" (933a).

But to reconsider Plato's metaphysical critique of representation in the light of the tradition of image magic is to recognize that the former is, so to speak, a reversal of the latter: Plato's philosophic project is grounded in a magisterial assertion that truth must control representation rather than vice versa. He seems to see the folk belief in image magic as another characteristic instance of that pernicious representation which, in his familiar double formula, is both socially and metaphysically subversive of good government. For the witch or magician, access to a person's image is believed to give power over that person's real self. For Plato, access to the Forms and Ideas of absolute reality gives power (in the shape of political authority) over the irrational multitude—both literally, because "the scrutiny of such objects gave the philosopher kings a right to make decisions and issue commands," and philosophically, because "the ideas become the unwavering, 'absolute' standards

[6] *Herodotus*, trans. A. D. Godley (London: William Heinemann, 1926), bk. 2, 48.

[7] E. R. Dodds, *The Greeks and the Irrational* (Berkeley: University of California Press, 1951), 194, 205 n.96. See also John J. Winkler, *The Constraints of Desire: The Anthropology of Sex and Gender in Ancient Greece* (New York: Routledge, 1990), 79, 93–98, for other references to the use of erotic figurines in Greek magic. The Greeks apparently associated this form of magic with the Egyptians, just as Americans today are likely to refer to the same kind of images as "voodoo dolls," thus associating them with a contemporary form of social and cultural alterity.

for political and moral behavior and judgment."[8] The state's political structure must resemble, because it reflects, the ontological structure of reality and the structure of the individual human soul.[9] The hierarchy of representation also enfolds that binarism of flesh and spirit of which Plato is perhaps the earliest formal source: truth must rule over image as, in other of Plato's formulations, the soul must rule the body (see, for example, *Phaedo* 67a), or the stronger part of the soul must rule the weaker.

Nevertheless, in an irony much noted by commentators, and exemplified perhaps most clearly of all in the celebrated allegory of the Cave, Plato critiques representation in dialogic texts that are themselves filled with poetic metaphor and myth. This irony, scholars often conclude, has its own social resonance: Plato believed that the "rabble" were incapable of pure reason and required the more tangible illumination of parable and poetry.[10] But if the rhetorical strategies of Plato's dialogues emerge, at least in part, as a concession to the limited capacities of his audience, they reveal at the same time an even more fundamental irony. For Plato, histrionic performance must be rejected (in the social world) precisely because its theoretical structure and institutional conditions may be said to resemble the ontological structure of universal reality. The chain of imitation descending downward from the poet into the various actions, utterances, and signs of theatrical performance is thus a secondary and subordinate version of the vaster chain of representation descending from the Forms and Ideas of absolute reality into the sensory multiplicity of the world. As Socrates had suggested in the *Ion* with another famous metaphor (the "loadstone" cited in this section's epigraph), the "rhapsodist and actor" is the middle ring on a chain of magnetic or spiritual transmission that extends downward to the spectator but also upward—first to the poet, and finally to "the deity." True enough this metaphor (like the *Ion* as a whole) is at least partly intended as a deliberately ironic mockery of the rhapsode's claims to a spiritual and poetic efficacy. Yet even such irony itself further constructs this figure in the same metaphoric terms as a kind of

---

[8] The first quotation is from R. S. Peters, "Authority," in *Political Philosophy*, ed. Anthony Quinton (Oxford: Oxford University Press, 1967), 88; the second is from Hannah Arendt, "What Is Authority?" in *Between Past and Future: Six Exercises in Political Thought* (New York: Viking, 1961), 110.

[9] See, in particular, *Republic* 434c-435e, where the three-part division of the state into "the moneymakers, the helpers, and the guardians" corresponds to the three-part division of the soul into appetite, will, and reason.

[10] On the history of this familiar argument, see Jean-François Mattéi, "The Theater of Myth in Plato," in *Platonic Writings, Platonic Readings*, ed. Charles L. Griswold, Jr. (New York: Routledge, 1988), 66–83.

empty vessel, filled with an "in-spiration" that descends through him but is not *of* him.

In even larger terms as well, Plato's metaphysics are articulated within a sweeping critique of the literal institution of performance as he knew it, but at the same time, outside of the strict limits of his philosophic system, the same basic conceptual structure survives as a model for theatrical authorship. Jacques Derrida has aptly called this particular model, in a phrase I employ throughout this book, the "theological" theater. As Derrida writes:

> The stage is theological for as long as its structure, following the entirety of tradition, comports the following elements: an author-creator who, absent and from afar, is armed with a text and keeps watch over, assembles, regulates the time or the meaning of representation, letting this latter *represent* him as concerns what is called the content of his thoughts, his intentions, his ideas. He lets representation represent him through representatives, directors or actors, enslaved interpreters who represent characters who, primarily through what they say, more or less directly represent the thought of the "creator."[11]

In such a theater literal authorship and literary authority—an "inspiration" which is linguistically and philosophically derived from the primitive belief in a divine *spiritus* or "breath"—descend from the poet down to player-puppets, who represent in articulate multiplicity the singularity of the authorial intention.[12] As I suggest later in more detail, this theological model of authorship has been rhetorically constructed, upheld, and imposed on the theatrical enterprise from the humanist revival of the early Renaissance to our own century, even though it has seldom accurately described the theater's real conditions and social relations. For the moment I observe merely that the hierarchical and "theatrical" structure of Plato's ontology corresponds to the more specific hierarchy of the theological theater, and that this convergence may explain how Plato, in the allegory of the Cave, could figure forth the whole multilevel process of perception and representation as a puppet show—a pageant of movable implements and objects invested with the multitudinous meanings of an absent and inaccessible author.

[11] Jacques Derrida, "The Theater of Cruelty and the Closure of Representation," in *Writing and Difference* (Chicago: University of Chicago Press, 1978), 235–36.
[12] See Joseph R. Roach, *The Player's Passion: Studies in the Science of Acting* (Newark: University of Delaware Press, 1985), 26–27, for a historical discussion of how both classical rhetoric and classical theories of acting were conditioned by the ancient concept of "in-spiration."

In the light of all this, it is striking that Plato should return to the image of the puppet as one of his final metaphorical or allegorical images of the human subject. In the *Laws* the Athenian addresses the subject of proper education, just as Socrates had done in the first books of the *Republic*, and he eventually presents what he calls a "fable" that provides a particular figuration of the characteristic Platonic division of the self:

> Let us look at the whole matter is some such light as this. We may imagine that each of us living creatures is a puppet made by gods, possibly as a plaything, or possibly with some more serious purpose. That, indeed, is more than we can tell, but one thing is certain. These interior states are, so to say, the cords, or strings, by which we are worked; they are opposed to one another, and pull us with opposite tensions in the direction of opposite actions, and therein lies the division of virtue from vice. In fact, so says our argument, a man must always yield to one of these tensions without resistance, but pull against all the other strings—must yield, that is, to that golden and hallowed drawing of judgment which goes by the name of the public law of the city. . . . So a man must always co-operate with the noble drawing of law. . . . In this wise our moral fable of the human puppets will find its fulfillment. (644e-645b)

As in the *Republic*, Plato discovers in the puppet a paradigm of representation, so here he discovers in the puppet a paradigm of the human soul. Furthermore, just as Plato's theory of representation (which makes the idea more real than the object) reverses the intuitive apprehension of "reality," so here Plato reverses what seems to have been his culture's intuitive belief in the possible efficacy of the magical image. The vulgar magician claims to control the embodied self through its mere figure; but Plato suggests that we are always already mere figures, puppets of the gods.

At the same time, Plato seems deliberately to parade the thoroughly problematic character of his own metaphor, which here confuses the inner and outer motive forces that the whole idea of a puppet in its subsequent cultural usage would generally divide. Thus, Plato suggests that the gods manipulate us like marionettes; but then he suggests that "the cords, or strings, by which we are worked" are *internal*, and that humanity must *choose* to "co-operate with the noble drawing of law." Familiar colloquial phrases still surviving in English such as "puppet state" or "pulling strings" depend figurally on an exteriority of power: the puppet as an object that is moved or manipulated by someone else. By contrast, Plato's fable evokes that complex middle ground of political discourse in which pure domination becomes *authority*—a formalized concept of the propriety of power, something invested with the aura of myth and morality and consequently internalized by those on whom it is imposed. This is precisely the point of Plato's parable, in which the soul's self-mastering, internal "judgment" not only is equivalent to but is finally *renamed* Law. Plato thus once again appropriates a particular kind of contemporary popular culture linked (socially) to the "rabble" and (metaphysically) to the hierarchical structure of all representation; and he does so within a text concerned with the discursive construction of "proper" and "appropriate" subjects for "the public law of the city." This double strategy was to recur across a wide range of ensuing Western discourse.

Mammets, Marmosets, and Marionettes: Iconophobia and the Embodied Sign

> Man's nature, so to speak, is a perpetual factory of idols.
> —John Calvin, *Institutes of the Christian Religion* 1.11.8

The Platonic hierarchy of representation eventually influences and merges with the iconophobia of the Judaeo-Christian theological tradition: the prohibition or suspicion of the making and worshiping of "graven images."[13] First articulated by the ancient Hebrews, an attack on idolatry reemerges in the church fathers as a critique of paganism, and centuries later becomes one of the the the foundations of the Reformation attack on the Catholic church. Here I want to glance briefly at a few highlights of the long history of Christian iconophobia, which constitutes one more discursive source for the cultural associations that would cling to the puppet in the early modern period and beyond. Most broadly, a recurrent theological anxiety about icons, idols, and imitation in general will prove to be discursively and linguistically related to the idea of the puppet—the inanimate object invested with histrionic "life." I move outward from this central observation, through the linguistic genealogies of several key words, to consider how the theological valence of the puppet underlies a much broader cultural process in which a particular cultural practice (designated along with other paratheatrical modes

[13] I take the term "iconophobia" from Christopher Collins, *Reading the Written Image: Verbal Play, Interpretation, and the Roots of Iconophobia* (University Park: Pennsylvania State University Press, 1991).

of performance as forms of low or popular culture) becomes a rubric or figure for other forms of social and cultural subordination. Specifically, I observe a few examples in which the puppet figures within the interrelated discourses of Christian misogyny, the "antitheatrical" prejudice, social mobility, witchcraft, religious reformation, and the like. In such discourses a persistent iconophobia joins with the idea of the puppet to locate gender and class in a representational hierarchy that subordinates the bodily and the material to the formal and the spiritual. Writers over many centuries thus appropriated in discourse a particular mode of performance they simultaneously constructed as popular even as they envisioned a variety of discursive categories in the terms of a broadly Platonic metaphysics marked by its "acute suspicion of embodied signs."[14] The historical pattern is itself hierarchical, in that the puppet may be seen, by turns and at once, either as diminutive and trivial, a mere doll or plaything, or as mysterious and efficacious, the very epitome of performance in all its supposedly transformative power.

In the Old Testament the rejection of idolatry grounds itself in questions of representation and agency. That is, an idol was pernicious both because it was a grossly inadequate attempt to represent the deity ("They changed their glory into the similitude of an ox," laments Psalm 106, describing the exodus from Egypt), and in its presumptuous belief that human hands might invest a material figure with animate life.[15] So to believe is, on the one hand, to credit human authorship with powers reserved for the divine Author and, on the other hand, to relinquish one's own agency, to disfigure the image of God within one's self:

The idols of the heathen are silver and gold, the work of men's hands.
They have mouths, but they speak not: eyes have they, but they see not;
They have ears, but they hear not; neither is there any breath in their mouths.
They that make them are like unto them: so is every one that trusteth in them.

(Psalm 115)

---

[14] R. Howard Bloch, *Medieval Misogyny and the Invention of Western Romantic Love* (Chicago: University of Chicago Press, 1991), 37.

[15] Edwyn Bevan, *Holy Images: An Inquiry into Idolatry and Image-Worship in Ancient Paganism and Christianity* (London: Allen & Unwin, 1940), 17–18.

This much-cited passage would introduce into theological discourse a formula broadly similar to Plato's equation of the subject and object of representation. As, for Plato, the loss of self suffered by the actor or mimic corresponds to the feeding and watering of his audience's passions, for the psalmist, more simply, he who worships idols is like what he worships.

In early Christianity this conventional understanding of the idol as a pernicious image suspended between identity and resemblance, between the wonder and the trick, is enfolded within a more complex representational hierarchy, one that itself enfolds the Platonic binarism of flesh and spirit. Saint Paul argues that those who "changed the glory of the uncorruptible God into an image made like to corruptible man . . . God also gave them up to uncleanness through the lusts of their own hearts, to dishonour their own bodies between themselves" (Romans 1.23–24). In Paul's construction, to worship the inanimate matter of the graven image is to degrade not just one's spiritual understanding but one's material flesh. The presumptuous attempt to represent God's transcendent truth in a merely human image, like the promiscuous sexuality which is both a mirror and a consequence of that attempt, is a subversion of the hierarchy of being and creation, serving "the creature more than the Creator" (1.25). Saint Paul has forced the opposition of animate and inanimate into a somewhat uncomfortable analogy with the opposition of spirit and flesh: the body is but a container for the soul and is thus itself mere matter, the dust of the ground.

This same theological and philosophical strategy would, of course, have profound consequences for Western ideas of gender and sexual morality. In polemical works of the early Christian fathers such as Tertullian's *De Spectaculis* (a text that, by the way, also strikes what would be an enduring parallel between idolatry and theatrical performance), the general Christian vision of the body as mere inanimate matter inhabited by a soul would produce a corresponding vision of the idol. Citing one of Saint Paul's other rhetorical attacks on the idol worshiper (1 Corinthians 10:19–20), Tertullian casually adds a further crucial point: " 'Not that an idol is anything,' says the apostle, 'but what they do, they do in honour of demons,' who plant themselves in the consecrated images of—whatever they are, dead men, or, as *they* think, gods."[16] Note that here the idol has become, in effect, a genuinely magical image, one literally inhabited by a demonic presence. This, as commentators have remarked, is actually a radical departure from earlier Judaic thought, for

---

[16] *De Spectaculis*, sec. 13, in Tertullian, *Apology and De Spectaculis*, trans. Gerald H. Rendall (London: William Heinemann, 1931), 267.

idol worship is here construed as wrong not because it mistakes inanimate matter for divine life but because it is the positive worship of a "real" but evil spirit.[17] Tertullian similarly envisions theatrical performance as a sort of spiritual possession, telling the now celebrated story of a woman "who went to the theatre and returned devil-possessed. So, when the unclean spirit was being exorcised and was pressed with the accusation that he had dared to enter a woman who believed; 'and I was quite right, too,' said he boldly, 'for I found her on my own ground.' "[18] We can hardly fail to notice in passing that Tertullian's puppetlike victim of demonic possession is female, and to be reminded accordingly that, as several recent commentators have argued, the whole polemical project of the patristic fathers constantly links prejudice against the theater with prejudice against women.[19]

Lactantius similarly inveighs against idolatry and repeats what had become the conventional analogy of the idol worshiper and his object. "What can you say of those who worship such things," asks Lactantius, echoing the psalmist, "except that they themselves are stones and blocks of wood."[20] In perhaps the most celebrated passage of his *Divine Institutes*, Lactantius appropriates from Persius a rhetorical conceit that would itself be incessantly repeated by later writers: "Persius . . . subjected to ridicule the fact that there is 'gold in temples, that puppets are donated by a maiden to Venus.' Persius . . . did not see that the statues themselves and the likenesses of the gods, made by the hands of Polycleitus, Euphanor, and Phidias, from gold and ivory, were nothing other than grand puppets, not given by maids to whose play pardon can be given, but dedicated by bearded men."[21] Here the traditional link between the subject and the object of idolatry takes on a sexual and familial dimension: the "bearded men" with their grand divine images are like girls with their dolls. Lactantius' rhetorical conceit projects a kind of ironically double spatial symmetry: the idols are both overgrown puppets and incongruously diminutive images of the deities they are presumed to

---

[17] Bevan, *Holy Images*, 90–93.

[18] *De Spectaculis*, sec. 26, 291.

[19] Jonas Barish, *The Anti-Theatrical Prejudice* (Berkeley: University of California Press, 1981), 50. See also Bloch, *Medieval Misogyny*, 37–46; and William B. Worthen, *The Idea of the Actor: Drama and the Ethics of Performance* (Princeton: Princeton University Press, 1984), 24–25.

[20] Lactantius, *The Divine Institutes*, ed. Roy Joseph Deferrari, trans. Sister Mary Francis McDonald, 2 vols. (Washington, D.C.: Catholic University of America Press, 1964), 1.21.

[21] Ibid., 2.4. Cf. Persius (2. 69–70): "Dicite, pontifices, in santo quid facit aurum? / nempe hoc quod Veneri donatae a uirgine pupae," which Guy Lee translates as "But say, you Pontiffs, what's gold in the sanctum doing? / No more than those dolls do that virgins give to Venus." *The Satires of Persius*, trans. Guy Lee (Liverpool: Frances Cairns, 1987), 25.

represent. But Lactantius also subdivides the basic binary distinctions between large and small, animate and inanimate, human and divine, on which
his rhetorical conceit depends, into a full hierarchy of social and sexual difference. Lactantius' irony implicitly affirms that the (male) sculptors and
dedicators ought to be both socially and ontologically "higher" than the
female figures here envisioned either as girls at play or as maidens taking
part in a sexual or procreative ritual (bringing magic images to the goddess
of love). The act of idolatry—the specific confusion of presence and
representation—induces an analogous cultural or psychological confusion
between the child and the man, the man and the maid. This passage would
often be cited or paraphrased in much later Protestant discourse attacking an
alleged Roman Catholic worship of images; it is thus a crucial site in which
the physical representation of the human figure, with its aura of potential
magic, would be enlisted within a discourse that constantly evokes and depends on shifting but interrelated forms of otherness.

Now, Lactantius is probably thinking of the idolatrous images as dolls
rather than as puppets or performing objects in the theatrical sense. The
word translated as "puppet" in the passage from Lactantius is *pupa*, which in
classical Latin meant either "little girl" or "doll."[22] The latter, secondary
sense presumably derives from the fact that dolls are given to little girls—
although even so, the etymology reflects a complex process of socialization
rather than some natural or essential connection. Nevertheless, Lactantius'
rhetorical point is precisely that the idol worshiper takes mere dolls, mere
play*things*, as the possessors of animate life, a perceptual confusion that literal
puppet theater strives quite specifically to achieve. Lactantius, like Plato before him, presumably knew of some kind of manipulable figure that can
meaningfully be called a puppet; and his rhetorical conceit depends precisely
on the (illusory) attribution of spirit to the merely inanimate material image.
Similarly, the practical histrionic conditions of puppet theater underlie a
complex historical and etymological process that links the cultural discourses
of biology and theology and embodies a continuing rhetorical and semantic
link between the doll, the puppet, the idol, and the (female) child.

By the sixteenth century a common alternative word for puppet in the
theatrical sense would be *maumet* or *mammet*, which originally meant

[22] For the etymological discussion that follows, I have consulted, in addition to the *Oxford English
Dictionary*, Robert K. Barnhart, ed., *The Barnhart Dictionary of Etymology* (New York: H. W. Wilson,
1988); Joseph T. Shipley, *The Origins of English Words: A Discursive Dictionary of Indo-European Roots*
(Baltimore: Johns Hopkins University Press, 1984); and Walter W. Skeat, ed., *An Etymological Dictionary
of the English Language*, 2d ed. (Oxford: Clarendon Press, 1924).

"idol." This word entered the English language from Old French as a corruption of the name Mahomet (Muhammad), a fictionalized figure referred to in a variety of medieval discourse (including an extensive religious drama) not as the historical prophet of the Islamic religion but as an imagined deity whom Turks, Moors, "paynims," and even Jews were said to worship. By extension, *maumet* could refer in a general way to a false god or, more specifically, to a false or deceiving image. The Lollards, at the end of the fourteenth century, initiated what would be a recurrent theme in later Protestant discourse in contending that "al that worshipen the crosse or ymages ben cursed and done mawmentri."[23] About 1426, in John Lydgate's translation of Guillaume de Deguileville's *Pilgrimage of the Life of Man*, the pilgrim observes a carpenter worshiping an idol and comments:

> Se hoy thus fool, off hys folye,
> Seth how hys Mawmet, foul off chere,
> Herys hath, and may nat here;
> And syttynge also in hys se,
> Eyen hath, and may nat se;
> But is as dowmb as stok or ston.
> (10,917–21)[24]

Expressing here the ancient Judaic attack on the attribution of divinity to mere matter, the pilgrim a few lines later refers to the contradictory Christian belief that the idolator is actually worshiping the devil:

> But off thy mawmet, I wolde here,
> Wyche may thé no thyng socoure,
> Why thow shouldest hym honoure.
> For (who that any resoun kan),
> With-Inne, enclosy ys Sathan,
> And ther hym-sylff hath mad a se.
> (21,016–21)

The "mawmet" or idol is both a mere "stok or ston" (an alliterative combination that regularly recurs in later invective against idol worship) and a site for the literal presence of an indwelling spirit.

[23] Anne Hudson, ed., *English Wycliffite Writings* (Cambridge: Cambridge University Press, 1978), 19.
[24] John Lydgate, *The Pilgrimage of the Life of Man: From the French of Guillaume de Deguileville*, ed. F. J. Furnivall (London: Kegan Paul, 1901). Citations are given parenthetically by line number in the text.

The word *mammet*, then, descends from this primary sense of "idol" into several other quasi-figural meanings. By the sixteenth century the term had assumed the meaning of "puppet" both in the general sense of a child's plaything and in the strict sense of a performing object.[25] In the anonymous comedy *Every Woman in her Humor* (1607) the naive Getica, a bawd, asks, "What showe will be heere to night?" and goes on to mention her familiarity with several other forms of popular entertainment: "I have seen the Babones already, the Cittie of new Ninivie, and Julius Caesar acted by the Mammets" (5.1.6–9).[26] Through the semantic senses of "doll" or "puppet," however, the word also could be applied colloquially to a subordinate person, usually a female, as a term either of condescending affection or of abuse and contempt. In accordance with its etymological roots, however, the term seems to convey in such usages not just the semantic sense of mastery or dominance figurally suggested by the conditions of puppet performance but also a reversal of that relationship. After all, the basic semantic connection between the idol and the puppet turns on the idea of an image that deceives the viewer and is thus *itself* powerful. In this sense "mammets" also resemble a particular misogynist image of woman, who, as described in a discursive tradition descending from the church fathers all the way to the pamphlet controversies of early modern England, uses her "fair, glozing countenance" to cause men to be "deceived . . . where they most trust."[27] Two contradictory meanings (the mastered object versus the powerfully deceptive image) thus converge in the word *mammet*. "This is no world," says Shakespeare's Hotspur, as he bids a loving farewell to his wife on his way to destiny and death, "to play with mammets and to tilt with lips" (*1 Henry IV* 2.3.91–92).[28] In a very different context, the bitterly angry Capulet refers to his daughter as "a wretched puling fool, / A whining mammet" (*Romeo and Juliet* 3.5.183–84). Note that Juliet is a "mammet" both because she is resisting the father's patriarchal right to give her in marriage to whomever he chooses, and

---

[25] *Oxford English Dictionary*, s.v. "mammet," 2.

[26] *Every Woman in her Humor*, ed. Archie Mervin Tyson (New York: Garland, 1980). Here, as when quoting all other dramatic texts from the early modern period, if necessary I silently modernize "u," "v," "j," "i," and scribal contractions. All dates cited for plays up to 1700 are from Sylvia Stoler Wagonheim, ed., *Annals of English Drama, 975–1700*, 3d ed. (London: Routledge, 1989).

[27] *The Schoolhouse of Women* (1541), quoted from Katharine Usher Henderson and Barbara F. McManus, eds., *Half Humankind: Contexts and Texts of the Controversy about Women in England, 1540–1640* (Urbana: University of Illinois Press, 1985), 154.

[28] Quotations from Shakespeare's works are from *The Riverside Shakespeare*, ed. G. Blakemore Evans (Boston: Houghton Mifflin, 1974). All citations are given parenthetically by act, scene, and line number in the text.

because her father alleges her tears to be merely a deceptive and manipulative histrionic performance. As I will suggest in more detail with later examples, woman is discursively constructed as puppetlike both in her general diminution and manipulability (a kind of materiality that opposes or conjoins a mastering masculine form) *and* in her alluring dissimulation and pernicious duplicity.

Thus, the semantic spectrum ranging from idol to puppet to woman by way of the associated senses of deception and false imitation once again stretches from the wonder to the trick, from the top to the bottom of the hierarchy of representation. A similar convergence of social and theological meaning is manifest in the history of another word, despite its wholly different etymological origins. In that same passage from Lydgate's *Pilgrimage* that I have already cited, the pilgrim also laments that the idolator's "hertë" was so set / To worshepë A Marmoset" (20,953–54). This word derives from the Old French root *marmouset*, which originally meant "grotesque image," and which developed into the modern French sense "little man." By the sixteenth century the English word had the meaning "ape" or "monkey" (which the *OED* claims is still in French provincial use). In *The Tempest*, for example, Shakespeare includes "the nimble marmazet" (2.2.174) among the wildlife of the island; and the same word survives in English as the formal name of a small tropical New World monkey.

The incongruous connection of the idol and the monkey operates on two semantic levels. As idols are often characterized as merely diminutive images, ridiculous in their physical smallness relative to the divine figure they claim to represent, so monkeys could be seen as a smaller or parodic version of human beings. More specifically, idols "pretend" to be something they are not; and monkeys, similarly, were proverbially understood clownishly to imitate or "ape" human behavior ("monkey see, monkey do"). The proverbial image of the imitative monkey already evoked entwined theological and social meanings in medieval and early modern Europe. On the one hand, the ultimate source of all false and deceiving imitation was the devil, whom the author of the medieval *Ancrene Riwle* calls the "olde ape," and whose primal sin was often seen as an attempt to *imitate* God.[29] In the conventional Renaissance vision of universal order, man (whom Aristotle had described in

[29] *The English Text of the Ancrene Riwle*, ed. Mabel Day (London: Early English Text Society, 1952), 110. In the "Creation and Fall of the Angels" play from the Wakefield cycle, Lucifer stands up immediately after the divine creation to declare that "this mastré belongs to me" and "Of me commys all this light" (l. 81). Cited from David Bevington, ed., *Medieval Drama* (Boston: Houghton Mifflin, 1975), 261.

the *Poetics* as the most imitative of creatures) was sometimes called "the ape of Nature." For example, in one of the illustrations in Robert Fludd's *Utriusque Cosmi Historia* (1617–19), a puppetlike Nature (envisioned as a naked female) is manipulated by a chain descending from God's hand and attached to a manacle on her wrist, while she herself holds a chain attached to a diminutive and even more puppetlike monkey sitting on the globe of the earth (see Figure 1).

The "apishness" of humanity manifests itself, most obviously and directly, in theatrical representation. Correspondingly, the "marmoset" was also, by the sixteenth century and probably earlier, a kind of literal performing object. As various historical records attest, trained monkeys or "baboons" were a popular form of entertainment in the streets and marketplaces of early modern England, performing various acrobatic tricks and comically miming human behavior. One of the few surviving handbills from the London Beargarden, a neighbor of Shakespeare's Globe Theatre on Bankside, mentions among its attractions "plasant sport with the horse and ape"; and as late as the eighteenth century "a little *Marmazet* from *Bengal,* that dances the *Chesire Rounds,* and exercises at the word of command," was performing at Bartholomew Fair.[30] Such performing monkeys were rhetorically lumped together with puppets, "motions," jugglers, and freak shows as similar forms of crude, carnivalesque entertainment. In the passage already cited from *Every Woman in her Humor,* Getica mentions seeing both "the Babones" and "Julius Caesar acted by the Mammets" (5.1.6–9). In *The Alchemist* Ben Jonson's Lovewit returns home unexpectedly and questions his neighbors about the strange goings-on at his house:

> *Lovewit.* . . . You saw no Bills set up, that promis'd cure
> Of agues, or the tooth-ach?
> *2. Neighbor.*   No such thing, sir.
> *Lovewit.* Nor heard a drum strooke, for Babions or Puppets?
> (5.1.12–14)[31]

---

[30] Andrew Gurr, *The Shakespearean Stage, 1574–1642,* 3d ed. (Cambridge: Cambridge University Press, 1991), 11; Henry Morley, *Memoirs of Bartholomew Fair* (London, 1859), 330–31. For more on performing monkeys in early modern England, see E. K. Chambers, *The Elizabethan Stage,* 4 vols. (Oxford: Clarendon Press, 1923), 4:11; Thomas Frost, *The Old Showmen and the Old London Fairs* (London, 1881), 20; and Tyson's introduction to his edition of *Every Woman in her Humor,* 16.

[31] Ben Jonson, *The Alchemist,* in *Ben Jonson,* ed. C. H. Hereford and Percy Simpson, 11 vols. (Oxford: Clarendon Press, 1925–63).

Figure 1. Nature, herself manipulated by God, manipulates Man, the "ape of Nature." Detail of an engraving from Robert Fludd, *Utriusque Cosmi Historia* (1617–19). Reproduced by permission of the Department of Printing and Graphic Arts, Houghton Library, Harvard University.

Similarly, in one of his epigrams Sir John Davies satirizes a poor poet who is reduced to writing for "him which Puppets represents / And also him which with the Ape doth play."[32]

In these examples the linked semantic senses of diminution and parodic imitation apply both as mere metaphor and as social description: baboons and puppets alike are instances of an imitation that degrades or parodies its object and of low, degraded practices common to the margins of urban life and the field of culture. And so, just as one might expect, "marmoset" could also be used as a virtual synonym for "ape" or "mammet" in the last of its senses, as a term of reproach to that proverbial archdeceiver woman. "O dissembling marmaset!" says Sir Gregory to his fiancée in Middleton and Rowley's *Wit at Several Weapons* (3.1.335).[33] As the *OED* documents, the word could also be applied to a male with the related connotation of "ingle," or homosexual favorite. "Thou manticore, ye marmoset, garnished like a Greek," writes John Skelton in one of his sequence of poems "Against Garnesche."[34] Jonson's Crites, the authorial voice in *Cynthia's Revels*, similarly refers to a courtier who

> appeares some mincing marmoset
> Made all of clothes, and face; his limbes so set
> As if they had some voluntarie act
> Without mans motion, and must moove just so
> In spight of their creation.[35]

Here the image of a literal puppet seems to underlie this description of a "marmoset" whose limbs enact a kind of "motion" which is pointedly other than the "natural" motion of essential humanity. Jonson's image is Plato's puppet of the gods turned inside out, so to speak: the courtier has literally internalized his external affectations, enslaving himself to himself in a manner that implicitly subverts the biological aspect of the theological hierarchy of creation.

[32] Epigram 30, "In Dacum," in *The Poems of Sir John Davies*, ed. Robert Krueger (Oxford: Clarendon Press, 1975), 142.

[33] Thomas Middleton and William Rowley, *Wit at Several Weapons* (1613), in *The Dramatic Works in the Beaumont and Fletcher Canon*, ed. Fredson Bowers (Cambridge: Cambridge University Press, 1966–89).

[34] "Skelton, Laureate, Defender, against Master Garnesche," *The Complete Poems of John Skelton*, ed. Peter Henderson (London: J. M. Dent, 1959), 153. The general interconnection of the words and meanings I have been considering is also manifest in Palsgrave's English-French dictionary of 1530, which defines *maument* as "marmoset" or "poupee."

[35] Ben Jonson, *Cynthia's Revels*, 3.4.22–26, in Hereford and Simpson, *Ben Jonson*, 4:90.

In a similar but more extensive use of the same comparision, Thomas Dekker makes clear how the topos of the "ape" emerges from and embodies the gendered theological and social hierarchies of early modern England. Identifying "apishness" as one of the "Seven Deadly Sinnes of London," which he discusses in the pamphlet of that name, Dekker concludes that

> Man is Gods Ape, and an Ape is *Zani* to a man, doing over those trickes (especially if they be knavish) which hee sees done before him: so that *Apishness* is nothing but counterfetting or imitation. . . . For as man is Gods ape, striving to make artificiall flowers, birdes, &c. like to the naturall: So for the same reason are women, Mens *Shee Apes*, for they will not bee behind them the bredth of a Taylors yard (which is nothing to speake of) in anie new-fangled upstart fashion.[36]

The familiar misogynist note at the end of this passage emerges rhetorically from, as it philosophically reflects, the conventional ideas of theological and biological order described in the preceding lines.

I will later pursue in more detail the psychosocial habit of thought that links the puppet, the doll, the woman, and the effeminate social climber in an implicit hierarchy of representational and social subordination. For the moment I want to shift directions to explore how the theological and cultural connotations of the puppet also reemerge both in the voluminous literature on witchcraft produced from the late fifteenth through the seventeenth centuries and in the homiletic, polemical, and theological texts of the Protestant Reformation. This is not the place to join the complex historical debate about whether these two profound cultural phenomena of roughly the same period were themselves causally related.[37] For my purposes I simply observe that the discourses of witchcraft and of Protestantism collectively envision the puppet as both wonder and trick, a potentially magic figure invested with a self-present representational power or, conversely, a site for representation construed as a degradation of some transcendent "truth." At the same time, both discourses locate themselves on an axis of implicit cultural (and class)

---

[36] *The Non-Dramatic Works of Thomas Dekker*, ed. Alexander B. Grosart (New York: Russell & Russell, 1962), 2:59. All further references to Dekker's pamphlets are from this edition and are cited parenthetically in the text.

[37] Ioan P. Couliano, in *Eros and Magic in the Renaissance* (Chicago: University of Chicago Press, 1987), asserts that "there is an immediate connection between the witch craze and the European Reformation" (191).

distinction, and thus focus the interrelation of hierarchies of authority, representation, and power.

The idea of image magic, as I have suggested, goes back at least as far as Plato, who implicitly attributed a different sort of power to the represented image even as he dismissed the belief in its literal magical efficacy. Over the long history of the witchcraft debate centuries later, it was always assumed that the manipulation of magically animated images was a crucial part of the witches' *maleficia*, an assumption that thus descends into new cultural contexts all the way from ancient ritual beliefs and practices.[38] In the *Daemonologie* of King James I, a work that itself primarily recites the claims made by a variety of earlier texts, witches are said to "make Pictures of waxe or clay: That by the rosting thereof, the persones that they beare the name of, may be continuallie melted or dryed awaie by continuall siknesse."[39] These magical figures, used in a process of homeopathic magic, were frequently referred to as "puppets" and sometimes confused with the demonic "familiars" that witches also were said to employ (see Figure 2). To cite one example from the long succession of Elizabethan and Jacobean pamphlets on the subject, during an extensive witchcraft investigation in Essex in 1582, one suspect "denied having any puppets, spirits, maumettes, and all charges," while another confessed to having "four imps called Robin, Jack, William, and Puppet alias Mamet, two hes and two shes, all like unto black cats, kept in wool in a box."[40] Here again, although their active semantic sense may be "doll," the words "puppet" and "mammet" clearly invoke both the sinister incongruity of a mere child's plaything used as a demonic tool and the possibility of magical life in the material image.

[38] My thinking about the discourses and practices of witchcraft in the early modern period has been primarily shaped by Stuart Clark, "King James' *Daemonologie:* Witchcraft and Kingship," in *The Damned Art: Essays in the Literature of Witchcraft,* ed. Sydney Anglo (London: Routledge & Kegan Paul, 1977), 156–81; Frances E. Dolan, *Dangerous Familiars: Representations of Domestic Crime in England, 1550–1700* (Ithaca: Cornell University Press, 1994); Clive Holmes, "Popular Culture? Witches, Magistrates, and Divines in Early Modern England," in *Understanding Popular Culture: Europe from the Middle Ages to the Nineteenth Century,* ed. Steven L. Kaplan (Berlin: Mouton, 1984), 85–111; Karen Newman, *Fashioning Femininity and English Renaissance Drama* (Chicago: University of Chicago Press, 1991); and David Underdown, *Revel, Riot, and Rebellion: Popular Politics and Culture in England, 1603–1660* (Oxford: Clarendon Press, 1985).

[39] James I, *Daemonologie,* ed. G. B. Harrison (New York: Barnes & Noble, 1966), 44 (bk. 2, chap. 5).

[40] *A true and just Recorde of the Information, Examination and Confession of all the Witches, taken at S. Oses in the countie of Essex* (London, 1582), cited in C. L'Estrange Ewen, *Witchcraft and Demonism* (London: Heath Cranton, 1933), 159. Cf. Cotton Mather's reference to the "Pictures, Poppets, and other Hellish Compositions" allegedly used by New England witches, in *The Wonders of the Invisible World* (1692), reprinted as *On Witchcraft* (Mt. Vernon, N.Y.: Peter Pauper Press, n.d.), 32.

Figure 2. Witches receive demonic "puppets" from Satan. From "The Witch of the Woodlands," an undated eighteenth-century chapbook reprinted in John Ashton's *Chap-Books of the Eighteenth Century*. Reproduced by permission of the Peabody & Essex Museum, Salem, Massachusetts.

The witches' supposed use of puppetlike images also corresponds to the belief that the witch herself was the puppetlike servant of Satan. In the voluminous literature on witchcraft from the end of the fifteenth century to the mid-seventeenth century, the magical image is often envisioned precisely as a mediating term within a hierarchy of demonic power. The authors of the *Malleus Maleficarum*, for example, argue that

> when a witch makes a waxen image or some such thing in order to bewitch somebody . . . and some injury is done upon the image, such as piercing it or hurting it in any other way . . . although the injury is

actually done to the image by the witch or some other man, and the devil in the same manner invisibly injures the bewitched man, yet it is deservedly ascribed to the witch. For, without her, God would never allow the devil to inflict the injury, nor would the devil on his own account try to injure the man.[41]

Commentators have often noticed the sinister logic whereby the human servant of Satan, who provides merely one link in an intricate theological chain of causation, nevertheless retains central responsibility for its results. Witches were also commonly said to suckle and nourish the devil through infernal "paps," which were sometimes alleged to have been discovered on their bodies after examination.[42] Thus, in the elaborate cultural construction of witchcraft as psychic fantasy and theological belief, the devil himself (the "Father" of Evil) becomes a surrogate child at the breast; and witchcraft inquisitors envisioned the female body as a conduit, at once passive and active, through which infernal sustenance descends into the childlike "puppet," and from there to the witch's victims (and accusers).

As several recent scholars have also suggested, the belief in witchcraft accordingly served as a perverse confirmation of the interrelated hierarchies of theological, political, and representational authority. The whole institution of witchcraft, with its supposed rituals of initiation and confirmation, was commonly declared to to be a parodic and degraded version of the holy church. "The devill as Gods Ape," writes King James, "counterfeites in his servantes this service & forme of adoration, that God prescribed and made his servantes to practise."[43] Witches both use puppets and are themselves puppetlike tools within a kind of metahierarchical system in which the "true" hierarchies of representation and power are inextricably linked to a subordinate, secondary hierarchy that re-presents them in parodic form. Moreover (as Clive Holmes has suggested), the accepted doctrine of the demonic puppet was the product of a complex mutual appropriation of relatively more popular and elite beliefs about witchcraft, and was also in itself inseparable from the entwined hierarchies of representation and social class. One legal theorist of the mid-seventeenth century, for example, responding

[41] Jakob Sprenger and Heinrich Kramer, *Malleus Maleficarum*, ed. Montague Summers (New York: Benjamin Blom, 1970), 135.

[42] "The Devil by sucking blood makes a pap or dug in a short time," confessed Margaret Johnson in the Lancashire witch investigation of 1634 (cited in Ewen, *Witchcraft and Demonism*, 248). On the searching of the Lancashire witches for these demonic "paps," see also Wallace Notestein, *A History of Witchcraft in England from 1558–1718* (New York: Russell & Russell, 1965), 154–55.

[43] King James I, *Daemonologie*, 35 (bk. 2, chap. 3).

to skeptics who questioned whether mighty demonic spirits would really manifest themselves in paltry domestic objects, argued that Satan appeared as human to educated people but appeared in "baser formes" to the "base, sordid, filthy and blockish."[44]

Individual instances of witchcraft prosecution were also frequently appropriated in popular literary forms such as ballads, pamphlets, and plays, and also within the current of collective social belief, inspiring not only their own representation but also subsequent "real" events. For example, in Jacobean England there were two major witchcraft scares in the county of Lancaster about twenty years apart, each producing its respective pamphlet account. During the first episode (1613), Elizabeth Sowtherns, an elderly woman, was induced to make the conventional confession about her use of image magic. "The speediest way to take a mans life away by Witchcraft," she reportedly told her interrogators, "is to make a Picture of Clay, like unto the shape of the person whom they meane to kill . . . then take a Thorne or Pinne, and pricke it."[45] Twenty years later in the same county a young boy initiated a new witchcraft scare with an outlandish tale of demonic apparitions which he later confessed was a fabrication. But the temporary acceptance of the story, itself a feigned narration, was at least an indirect consequence of the first persecutions and the published accounts of them. Those accused in the second Lancashire witch scare were thus the victims of a historical and cultural version of the homeopathic *maleficium* of which they were accused, a process in which a mere representation becomes the conduit for a deferred and secondary agency. This second persecution became the subject of a play by Thomas Heywood and Richard Brome, *The Late Lancashire Witches* (1634); and in the same year a puppet show called "The Witches of Lancaster" was reported at Oxford.[46] Here, as though coming full circle in a vertiginous descending cycle of fantasy and theater, the same "puppets" supposedly used by witches finally themselves reenacted the imagined (and twice represented) events in which they had already played their conventional mediating role.

In broadly similar fashion, and in roughly the same period, the puppet emerges in Protestant discourse as a crucial mediate term within a doctrinal revolution focusing by turns on questions of divine representation and theological authority. From Wycliffe and his Lollard followers in the late four-

---

[44] Richard Bernard, *A Guide to Grand Jury Men* (1627), quoted in Holmes, "Popular Culture?" 97.

[45] Thomas Potts, *The Wonderfull Discoverie of Witches in the Countie of Lancaster* (London, 1613), B3v.

[46] Gerald Eades Bentley, *The Jacobean and Caroline Stage*, 3 vols. (Oxford: Clarendon Press, 1941–68), 3:75–76.

teenth and early fifteenth centuries, through Luther, Calvin, and the English Protestants of the sixteenth century and beyond, the critique of Roman Catholicism questioned at once the miracle of the Eucharist and the nature of the church hierarchy. To Protestants, even as papal authority had degraded spiritual grace by claiming to dispense it through a quasi-secular system of material privilege and power, so the Catholic belief in the transubstantiation of the Host mistakes a mere representation, a figure or symbol, for a literal magic transformation. Lactantius' famous comparison of the idol and the puppet reemerges in a wide range of later Protestant discourse to suggest that Catholic ritual transforms the mere process of figuration, mere *play*, into the objects of worship. Here, for quick comparision, are three passages covering about half a century from the Lutheran revolt against Rome to the English Reformation:

> If these things [i.e., Roman Catholic ritual observances] had been left as child's play for youth and young pupils, so that they would have had a childlike image of Christian teaching and life, as one must give children dolls, puppets, hobby-horses, and other kinds of children's toys . . . then it would be possible to tolerate the palm-ass, Ascension, and many similar things. (Martin Luther, *Exhortation to All Clergy Assembled at Augsburg*, 1530)

> Thou seest how they with Idols play, and teach the people to,
> None otherwise then little gyrles with Puppets use to do.
> (Barnabe Googe, *The Popish Kingdome, or reigne of Antichrist*, 1570)

> Whefforth it followeth, that there is like foolishnesse and lewdnesse in decking of our images, as great puppets for old fooles, like children, to play the wicked play of idolatry. . . . Our Churches stand full of such great puppets, wonderously decked and adorned. (*Certain Sermons or Homilies . . .* , 1623)[47]

As this conventional rhetorical conceit reemerges in the doctrinal controversies of early modern England, the children's doll becomes, through the rhetorical momentum of the figure itself, a genuinely histrionic figure: a "pup-

[47] The first passage is from *Luther's Works*, ed. Helmut T. Lehmann, vol. 34, trans. Lewis W. Spitz (Philadelphia: Muhlenberg Press, 1960), 59; the second, a verse translation of *Regnum Papisticum* (1554) by Thomas Kirchmayer or "Naogeorgus," is from Karl Young, *The Drama of the Medieval Church*, 2 vols. (Oxford: Clarendon Press, 1933), 2:537; the third is from *Certain Sermons or Homilies appointed to be read in Churches in the time of the late Queene Elizabeth of famous memory* (London, 1623), bk. 2, 71; ff.6r.

pet" employed in a process of doctrinal trickery. The Host of the Catholic Eucharist, manipulated with ritual gestures and supposedly embodied with the divine spirit, could as such be dismissed as a kind of grotesque performing object. In John Bale's *King Johan* (ca. 1538), for example, the titular character admonishes the allegorical figure Clergy for corrupting England "with your latyn howrs, serymonyes & popetly playes."[48] Here the speaker is clearly referring not just to doll-like images but specifically to puppet performance; indeed, he is making a near-pun on "puppetry" and "popery" which rhetorically reenacts the very situation it condemns by linking and confusing the opposing poles on the same hierarchy of representation and authority which the Catholic church allegedly subverts.

This early modern iconophobia here again clearly interpenetrates an ongoing process of social and cultural subordination. Reformation thinkers often felt called upon to refute a commonly cited idea that Catholic images served as the equivalent of books for the uneducated. John Calvin, for example, dismisses this idea as a rationalization for the failures of the clergy, asserting that "those in authority in the church turned over to idols the office of teaching for no other reason than that they themselves were mute."[49] John Veron, an English Protestant writing in the mid-sixteenth century, complains similarly that ministers, "so they might live at ease, and in continual idlenesse . . . have appointed unto us meete vicares for to supply their roumes, and to preache unto the people for theym, that is, dumme ymages, domme stockes and stones, which have mouthes and speake not, which have eyes and see not, which have ears and heare not."[50] In a different but finally interrelated strategy of Protestant discourse, reformers also tended to associate the idolatrous image with the alluring female body, and thus attempted (as Huston Diehl argues) "to incite iconophobia through appeals to gynophobia."[51] "The pictures or statues that [the Catholics] dedicate to saints," complains Calvin, are "but examples of the most abandoned lust and obscenity" (1.11.7). The Elizabethan homily cited earlier goes on to allude to the Pauline

[48] John Bale, *King Johan*, ed. John Johnson (Oxford: Oxford University Press, 1931), 21. This edition transcribes the manuscript of Bale's play; I have modernized scribal contractions but left the original spelling "popetly."

[49] John Calvin, *Institutes of the Christian Religion*, ed. John T. McNeill, vols. 20–21, trans. Ford Lewis Battles (Philadelphia: Westminister Press, 1950), 1.11.7, henceforth cited parenthetically in the text.

[50] John Veron, *A Strong battery against the Idolatrous invocation of the dead Saintes* (London, 1562), unpaginated. I have corrected two apparent typographical errors in the passage.

[51] Huston Diehl, "Bewhored Images and Imagined Whores: Iconophobia and Gynophobia in Stuart Domestic Tragedy," *English Literary Renaissance*, forthcoming. I am grateful to the author for generously sharing the manuscript of this essay.

equation of idolatry and fornication, and insists that the "decking of Images and Idoles" is intended "but for the further provocation and inticement to spiritual fornication, to decke spiritual harlots most costly and wantonly."[52] Many more examples could be cited to confirm how Protestant discourse operates within a sort of constellation of interrelated hierarchies which associate the image, the idol, the child, the woman, and the puppet as instances at once of a sinful corporeality and a pernicious spiritual representation.

I want to mention, finally, one more synonym for *puppet* whose obscure etymology seems nevertheless obvious from its own verbal form, and which further suggests the entwined theatrical and theological valence of the performing object. The word *marionette* enters our language from French as a diminutive of Marion, itself a diminutive of the female name Marie (Mary). Thus, it seems safe to assume, as several scholars have, that the "marionette," or "little Mary," must have referred originally to the sculpted figures of the Virgin used in stationary Nativity scenes—the "crèches" that still survive today as a custom in many American cities and homes. The histrionic sense that eventually attaches to the word *marionette* presumably derives from the fact that some of the figures in medieval crèches were automata, capable of some form of limited mechanical movement. The actual existence of such mechanized ritual figures also goes hand in hand with legends of statues that miraculously come to life: a crucified Christ that nods its head, a Mary that blesses the assembled multitude.[53]

During the Middle Ages, the "three Marys" who question and announce the resurrection of Jesus in the "Quem Quaeritis" tropes were becoming the first "characters" in the liturgical drama of the church. This "visit to the sepulcher" scene also seems to have been performed at Easter with puppets.[54]

---

[52] *Certain Sermons*, bk. 2, 69, ff.5r. This passage, and the general equation of Catholic ritual with theatrical performance, is also discussed in C. L. Barber and Richard P. Wheeler, *The Whole Journey: Shakespeare's Power of Development* (Berkeley: University of California Press, 1968), 22.

[53] *Marionette* in the specific sense of a puppet manipulated by strings is first cited by the *OED* in 1620. On medieval religious automata, see Henryk Jurkowski, "Transcodifications of the Sign System of Puppetry," *Semiotica* 47.1–4 (1983): 132; Charles Magnin, *Histoire des marionettes en Europe: depuis l'antiquité jusqu'à nos jours* (1861; rpt. Paris: Slatkin, 1981), 54–63, 208–10; and George Speaight, *The History of the English Puppet Theatre*, 2d ed. (London: Robert Hale, 1990), 32–34. For more general critical speculation on the animated figure in Western culture, see Kenneth Gross, *The Dream of the Moving Statue* (Ithaca: Cornell University Press, 1992).

[54] Wagonheim, *Annals of English Drama*, records what seems to be a very late puppet version of the "Quem Quaeritis" play in Leicester churches in 1491 or later.

Historians of puppet theater frequently cite a passage from William Lambarde, a sixteenth-century antiquary:

In the Dayes of ceremonial religion they used at *Wytney* to set foorthe yearly in maner of a Shew, or Enterlude, the Resurrection of our Lord and Saviour *Chryste*, partly of Purpose to draw thyther some Concourse of People that might spend their Money in the Towne, but cheiflie to allure by pleasant Spectacle the comon Sort to the Likinge of Popishe Maumetrie; for the which Purpose, and the more lyvely thearby to exhibite to the Eye the hole Action of the Resurrection, the Preistes garnished out certein smalle Puppets, representinge the Parson of the *Christe*, the Watchmen, *Marie*, and others, amongest the which one bare the Parte of a wakinge Watcheman, who (espiinge *Christ* to arise) made a continual Noyce, like to the Sound that is caused by the Metinge of two Styckes, and was therof comonly called, *Jack Snacker* of *Wytney*.[55]

These "smalle Puppets"—at least one of which was, in the primal sense of the word, a "marionette"—evoke for Lambarde that characteristic link between the puppet and the idol that I have observed throughout. Indeed, the use of literal puppets in religious drama lends a curious circularity to the conventional attack on theater as a form of idolatry, a topos that recurs from the patristic fathers, to the famous Lollard "Treatise of Miraclis Pleyinge" in the fourteenth century, through the polemical attacks of Gosson, Stubbes, Prynne, and others in the late sixteenth and early seventeenth centuries.

More specifically, however, I want to observe how Lambarde's discourse again links the supposedly pernicious effects of representation to an assumed social and cultural hierarchy. The puppets are said to represent (and diminish) the transcendent spiritual "truth" by transforming it into the tangible figures of "Popishe Maumetrie," even as the same puppets implicitly correspond to the "comon Sort" of people they are intended to "allure by pleasant Spectacle." This passage also clearly reveals a complex pattern of mutual appropriation between relatively more popular and elite forms of discourse and practice. Lambarde envisions a situation in which the priests appropriated something that was not quite "their" culture, and in which the townpeople then transformed the spectacle "exhibited" to their eyes into a site of cultural resistance. Onto the watchman-puppet they seem to have displaced precisely the fear and trembling that the show itself was presumably intended to

<hr>

[55] *Dictionarium Angliae Topographicum et Historicum: An Alphabetical Description of the Chief Places in England and Wales* (London, 1730), quoted in Young, *Drama of the Medieval Church*, 2:542–43.

evoke; and this ostensibly marginal but theatrically central figure finally re-emerges as "Jack Snacker of Wytney," a grotesque embodiment of carnivalesque comedy and civic profit. Lambarde, however, reappropriates the scene for wholly different purposes. His Protestant skepticism concedes the constructedness of the initial "Popish" appropriation even as his antiquarian nostalgia recontextualizes the ensuing popular resistance within his own relentlessly elite discourse. The passage thus instantiates the inextricable connection between the various modes of discourse and practice that it is also at pains to distinguish, and thus also represents in miniature the cultural process I consider in the chapters that follow.

Two

Authorship and Culture in Early Modern England

In the last few decades students of early modern literature have investigated its dynamic relation to a range of other social and cultural activities. In the rituals of kingship, in civic ceremonies and public executions, in carnivals and seasonal celebrations, even in the architecture and topography of London and its suburbs, critics have discovered patterns of meaning that shaped and were shaped by a wide range of early modern discourse—including, of course, the rich tradition of drama produced just before and just after 1600. Such work accords with the historical and cultural tendencies of recent literary theory, which have led many scholars to focus on the interactions of social practice and literary textuality and the interrelationship of canonical texts with relatively more popular modes of discourse. Yet scholarship of the early modern period has neglected an obvious target for such analysis: a whole alternative tradition of dramatic performance that thrived in the same years as the so-called literary drama. I refer, of course, to puppet theater, a mode of culture noted more frequently by early modern playwrights and pamphleteers than by modern students of the period. As I have suggested, the practical conditions of the puppet seem often to suggest or determine not just its abundant figural applications but also its reception. As an oral and ephemeral mode of performance puppet theater remains an elusive critical object, for one must consider the early modern puppet, as I do here, almost exclusively as reflected in texts whose own conditions both guarantee their availability for study and instantiate their "literary" status. More broadly, the relative neglect of early modern puppets within the contemporary retheorization of the Renaissance also confirms the cultural subordination to which puppetry was subjected in that period.

In this chapter I observe the discursive and theatrical appropriation of the puppet—as metaphor, metadramatic device, or discursive standard of reference—by writers who also define puppet theater as a mode of culture somehow "lower," less literary and more popular, than their own texts. In the first section I trace some of the outlines of the cultural landscape addressed throughout the chapter by considering the conventions and conditions of early modern puppet theater itself. In the second section I go on to consider how the puppet figures within the rhetorical construction of a particular vision of theatrical authorship, one grounded in the hierarchical view of representation that I have called the theological theater. Here I also begin to trace the frequent allusions to puppetry in the works of Ben Jonson, who is now commonly conceded to be a pivotal figure in the construction of authorship, and who proves to be the central figure of my investigation as well. In the third section I attempt perhaps my hardest task in this chapter: to sketch the intricate pattern of associations by which, in a wide range of early modern discourse, the puppet illuminates various forms of social difference and subordination, on the axes of both gender and class. Such associations I will suggest, merge with the hypothetical structure with which some contemporaries envision the process of histrionic embodiment, and collectively constitute a complex, multihierarchical system of representational, cultural, and social distinction. I conclude by applying these observations to Shakespeare's *Tempest* and Jonson's *Bartholomew Faire*, two roughly contemporaneous and subsequently canonical works which also appropriate the puppet as a central image and metadramatic device.

"In Despight of the Players":
Early Modern Puppetry and the "Popular" Voice

> . . . you shall see it your self, 'tis in this house, 'tis called a motion; there's first the Master of the motion, then the Master's Mate, the Mate's Consort, the Consort's Cabin-fellow, the Cabin-fellows Hangby, the Hangby's Man, the Man's Boy, the Boy's Page, the Page's Wench, and all these live upon the motion.
> —John Chettle and Henry Day, *The Blind Beggar of Bednal Green*

Tramplers of time, Motions of Fleete-streete, and Visions of Holborne.
—Thomas Middleton, *A Trick to Catch the Old One*

The writers I consider in this chapter had every reason to be familiar with puppet theater, which was a pervasive presence in the streets and market-places of early modern England. Historical records confirm that puppeteers, or "motion men," accompanied the jongleurs, jugglers, tumblers, minstrels, "histriones," "mimi," "ioculatores," "pleyers," "beare or bull bayters," and all the other itinerant entertainers who performed regularly in provincial towns and rural villages.[1] Shakespeare's Autolycus is a literary reimagining of these familiar social practices: an out-of-work servant who travels the countryside picking pockets and selling ballads, and who claims to have also been "an ape-bearer" and a puppeteer who "compass'd a motion of the Prodigal Son" (*The Winter's Tale* 4.3.95–97). Jonson's Lord Frampul, the Host of *The New Inne,* reminisces similarly about his younger days when he traveled with the

> Pipers, Filers, Rushers, Puppet-masters,
> Juglers, and Gipseys, all the sorts of Canters,
> And Colonies of beggars, Tumblers, Ape-carriers. (5.5.96–98)[2]

These itinerant puppeteers were also active in London at the yearly fair in Smithfield, on Holborn Bridge and Fleet Street in the heart of the legal dis-

---

[1] Peter Burke, *Popular Culture in Early Modern Europe* (New York: New York University Press, 1978), 94; see also 96–98 and 111 for other references to itinerant puppeteers. On the varieties of popular and itinerant entertainment in the early modern period, see also George Speaight, *The History of the English Puppet Theatre,* 2d ed. (London: Robert Hale, 1990), 53–57; and A. L. Beier, *Masterless Men: The Vagrancy Problem in England, 1560–1640* (London: Methuen, 1985), 96–99. The *Records of Early English Drama* series also records a thriving tradition of puppetry in the sixteenth century; see, among many other examples, the volumes *Herefordshire and Worcestershire,* ed. David N. Klausner (1990), 524; *Devon,* ed. John M. Watson (1986), 280; *Cumberland, Westmorland, Gloucester,* ed. Audrey Douglas and Peter Greenfield (1986), 308; *Coventry,* ed. R. W. Ingram (1981), 353; and *Cambridge,* ed. Alan H. Nelson, 2 vols. (1989), 1:710 (all volumes Toronto: University of Toronto Press).

[2] All quotations from Shakespeare are from *The Riverside Shakespeare,* ed. G. Blakemore Evans (Boston: Houghton Mifflin, 1974); all quotations from Jonson are from *Ben Jonson,* ed. C. H. Hereford and Percy Simpson, 11 vols. (Oxford: Clarendon Press, 1925–63). Citations are given parenthetically in the text, where possible by act, scene, and line number, otherwise by volume and page. When citing the Hereford and Simpson edition, I have silently modernized "i," "j," "u," "v," and scribal contractions, and have occasionally regularized speech prefixes.

trict, and at Paris Garden on Bankside, joining with a variety of other paratheatrical entertainers in what Peter Burke describes as "a nearly continuous performance."[3] The figural and theatrical meaning that the puppet evokes in early modern texts must thus derive in part from the obvious contrast between a drama of direct human representation and a theater of objects, each of which, by the turn of the seventeenth century, was performing in similar urban venues, and joining in a cultural field structured by mutual parody, allusion and influence.

The early modern puppet obviously emerges from that realm of social practice and discursive formulation which Bakhtin and many succeeding writers call the carnivalesque.[4] In light of the salutary warnings of critics such as Peter Stallybrass and Allon White—who point out how the Bakhtinian celebration of the carnival impulse itself "mystifies the conditions which determined the fair's existence"—I use the term in its simplest sense, to refer to discourse or practices that express a general sense of social license and a parodic mockery of accepted authority.[5] Most obviously, puppets were carnivalesque in that they were among the attractions to be found at the market fairs of early modern England. As we shall see, discourse either about the fair itself or specifically about puppets almost consistently invokes the other term in this conventional associative pair. More broadly, puppets also carnivalized the subject matter of the human stage, performing a mélange of biblical, historical, and conventional dramatic stories such as Jonah and the Whale, the Gunpowder Plot, and Doctor Faustus, mixed up with topical allusions, music and dance, and the kind of farcical violence that the mere materiality of the performing object seems always to invite. The fully realized puppet show included by Jonson in *Bartholomew Faire* (1614), which I will discuss in more detail later in this chapter, is a farcical version of Marlowe's "Hero and Leander," combined incongruously with the story of Damon and Pythias, and then further debased by recasting these classical characters as watermen and whores of contemporary London. Similarly, in Henry Chettle and John

[3] Peter Burke, "Popular Culture in Seventeenth-Century London," in *Popular Culture in Seventeenth-Century England*, ed. Barry Reay (New York: St. Martin's, 1985), 36–39; see also Speaight, *History of the English Puppet Theatre*, 56–60.

[4] See Mikhail Bakhtin, *Rabelais and His World*, trans. Helen Iswolsky (Bloomington: Indiana University Press, 1984). For discussions of the "carnivalesque" that follow and comment on Bakhtin's analysis, see Michael Bristol, *Carnival and Theater: Plebeian Culture and the Structure of Authority in Renaissance England* (New York: Methuen, 1985); Natalie Zemon Davis, "The Reasons of Misrule," in *Society and Culture in Early Modern France* (Stanford: Stanford University Press, 1975), 97–123; and Peter Stallybrass and Allon White, *The Politics and Poetics of Transgression* (Ithaca: Cornell University Press, 1986).

[5] Stallybrass and White, *The Politics and Poetics of Transgression*, 34.

Day's *Blind Beggar of Bednal Green* (1600), the rogue Canby gets temporary work as a puppeteer, and the audience briefly sees him in action, introducing the onstage spectators to a ludicrous mixture of pseudohistory and contemporary farce: "You shall likewise see the famous City of *Norwitch*, and the stabbing of *Julius Caesar* in the French Capitol by a sort of Dutch *Mesapotamians*. . . . You shall likewise see the amorous conceits and Love Songs betwixt Captain *Pod* of *Py-corner*, and Mrs. *Rump* of *Ram-Alley*, never described before. . . . Or if it please you shall see a stately combate betwixt *Tamberlayn* the Great, and the Duke of *Guyso* the less, perform'd on the *Olympick* Hills in *France*."[6]

This description, which pointedly mixes parodic versions of contemporary drama with the social marginality of urban locales such as "Py-corner" and "Ram-Alley," perhaps exaggerates the outlandish qualities of the puppet show for satiric effect. Whether as social observation or as parody, however, such a passage participates in the cultural construction of puppet theater as a debased version of the human stage—which is here implicitly assumed to be the "original" source of plays about Julius Caesar, Tamburlaine, or the Duke of Guise. In its content and conditions alike, the early modern puppet theater is thus an obvious example of the "two-way traffic" between so-called high and low forms of culture.[7] On the one hand, puppet performance adapts and carnivalizes the material of the human stage. On the other hand, Elizabethan and Jacobean drama was itself, as scholars have long recognized, a flexible synthesis of popular and learned modes of performance, and the playwrights who created it sometimes exploited the conventions of puppet theater for rhetorical or theatrical effect.[8]

[6] John Day [and Henry Chettle], *The Blind Beggar of Bednal Green* (London, 1659), G2r. Other texts of the period similarly mention puppet shows named for cities. Lantern Leatherhead in *Bartholomew Faire*, mentions puppet shows of "Jerusalem . . . Ninive . . . the citty of *Norwich*, and *Sodom* and *Gomorrah*" (5.1.8–10). Asper, in the induction of *Every Man out of his Humour*, refers to "motions" of "the new *London, Rome*, or *Nineveh*" (164). Hereford and Simpson speculate that these were puppet versions of plays from the regular stage, "Ninive" being based on Thomas Lodge and Robert Greene's *Looking Glasse, for London and England* (which recounts in part the story of Jonah and the Whale), Rome being based on *Julius Caesar*, and so forth (*Ben Jonson*, 9:420). This explanation seems to be supported by the Citizen's reference in Francis Beaumont's *Knight of the Burning Pestle* (1607) to a show called "Ninivie" which his wife claims told "the story of Joan and the wall"—presumably a mistake for Jonah and the Whale (3.289). Speaight, by contrast, suggests that the city shows may have been exhibits "painted in aerial perspective like Visscher's familiar view of London," with some kind of movable figures (*History of the English Puppet Theatre*, 57).
[7] Burke, *Popular Culture in Early Modern Europe*, 58.
[8] Among the works that address the popular roots of early modern drama, see S. L. Bethell, *Shakespeare and the Popular Dramatic Tradition* (1944; rpt. New York: Octagon, 1970); Bristol, *Carnival and*

Thus, puppets are typically carnivalesque in their literal social conditions, in their presumed subordination to the human drama they parody, and in the way their conventional protruding noses, humped backs, and wooden movements join to form an iconic image of what Bakhtin calls the "grotesque body."[9] By extension, the poets of the human stage construe the puppet theater as a crude and parodic Other, a terminus of that hierarchy of cultural sophistication that resembles and derives from a master system of representation similarly conceived as a descent of primary to secondary, "truth" to image. "A man cannot imagine that thing so foolish, or rude, but will find, and enjoy . . . a Reader, or Spectator," Ben Jonson complains in *Discoveries*. "The Puppets are seene now in despight of the Players" (8:582). Here, Jonson confirms the contemporary popularity of puppet theater even as he opposes the performing object to a human drama assumed to be both socially and aesthetically "higher." Correspondingly, in the hypothetical structure of a theological theater, the puppet would be to the player as the player is to the author: one step closer to formless materiality, and one step farther from that postulated if irretrievable "truth" from which is said to spring the multitudinous re-creations of theatrical performance. Located figurally at the bottom of the hierarchy of representation and literally in the marginal social spheres of carnival, fairground, and marketplace, the puppet could be seen at once as ontologically, culturally, and socially low.

At the fair itself the puppet was also a cultural site in which histrionic illusion merged with the commercial power of the marketplace. As the parodic quality of puppetry corresponds to the general license of the carnival experience, so does the puppet's social existence as a tangible iconic figure link it to the other unusual, luxurious, or fetishistic objects that were exhibited, bartered, and sold at the market fairs of early modern England—toys, "hobbyhorses," "bartholomew babies" or dolls, gilt gingerbread figures, religious paintings, and so forth. In the middle of the sixteenth century, Sir Thomas Smith in his *Discourse of the Commonweal* argued against the import into England of luxury consumer goods, listing as examples "glasses, puppets,

---

Theater; and Robert Weimann, *Shakespeare and the Popular Tradition in the Theater: Studies in the Social Dimension of Dramatic Form and Function* (Baltimore: Johns Hopkins University Press, 1978).

[9] On the grotesque body, see Bakhtin, *Rabelais and His World,* esp. pp. 25–27. Without knowing precisely what English puppets of the early seventeenth century looked like, we can assume they contributed to, and thus probably resembled, the celebrated and familiar later heroes of the European puppet stage such as Polichinelle, Casper, and Punch. For illustrations of European puppets, in addition to books otherwise cited, see René Simmen, *The World of Puppets* (New York: Thomas T. Crowell, 1972).

rattles, and such things" (69).[10] By the seventeenth century the ancient cultural associations of magic or ritual efficacy that cling to dolls, puppets, and iconic images were in effect being repackaged for bourgeois consumption. An anonymous pamphlet of 1641 describes Bartholomew Fair in its title as "a faire of wares, and all to please your mind." In the text the author recalls his entrance to the fairgrounds, where he was initially struck by the commodification of the religious image: "First let me enter in to Christ Church Cloysters, which are now hung so full of pictures, that you would take that place or rather mistake it for Saint *Peters* in *Rome*, onely this is the difference, these there are set up for worship, these here are for sale." He goes on to enumerate, in a passage frequently cited by historians of popular culture, the rich variety of amusements available at the fair: "Here a Knave in a fooles coate, with a trumpet sounding, or on a drumme beating, invites you and would faine perswade you to see his puppets; there, a rogue like a wild woodman, or in an antick shape like an Incubus, desire your company to view his motion: on the other side Hocus Pocus with three yards of tape or ribbin in's hand, shewing his art of Legerdemaine."[11] One observes quite clearly how a sense of magic and social alterity—the puppet master as "wild woodman" or "Incubus"—is at once invoked and domesticated. The puppet's cultural and etymological roots in idolatry, witchcraft, and image magic seem to be at once expressed and repressed. The persuasion of the carnival huckster merges with the "desire" of a spectator who reconstrues his own evident presence at the fair into the absent "you" of narrative convention.

Throughout the seventeenth century and well beyond, the performing object would continue to evoke its ancient associations of the magical and the monstrous, even as it also descended into the nostalgic comfort of bourgeois domesticity. In the late eighteenth century a visitor to Stourbridge Fair in Cambridgeshire was still observing "Puppet Shews" in literal and rhetorical proximity to practitioners of "Legerdemain," "Mountebanks, Wild Beasts, Monsters," and "Giants."[12] William Wordsworth, in a celebrated passage, similarly observed at Bartholomew Fair

[10] *A Discourse of the Commonweal of this Realm of England,* ed. Mary Dewar (Charlottesville: University Press of Virginia, 1969), 69.

[11] *Bartholomew Faire or Variety of Fancies, where you may find a faire of wares, and all to please your mind* (London, 1641). This brief pamphlet is cited nearly in its entirety in Henry Morley's *Memoirs of Bartholomew Fair* (London, 1859), 187, and in John Brand, *Observations on the Popular Antiquities of Great Britain,* 3 vols. (London, 1849), 2:459–60.

[12] Robert W. Malcolmson, *Popular Recreations in English Society, 1700–1850* (Cambridge: Cambridge University Press, 1973), 20.

The Bust that speaks, and moves its goggling eyes,
The wax-work, Clock-work, all the marvelous craft
Of modern Merlins, wild Beasts, Puppet shows.

(*The Prelude* 7.682–86)

I want to emphasize the puppet's recurrent centrality among these bourgeois observations of the monstrous and magical world of carnival. The fair would persist as a site for the ineluctable expression of the purest and crudest forms of corporeal presence (roast meat, intoxication, the "open" grotesque body) and a site for re-presentation in virtually all of its multitudinous social shapes: dolls, puppets, theater, magic tricks, images of every kind. This curious symmetry, on the level of social practice, resembles and corresponds to the puppet's discursive association with both crude corporeality and histrionic illusion. The latter, I also suggest, exerts a certain pressure on the former by adding to the cultural equation precisely that (apparent) spirituality which is otherwise abnegated within the conventional image of the carnivalesque puppet. The same binary model that paradoxically sees the flesh as *inanimate* (in contrast to the animating "breath" or "spirit" of life), and that to Bakhtin and other scholars is overturned in the festive inversions and corporeal indulgence of carnival, yields to the puppet a certain paradoxical purity—a freedom from the flesh—in contrast to that drama of living actors which contemporary puppeteers sometimes derisively call "meat theater." Much later in Western culture puppets would often be extolled as exemplary vehicles of performance precisely and paradoxically because they are free from the supposedly paralyzing effect of self-consciousness on corporeal being. This cultural reversal itself confirms how the puppet (like carnival itself) would continue to reflect for bourgeois culture what Stallybrass and White call "its own uneasy oscillation between high and low."[13]

"Puppets That Speake from Our Mouths": Authors and Objects on the Early Modern Stage

If you please to conferre with our Author, by atturney, you may, sir: our proper selfe here, stands for him.

—Ben Jonson, *Cynthia's Revels*

---

[13] Stallybrass and White, *The Politics and Poetics of Transgression*, 31.

Writing in 1592, at the end of his life, the playwright Robert Greene complained to "those Gentlemen his Quondam acquaintance, that spend their wits in making Plaies," usually identified as Christopher Marlowe, Thomas Nashe, and George Peele, about the new generation of playwrights then beginning to write for the popular stage. Greene's bit of rhetorical grumbling would become one of the single most frequently cited of Elizabethan texts:

> Based minded men al three of you, if by my miserie ye be not warned: for unto none of you (like me) sought those burres to cleave: those Puppits (I meane) that speake from our mouths, those Anticks garnisht in our colours. . . . Yes trust them not: for there is an upstart Crow, beautified with our feathers, that with his *Tygers hart wrapt in a Players hide*, supposes he is as well able to bumbast out a blanke verse as the best of you: and being an absolute *Johannes fac totum*, is in his own conceit, the only Shake-scene in a countrie.[14]

This passage, commonly acknowledged to be the first printed reference to William Shakespeare, has attracted considerable commentary over the last century. Scholars still debate the terms of Greene's attack, which remain ambiguous despite the violence of the rhetoric. Is Greene charging Shakespeare with stealing his own work, and is the passage evidence, as some have argued, that the youthful Shakespeare began his career as a reviser of existing plays? Or is Greene simply attacking the presumption of a mere player now assuming the role of poet? Even the infamous image of the "upstart Crow" makes sense as an expression of either accusation. The phrase alludes either to the fable of Rocius and the cobbler's crow who was taught, like a parrot, to speak, or to Horace's image of a crow "divested of its plundered lustre," a metaphor for literary plagiarism.[15] In any case, these two different accusations are implicitly related in that both refer to trangressions of the presumed sovereignty and propriety of theatrical authorship.

A few lines earlier, correspondingly, Greene compares Shakespeare and the

[14] Robert Greene, *The Life and Complete Works in Prose and Verse of Robert Greene*, ed. Alexander B. Grosart, 15 vols. (1881–1886; rpt. New York: Russell & Russell, 1966), 12:144. All subsequent references to Greene's work are to this edition, and are cited parenthetically in the text.

[15] For a summary of the debate, extending from Edmund Malone to Dover Wilson, over the significance of Greene's passage to Shakespeare's biography, see D. Allen Carroll, "Greene's 'Upstart Crow' Passage: A Survey of Commentary," *Research Opportunities in Renaissance Drama* 28 (1985): 111–27. On Greene's metaphor, see J. Dover Wilson, "Malone and the Upstart Crow," *Shakespeare Survey* 4 (1951): 65–67; and S. Schoenbaum, *William Shakespeare: A Compact Documentary Life*, 2d ed. (New York: Oxford University Press, 1987), 152–53.

popular playwrights collectively to "Puppits . . . that speake from our mouths." This metaphor also makes sense as an expression of either one of Greene's two possible accusations. Just as a literal puppet is an inanimate figure invested with and embodying the words and gestures of its "master," so Shakespeare might be considered a puppet because, whether as player or plagiarist, the voice of some external, absent author speaks through him. Greene's metaphor thus seems to depend on a shared understanding in his readers and fellow playwrights that representation is hierarchical, and that the theater is accordingly theological in the sense I have described. A few pages earlier in the same pamphlet, the love-struck Lucanio had been compared to "a plaier that being out of his part at his first entrance, is faine to have the booke to speake what he should performe" (12:116–17). Just so, Greene's satire of the popular playwrights assumes a theater in which a great gulf is fixed between the speaking player and the authorial Word. In other words, Greene is complaining that the mere "anticks," the interpretive slaves, are threatening the representational hierarchy by presuming to the role of author. In Shakespeare's case the apparent presumption of a player turned playwright (who thus subverts the power relations of the theological theater) corresponds to the social progress by which this "upstart" from the provinces now "supposes he is as well able to bumbast out a blanke verse as the best of you." The puppet or performing object thus serves as a figure both for theatrical authorship as Greene envisions it and for the hierarchy of social distinction assumed to be mutually transparent with the former.

Considered in the context of its actual conventions, conditions, and cultural associations, the puppet is a strikingly multivalent metaphor within this polemic of authorship and social distinction. In one sense Greene's metaphor calls on the puppet's conceptual status as a merely inanimate object, formless materiality available for the mastering form of authorial "inspiration." The players are puppets "that speake from *our* mouths," vehicles or vessels for the creator's voice. In another sense, however, Greene's satire also depends on the puppet's cultural lowness and social marginality, attributes here implicitly construed as analogous to its histrionic passivity and inanimate materiality. Elsewhere in the pamphlet, for example, Greene places the actual conditions of contemporary puppet theater within a spectrum of theatrical and paratheatrical performance. The semiautobiographical character Roberto encounters a player who appears by his "outward habit" to be "a gentleman of great living" (12:131). This player proceeds to boast of what seems to have been a long and successful theatrical career: "I am as famous for Delphrigus, and the king of Fairies, as ever was any of my time. The twelve labors of *Hercules* have

I terribly thundred on the stage. . . . Nay more (quoth the player) I can serve to make a prettie speech . . . for it was I that pende the Moral of mans wit . . . and for seven yeeres space was absolute interpreter of the puppets (12:131–32)."[16] These and many other similar references reveal that in Renaissance puppetry a kind of showman or "interpreter" provided the voices of and bantered comically with his cast of artificial players. The convention of the puppet interpreter—who serves quite literally, in the words of Jonson's Lantern Leatherhead, as "the mouth of 'hem all," a singular voice manifesting itself in histrionic multiplicity—suggests more specifically how the performing object could evoke the hypothetical structure of theatrical authorship. With a kind of inevitable figural duplicity, puppets are low, popular, and carnivalesque, and thus inevitably associated with what Michael Bristol calls "the promiscuous creativity of mimetic forms, with their dispersion of authority among multiple voices." Yet, in their passive materiality, their availability for mastering authorial form, they may also ironically and incongruously epitomize the opposite, those "philosophically unified forms that reveal a singular, sovereign voice."[17]

Once again, however, this philosophic or merely conceptual opposition converges, in Greene's rhetoric, with highly specific and implicitly related oppositions of culture and class; and the hypothetical power relations of a theological theater reveal themselves to be both mirror and consequence of much larger assumptions about social distinction. The player-poet whom Roberto meets is costumed as a "gentleman," as though such status were merely one more role instead of something practically achieved through his financial success in the theatrical enterprise. Thus, Greene's satiric image of the player as a literal puppeteer (who composes for the puppet stage the kind of morality play that had long been out of date on the human stage) corresponds to his later metaphoric image of player-as-puppet. That Greene himself was in fact a thoroughly commercial author of journalistic ephemera and collaborative popular plays, and who was moreover famous for the bohemian dissoluteness of his life, merely confirms that his implicit theatrical model is a construct upheld by rhetorical pretense rather than a summary of the institution's real conditions. Nearing his own death and, one assumes, genu-

---

[16] Professional players sometimes did apparently resort to puppetry in lieu of better professional opportunities. Gerald Eades Bentley records one case in which two minor players, William Cooke and Fluellen Morgan, got in trouble with provincial authorities for putting on puppet plays with a license leased from another player. Gerald Eades Bentley, *The Jacobean and Caroline Stage* (Oxford: Clarendon Press, 1941–68), 2:413, 480.

[17] Bristol, *Carnival and Theater*, 21.

inely bitter about this grammar school boy from the provinces now supplanting him on the commercial stage, Greene turns to the discursive terminology of an authorial ideal that had little connection to his actual social position. His celebrated pamphlet is, however, just one of many rhetorical sites in which an ideal of authorial sovereignty would be imposed on a theatrical enterprise whose real conditions and social relations it has seldom accurately described. A variety of recent theoretical and scholarly work converges in a consensus that the "author" is a cultural construction of the early modern period, a concept that replaced the improvisational, communal, and anonymous modes of literary production that prevailed in the Middle Ages. Both authorship itself and the related belief in the text as "a line of words releasing a single 'theological' meaning (the message of the Author-God)," Roland Barthes concludes in a celebrated essay, were the product of "the personal faith of the Reformation" and of the "capitalist ideology" which exalts the individual over the collective.[18] Michel Foucault, writing in retrospective commentary on this foundational insight, agrees that "the coming into being of the notion of 'author' constitutes the privileged moment of *individualization* in the history of ideas, knowledge, literature, philosophy, and the sciences." Foucault dates the construction of authorship as a literary phenomenon somewhat imprecisely to the "seventeenth or eighteenth century" and suggests that this belief in authorial singularity emerged just as the discourses of science were, conversely, beginning to be accepted in what he calls "the anonymity of an established . . . truth."[19] Many other critics have debated how and when the notions of authorship that still largely prevail in Western culture were codified.[20] In the broadest of terms authorship increasingly seems to have had no single or simple historical trajectory but instead appears to be a phenomenon constantly re-created at different historical mo-

[18] Roland Barthes, "The Death of the Author," in *Image, Music, Text* (New York: Farrar, Straus and Giroux, 1974), 142–43, 146.
[19] Michel Foucault, "What Is an Author?" in *The Foucault Reader*, ed. Paul Rabinow (New York: Pantheon, 1984), 101, 109.
[20] Raymond Williams, in *Marxism and Literature* (Oxford: Oxford University Press, 1977), suggests that "in its modern form the concept of 'literature' did not emerge earlier than the eighteenth century. . . . Yet the conditions for its emergence had been developing since the Renaissance" (46). Stephen Greenblatt, in his influential *Renaissance Self-Fashioning: From More to Shakespeare* (Chicago: University of Chicago Press, 1980), and Richard Helgerson in *Self-Crowned Laureates: Spenser, Jonson, Milton and the Literary System* (Berkeley: University of California Press, 1983), discuss how literary authorship became an entwined personal and social goal for a variety of Renaissance writers. Bristol, in *Carnival and Theater*, pursues the interrelationship of the carnivalesque with various modes of early modern discourse and describes how the concept of "a singular, sovereign voice" emerges out of the "diverse and energetic popular culture" of early modern England (21–22).

ments. I would argue, however, that the construction of authorship had a particular urgency and specificity in the early modern theater, a mode of culture that only in this period was emerging from conditions of itinerancy and improvisation to define itself as "legitimate" and its texts as "literature."[21]

In the same period, however, the real structures of financial ownership and authority in the theater continued to diverge from the rhetorical and philosophical vision of a theological theater. Moreover, the process of histrionic impersonation was susceptible to a variety of competing figural interpretations. If the players could be seen (in the terms of the nascent vision of authorship) as puppetlike slaves of a sovereign poet, wholly mastered by authorial intention, they could also be seen, especially by opponents of the theater, as "masterless men"—rogues and vagabonds standing outside the normative social hierarchy that resembles (but here also contradicts) the representational hierarchy.[22] Poets, from about the end of the sixteenth century, were increasingly demanding a figural sovereignty over text and performance, insisting that the players "speak no more than is set down for them" (*Hamlet* 3.2.39), and complaining about the degradation of dramatic texts in performance. The maintenance of a proper representational hierarchy within the theater was also commonly linked to the maintenance of social order and degree. In the words of the academic authors of *The Returne from Parnassus* (part 2, 1603), professional players are merely "leaden spouts / That nought down vent but what they do receive." This representational ventriloquism, correspondingly, tends to overturn the hierarchy of property and power: "With mouthing words that better wits have framed, / They purchase lands, and now Esquires are made."[23] Here, as in Greene's famous passage, players are "upstarts" in that the financial success of the theatrical enterprise allows them to subvert on a practical level their figural status as puppets of a sovereign author.

But however much the dramatic poets of early modern England attempted rhetorically to maintain their preeminent status within the theoretical do-

[21] In the 1590s, writes Richard Helgerson, "the players' theater was becoming what retrospectively looks like an authors' theater." See Richard Helgerson, *Forms of Nationhood: The Elizabethan Writing of History* (Chicago: University of Chicago Press, 1992), 199.

[22] Cf. Jean Christophe Agnew's similar contrast between Hobbes's concept of the "artificial" person—which meant a person subject to another's authority, and which could thus include players insofar as they were "mere hirelings"—and William Prynne's Puritan vision of players as artificial "precisely because they could claim no author, contractualism being an insufficient ground of authority." Jean Christophe Agnew, *Worlds Apart: The Market and the Theater in Anglo-American Thought, 1550–1750* (Cambridge: Cambridge University Press, 1986), 99–100.

[23] *The Returne from Parnassus, or The Scourge of Simony* (London, 1606), G2v (4.4); G3v (5.1).

main of representation, in concrete practical terms, as several recent scholars concur, the poets "were the servants of the players, in economic servitude to them." That is, "the authority represented by the text [was] that of the company, the owners, not that of the playwright, the author." And on stage, plays were "represented by the speaking actor as 'ours,' the possession and, indeed, the product of the actors."[24] Here again, however, these practical conditions of ownership were themselves susceptible to rhetorical inversion for different reasons. Because plays and texts could on some occasions offend the great and powerful—because, that is, authorship was in one sense a form of authority and in another sense subject to it—both poets and players were sometimes at pains to *renounce* ownership of the theatrical text. George Chapman, responding to accusations about the political content of his work, observed, "I see not myne owne Plaies; nor carrie the Actors Tongue in my mouthe."[25] The epilogue of a 1632 revival at court of Marlowe's *Jew of Malta* asks the "dread Sovereign" to remember that "if aught here offend your ear or sight, / We only act, and speak, what others write."[26] Sometimes, in other words, it suited the poets to envision themselves as the puppet masters of a theological theater; and sometimes it suited the players to envision themselves as merely passive vehicles of authorial intention.

One thus observes a certain anxiety about individual agency and institutional authority manifest in the literal conditions of the poets and performers of early modern drama. The image of the puppet—which epitomizes histrionic passivity and serves as a "living" image of theatrical illusion—seems both to assuage and to incite such anxieties in the period's discourse. As many scholars have suggested, a central figure in the early modern construction of theatrical authorship was Ben Jonson, who also reveals, throughout his career, a virtual obsession with the performing object.[27] There is even the

[24] The first quotation is from Andrew Gurr, *The Shakespearean Stage, 1574–1642*, 3d ed. (Cambridge: Cambridge University Press, 1991), 19; the second is from Stephen Orgel, "What Is a Text?" *Research Opportunities in Renaissance Drama* 26 (1981): 4; and the third is from Joseph Lowenstein, "The Script in the Marketplace," in *Representing the English Renaissance*, ed. Stephen Greenblatt (Berkeley: University of California Press, 1988), 266.

[25] Quoted in A. R. Braunmuller and Michael Hattaway, eds. *The Cambridge Companion to English Renaissance Drama* (Cambridge: Cambridge University Press, 1990), 57.

[26] Christopher Marlowe, *The Jew of Malta*, ed. Richard W. Van Fossen (Lincoln: University of Nebraska Press, 1964), 113.

[27] On Jonson and authorship, see Bristol, *Carnival and Theater*, 117, 201; Helgerson, *Self-Crowned Laureates*; Richard C. Newton, "Jonson and the (Re)invention of the Book," in *Classic and Cavalier: Essays on Jonson and the Sons of Jonson*, ed. Claude J. Summers and Ted-Larry Pebworth (Pittsburgh: University of Pittsburgh Press, 1982), 31–58; David Riggs, *Ben Jonson: A Life* (Cambridge: Harvard University Press, 1989); and Don E. Wayne, "Drama and Society in the Age of Jonson: An Alternative View," *Re-*

thinnest of historical evidence to suggest that the youthful Jonson may have had some personal experience as a writer for or performer with puppets. About 1601 Thomas Dekker brought the so-called War of the Theatres to its culmination with his *Satiromastix, or The Untrussing of the Humorous Poet*, which presents a thinly veiled caricature of Jonson as the character Horace— his own self-chosen persona from *The Poetaster* of the previous year. At one point in the play, as Jonson/Horace attempts to defend himself against a relentless tide of mockery, one of his tormentors responds: "Hold, silence, the puppet-teacher speaks" (4.3.175), a cryptic reference that might suggest Jonson's involvement with literal puppet theater.[28] Some recent critics have also speculated that Jonson (like his character Lord Frampul, the host of *The New Inne*) may at some point have tried "to turne Puppet-master / And travell with Yong Goose, the Motion-man" (1.3.61–62).[29] The biographical evidence is thin at best, but Jonson does demonstrate throughout his career a detailed knowledge of the conventions and conditions of puppetry, and he alludes to performing objects of all kinds in nearly every one of his major works: in his plays, his epigraphs, and his unfinished work of literary theory, *Timber, or Discoveries*. I will have occasion to return to Jonson periodically throughout this chapter, and will also close with a detailed analysis of *Bartholomew Faire*—which includes, of course, the most extensive and self-conscious literary appropriation of puppet theater in the canon of Western drama.

As I have suggested in general terms, puppet theater becomes for Jonson a paradigm of low, popular culture in its subordination to a drama newly conceived of as literary, and of histrionic performance itself in its subordination to the dramatic text. In *Discoveries* Jonson not only contrasts puppet theater to a human drama assumed to be both socially and aesthetically higher, but also uses it as a corresponding metaphor for "Imposture," that "specious thing" that "is ever asham'd of the light." He writes: "A Puppet-play must be shadow'd, and seene in the darke: For draw the Curtaine, *Et sordet gesticulatio*" (8:570).[30] Here and elsewhere, Jonson's figural use of the performing ob-

---

naissance Drama 13 (1982): 103–28.

[28] *The Dramatic Works of Thomas Dekker*, ed. Fredson Bowers (New York: Cambridge University Press, 1953). William Gifford, Jonson's nineteenth-century editor, suggested that Jonson merely incorporated into *Bartholomew Faire* an actual puppet show that he himself had written years earlier. See also Frances Teague, *The Curious History of Bartholomew Faire* (Lewisburg, Pa.: Bucknell University Press, 1985), 19–20.

[29] See Riggs, *Ben Jonson*, 306; Teague, *Curious History of Bartholomew Faire*, 24; and C. G. Thayer, *Ben Jonson: Studies in the Plays* (Norman: University of Oklahoma Press, 1963), 230.

[30] That is, the playing appears mean or sordid. Thomas Elyot's *Dictionary* (London, 1538) defines the word *gesticulator* as "he that playeth with puppetts." Jonson in *The Poetaster* uses the same word to refer

ject evokes the representational hierarchy of what Jonas Barish calls the "Christian-Platonic-Stoic tradition," a hierarchy in which "likenesse is alwayes on this side Truth" (*Discoveries* 8:590).[31] But to survey Jonson's many references to puppets throughout his works is also to recognize that his profoundly hierarchical concepts of theater and society never quite conceal the precariousness of his own position within a theater that was theological only in theory, and a society that only inconsistently rewarded him in ways he deemed appropriate.[32]

As early as *Every Man out of his Humour* (1599), Jonson seizes on the puppet as a central metaphor in a play that also announces his literary ambition. Here Jonson associates the puppet at once with the characters, the players, and the audience—all three crucially subordinate to himself as author, and all three inextricably entwined within the intricate metadramatic design of the play as a whole.[33] In the opening character sketches (which Jonson added to the text of the published quarto version), he describes Sogliardo, one of the comic butts of the play, as "an essentiall Clowne . . . [who] comes up every Terme to learne to take Tabacco, and see new Motions" (3:425). In the play itself Sogliardo verifies this description, at one point exclaiming: "They say, there's a new Motion of the city of *Niniveh*, with Jonas, and the whale, to be seene at Fleetbridge" (2.3.146–48). Earlier, however, Sogliardo himself had been compared to "one of these motions, in a great antique clock" (2.1.6). Later in the play as well, Sogliardo and Shift demonstrate one of the affectations of urban life they have acquired in the course of the play, announcing their intention to affect classical names for each other:

> *Sogliardo.* I, he is my Pylades, and I am his Orestes: how like you the conceit?
> *Carlo.* O, it's an old stale enterlude device: No, I'le give you names my selfe, looke you, he shall be your Judas, and you shall bee his Elder tree, to hang on.

---

to a particular kind of exaggerated theatrical performance, attacking his fellow satiric playwrights Marston and Dekker by questioning whether there is "any man so vile, / To act the crimes, these Whippers reprehend / Or what their servile apes gesticulate" ("To the Reader," 54–56, 4:319).

[31] Jonas Barish, *The Anti-Theatrical Prejudice* (Berkeley: University of California Press, 1981), 143, 135.

[32] This basic point, which I approach by way of Jonson's recurrent figural use of the puppet, is made in general terms by Don E. Wayne in "Drama and Society in the Age of Jonson: An Alternative View," *Renaissance Drama* 13 (1982): 103–28.

[33] On Jonsonian metadrama in this play and elsewhere, see Robert N. Watson, *Ben Jonson's Parodic Strategy: Literary Imperialism in the Comedies* (Cambridge: Harvard University Press, 1987), esp. 47–79.

Macilente. Nay, rather, let him be captaine Pod, and this his *Motion*;
for he does nothing but shew him.

(4.5.56–63)

(Captain Pod was apparently a real London puppeteer active in the late sixteenth century whom Jonson and other writers mention frequently, and
whose name was evidently familiar to the London theatrical audience.)[34]
Throughout the play, in other words, Jonson suggests that his comic characters are at once devoted spectators of puppet theater and themselves metaphoric puppets. Thus, he not only satirizes a particular kind of theatrical
taste as a distinct form of social behavior but also, correspondingly, allows
the performing object to convey its double association of cultural lowness
and social subordination.

Sogliardo is also, of course, a paradigm of the Jonsonian "humour" character, created by reference to that concept of comic psychology which the
fictional author in the play's induction describes at length. Jonson/Asper suggests that the word "humour, originally referring to the four bodily fluids,
"choller, melancholy, flegme, and bloud," which were believed to be the
causes of human personality and behavior,

> may, by *Metaphore,* apply it selfe
> Unto the generall disposition:
> As when some one peculiar quality
> Doth so possesse a man, that it doth draw
> All his affects, his spirits, and his powers,
> In their confluctions, all to runne one way.
>
> (Ind. 103–8)

There is something distinctly puppetlike about this Jonsonian "humour," which
he defines here as a particular form of focused, single-minded, and unbalanced
behavior, the consequence and index of a particular corporeal "quality" that
"possesses" and wholly masters the "spirits" and "powers" of the individual.

---

[34] Captain Pod is mentioned in *Bartholomew Faire* (5.1.8) as the master of Lantern Leatherhead, and
also in Jonson's Epigraphs 97 and 129. He is also mentioned as a character in the puppet show described
in *The Blind Beggar of Bednal Green* (G2). Thomas Dekker and George Wilkins, in *Jests to make you Merie*
(1607), refer to "*Bankes* his horse" (a famous "talking" animal act), "the *Baboones*," and "captain *Pold* [*sic*]
with his motion." *The Non-Dramatic Works of Thomas Dekker,* ed. Alexander B. Grosart (New York: Russell & Russell, 1962), 2:317. All further references to Dekker's pamphlets are from this edition, and are
cited parenthetically in the text.

Elsewhere, Jonson uses the puppet more specifically as a metaphor for "humourous" behavior thus conceived, and calls on some of the distinct cultural associations of the puppet in early modern discourse which I have observed. In Epigraph 88, "On English Mounsieur," for example, Jonson specifically invokes the conventional binarism of flesh and spirit that underlies his psychological theory of character:

> Would you beleeve, when you this Mounsieur see,
> That his whole body should speake *french*, not he?
> . . . is it some *french* statue? No: 't doth move,
> And stoupe, and cringe. O, then it needs must prove
> The new *french* taylors motion, monthly made,
> Daily to turne in Paul's and helpe the trade.
>
> (8:56)

Here, in a spiral of interrelated meanings, Jonson envisions the frenchified fop as a kind of mannequin or tailor's dummy, and thus as a figural "puppet" in two distinct senses: a passive tool used by the tailor to "help the trade," and an effeminate, doll-like figure whom the tailor dresses and adorns. The same "motion" that proves the courtier to be alive and declares him no mere "French statue," also confirms his commodification and social subjugation. Similarly, in Epigraph 98 Jonson asks:

> See you yond' Motion? Not the old *Fa-ding*,
> Nor Captayne Pod, nor yet the *Eltham*-thing;
> But one more rare, and in the case so new:
> His cloke with orient velvet quite lin'd through,
> His rosie tyes and garters so ore-blowne,
> By his each glorious parcell to be knowne!
>
> (8:62)[35]

Here again Jonson seems to be using the image of the "motion" or puppet to evoke at once the metaphoric sense of a doll-like effeminacy and a corresponding but different sense of empty, passive materiality.

---

[35] A "fading" is an Irish jig; the "Eltham-thing" was a kind of clockwork automaton claimed to be a perpetual motion machine which was exhibited to great acclaim in the early seventeenth century. The latter is also alluded to in *Epicoene* (5.3.63). See Hereford and Simpson's note to the latter passage (*Ben Jonson*, 10:43–44) for several other Continental and English references to the device.

At the end of the induction to *Every Man out of his Humour*, Jonson/Asper turns his satiric gaze on the audience, envisioning a particular kind of affected and falsely judicious spectator who

> Sits with his armes thus wreath'd, his hat pull'd here,
> Cryes meaw, and nods, then shakes his empty head,
> Will shew more several motions in his face,
> Than the new *London, Rome,* or *Nineveh.*
>
> (161–64)

The puppetlike "motions" of the spectatorial gaze betray its "empty" corporeality, the lack of those inner "motions" which the spectator's carefully chosen gestures are intended to suggest. By contrast, the "attentive auditors" for whom Asper (and Jonson) hopes to write will use the play to "feed their understanding parts." For them, says Asper, "Ile prodigally spend my selfe, / And speake away my spirit into ayre" (Ind. 204–5). Jonson here rhapsodically describes the dynamics of a hypothetical theater in which authorial inspiration flows into the breath of the histrionic voice and, from there, "in-spires" the auditor. As Jonson describes it, however, the author who claims to expend himself selflessly in the histrionic process, melting into invention, speaking himself into air, in so doing also fills the puppetlike bodies of his auditors with the mastering spirit of his own authorial design. If the affected and false spectator is like a puppet in his apparent gestural manifestation of an illusory inner spirit, the true spectator is equally puppetlike in that passive readiness for "profit" and "understanding" which the Jonsonian vision of authorship demands.

Jonson's own position in this hypothetical process remains suspended between explicit self-abnegation and a theoretical ideal of authorial mastery, the latter obviously corresponding more closely to his practical aspirations. In the astonishing final lines of *Every Man out of his Humour*, the character Macilente (played by Asper, the authorial figure of the induction) almost literally empties himself of the animating "spirit" that determines his character, even as he similarly dismisses the puppetlike objects of his satiric "envy" into the mere materiality of nonbeing:

> Now is my soul at peace.
> I am as emptie of all envie now,
> As they of merit to be envied at.

My humour (like a flame) no longer lasts
Than it hath stuffe to feed it, and their folly,
Being now rak't up in their repentant ashes,
Affords no ampler subject to my spleene.
. . . .
It grieves me
To thinke they have a being.
. . . .
But let them vanish, vapors.
(5.11.54–65)

The actual players, and the characters they represent, are equally puppetlike, the former as vehicles of authorial intention, the latter as mere containers for the humorous "vapors" exorcised through satiric ridicule.

If literal "playing," "humourous" behavior, and theatrical spectatorship are thus linked to one another as forms of imitation, so are all three similarly linked to authorship itself. In the induction Asper denounces:

the monstrousnesse of time,
Where every servile imitating spirit
(Plagu'd with an itching leprosie of wit)
In a meere halting fury, strives to fling
His ulc'rous body in the *Thespian* spring,
And streight leap's forth a Poet! but as lame
As Vulcan, or the founder of *Cripple-gate.*
(66–72)

Here Jonson/Asper envisions the negative and pernicious form of author-ship as corporeal deformity in lines that again implicitly evoke that binar-ism of flesh and spirit essential to his general view of character. He also suggests that the false author is "imitative" in multiple, involuted senses: (1) because, in that most conventional of Renaissance literary metaphors, he attempts to "mirror nature"; (2) because he writes for histrionic players; and (3) most of all because he aspires to be like (and hence often plagiarizes) the true poet. As a pernicious imitator, the false author is a close analogue of the "humourous" comic butt of Jonsonian comedy. Correspondingly, in a phrase that was perhaps first coined by Aristotle, and that also appears in Sidney's *Defence of Poesy,* and would later be bandied about in many texts from the War of the Theatres, the false author is merely a "poet-ape."[36]

An ironic similarity of "false" poet and "true" player is suggested by Jonson's character Envy, who, while speaking the prologue to *The Poetaster*, surveys the theater and asks hopefully:

> Are there no players here? no poet-apes,
> That come with basiliskes eyes, whose forked tongues
> Are steept in venome, as their hearts in gall?

> (4:204)

The false poet, in his multiple forms of apishness, collapses what should be the inviolable distinction between author and player. In his Epigraph 56, "On Poet Ape," Jonson describes such an author more specifically as a deliberate literary plagiarist:

> At first he made low shifts, would picke and gleane,
> Buy the reversion of old playes; now growne
> To'a little wealth, and credit in the scene,
> He takes up all, makes each mans wit his owne.
> And, told of this, he slights it. Tut, such crimes
> The sluggish gaping auditor devoures;
> He markes not whose 'twas first: and after-times
> May judge it to be his, as well as ours.

> (8:45)

Here Jonson's metaphors portray the author as a kind of usurer (like those dramatized in Jacobean city comedy), one who gradually engrosses personal wealth by exploiting others' losses ("the reversion of old plays") and his personal "credit." Authorship is identified with an almost literal sense of financial and legal propriety: like the usurer, the plagiarist achieves a form of nominal ownership which subverts the deeper social ties of inheritance and tradition. His success is also contingent, once again, on the "gaping" emptiness of the auditor, who "devoures" the stolen inspiration without regard for its "true" origins. Similarly, Jonson's Epigraph 129, "To Mime" (an attack on the scenographer Inigo Jones), associates the titular character with a broad

---

[36] Aristotle, *Poetics* 26.2. Philip Sidney, "The Defence of Poesy," in *Sir Philip Sidney*, ed. Katherine Duncan-Jones (Oxford: Oxford University Press, 1989), 249.

range of popular entertainment. Mime, says Jonson in mocking praise, can "out-dance the Babion," and "out-zany Cokely, Pod; nay Gue," the last three names referring, respectively, to a celebrated jester, a puppeteer, and an ape trainer.[37] All these figural meanings depend on the interrelated social and representational secondariness of the performing object, a form of performance for which Jonson recurrently reveals both his explicit contempt and his apparently inescapable fascination.

Now, on the one hand, Jonson's basic rhetorical vision of an imperious and virtuous author, secure in the sovereignty of an inspiration that is both ontologically and morally "true," would, by the same logic, seem capable of confronting at once both the object and the audience of his own histrionic art. On the other hand, the practical conditions of theater, even as they are metaphorically reinterpreted within this hierarchical system, tend to contaminate an authorial voice that must enter the descending spiral of representation in order to represent itself. For Jonson can set the complex multiple system of social and theatrical reform in motion only by splitting himself, by making himself a kind of puppet (as he does, almost literally, in each of his "comical satires") within a sphere whose inevitable multiplicity dilutes the purity of a voice and presence that only in such splitting can extend and express itself. In a difficult passage from *Cynthia's Revels*, one more of Jonson's authorial personae, the scholar Crites, seems once again to unite the object and the audience of Jonson's satiric reform within an implicit spectrum of histrionic effect:

> . . . such is the perversenesse of our nature,
> That if we once but fancie levitie,
> (How antike and ridiculous so ere
> It sute with us) yet will our muffled thought
> Choose rather not to see it, then avoide it:
> And if we can but banish our owne sense,

᠈ [37] In *Bartholomew Faire* Lantern Leatherhead (who may also be a satire of Inigo Jones) is said "to put downe *Coriat*, and *Cokeley*" (6:71); see Hereford and Simpson's note (*Ben Jonson*, 10:198). "Captain Pod" the puppeteer has already been discussed in this chapter. For Gue, see the induction of John Marston's *Antonio and Mellida*, ed. W. Reavley Gair (Manchester: Manchester University Press, 1991): " 'T had been a right part for Proteus or Gew. Ho! Blind Gew would ha' done't rarely, rarely" (137–39). Both Gair in his note to this line and Hereford and Simpson, in their note to Jonson's epigraph (11:28), cite William Guilpin's Satire 5, which refers to "my lord and foole, / One that for ape tricks can put *Gue* to school." Whereas Gair concludes that Gue must have been "an actor specializing in apelike mannerisms" (68), I think Guilpin's line more plausibly suggests a professional ape trainer; but that the phrase "ape tricks" might be susceptible of either interpretation is itself an index of the associations I have been observing.

We act our mimicke trickes with that free license,
That lust, that pleasure, that securitie,
As if we practiz'd in a paste-boord case,
And no one saw the motion, but the motion.

(1.5.55–66)

The "mimicke trickes" of pernicious social behavior result from the contagion of histrionic "levitie," and themselves constitute a terminally solipsistic
performance in which each individual becomes at once player and puppet,
actor, author, and audience.[38] Jonson's extraordinary final image of a social
being marked by a "natural" perverseness but also shaped by representation,
who then becomes a kind of self-mastered and self-mastering puppet, would
actually correspond to the impossible ideal of a theater unmediated either by
actors or audition: a theater uncontaminated, in short, by itself.

Thus, not only the character, the player, and the audience but even the
author himself are implicated in and contaminated by a system of representation within which they have taken crucially distinct and yet ultimately
analogous places, and for this reason they are all at moments susceptible to
description by the problematic and ambivalent metaphor of the performing
object. Jonson's vision of the histrionic process, as Richard Helgerson remarks, demands a recognition that "the Author is an actor, a role-player,
whose various parts depend on and refer back to his moral authority." By the
same token, as Stallybrass and White phrase a familiar critical insight, "Jonson found in the huckster, the cony-catcher and the pick-pocket an image of
his own precarious and importuning craft."[39] The first point conveys Jonson's chosen vision of authorship as something taking place within a quasi-
Platonic theoretical structure in which authorial access to the truths of inspiration and moral rectitude (like the philosopher-king's access to the Forms
and Ideas of true reality) justifies his literary authority, his creation and control of the multiple embodiments of his vision.[40] The second point, con-

[38] In this passage Jonson is, I believe, deliberately echoing Plato, who argues at the culmination of his
attack on theater in the *Republic* that an enjoyment of the *representation* of laughable objects will eventually lead to a kind of pernicious self-representation (606c).

[39] Helgerson, *Self-Crowned Laureates*, 138; Stallybrass and White, *The Politics and Poetics of Transgression*, 77.

[40] For Plato, argues R. S. Peters, "the scrutiny of such objects [i.e., the Forms] gave the philosopher
kings a right to make decisions and issue commands." R. S. Peters, "Authority," in *Political Philosophy*, ed.
Anthony Quinton (Oxford: Oxford University Press, 1967), 88. Hannah Arendt agrees that the eternal
ideas "become the unwavering, 'absolute' standards for political and moral behavior and judgment"
("What Is Authority?" in *Between Past and Future: Six Exercises in Political Thought* [New York: Viking,

versely, suggests Jonson's inescapable awareness of the sordid and practical social context of this vision: the author as mere "apish" imitator, himself implicated in the system of representation whose pernicious consequences he lays bare. Even more generally, as Don E. Wayne has argued, Jonson increasingly shows signs "that his own identity as poet and playwright—and therefore his personal transcendence of the still rigid social hierarchy in which he lived and wrote—depended on the same emerging structure of social relationships that he satirized in his plays."[41] I have been suggesting, by extension, that this personal dilemma is inextricably linked to Jonson's impassioned and impossible belief in the perfect transparency of the social and representational hierarchies, a belief that the figural meanings of the puppet must have seemed to confirm in ways his real social position could not.

As I will further suggest in the section that follows, Jonson and other early modern playwrights seized the puppet as a theatrical and discursive tool that figurally linked their nascent concepts of authorship to a variety of other cultural anxieties. Thus, the puppet became an incongruous participant in the construction of interlocking cultural hierarchies which themselves emerged from what I have called the hierarchy of representation. The literal conditions of puppetry—in which a performing object serves as the vehicle, index, or mouthpiece for the "motions" and voice of an absent and invisible author—not only underlie its specific figural meanings but also serve as metaphor for the larger cultural process I am describing, a process in which writers aspiring to "literary" status appropriated this particular form of low and popular performance. They did so in texts whose own existence as stable social commodities made possible their survival within the literary history they also constitute, texts that thus preserve this otherwise ephemeral cultural artifact, but only by making the literal performing object, so to speak, a puppet of itself—a discursive mouthpiece for another's voice.

"The Puppet's Part":
Cultural Hierarchy and Social Subordination

To seek your Ladyship, I have been in Cellars,
In private Cellars, where the thirsty Bawds

1961], 110). On the almost magical authority given to the Platonic philosopher-king by his access to the Forms, see also E. R. Dodds, *The Greeks and the Irrational* (Berkeley: University of California Press, 1951), 210–11.

[41] Wayne, "Drama and Society in the Age of Jonson," 107; cf. Riggs, *Ben Jonson,* 59–60.

Hear your Confessions; I have been at Plays,
To look you out amongst the youthful Actors,
At Puppet Shews, you are Mistress of the motions.
                              —John Fletcher, *Rule a Wife and Have a Wife*

You come with letters against the King, and take Vanity the puppet's
part against the royalty of her father.
                              —William Shakespeare, *King Lear*

So far I have argued that in early modern theater and discourse, the puppet
was enlisted in the construction of a particular vision of theatrical
authorship, one grounded in a hierarchical view of representation and a corresponding cultural opposition between popular and elite forms of
performance. The hierarchy of the theological theater—the hypothetical relationship of mastery and servitude between the poet and the player-
puppet—seems both to reflect and to confirm a purportedly transparent series of social, philosophic, and theological hierarchies. In this section I
continue to suggest that the performing object evoked in the early modern
imagination a broad pattern of cultural associations. My observations thus
converge with a recent critical consensus that the evident social anxieties of
seventeenth-century England were conditioned by the rapid development of
an institutionalized theater.[42] At about the turn of the seventeenth century,
as Lawrence Stone makes what has now become a familiar point, "the ideal
of a society in which every man had his place and stayed in it was breaking
down under a combination of material and ideological pressures."[43] In the
same period a London theatergoer had access to an intricate hierarchy of histrionic entertainment in which material puppets represented corporeal beings, boy players represented men and women, and adult players represented
kings and clowns—the whole spectrum of social distinction. The contrast
and potential incongruity between literal players and represented characters
in all their relative sizes, sexes, and roles, must inevitably have suggested an
analogy between the theatrical and the social "role." As an increasingly sophisticated system of theatrical representation tended to suggest that social

[42] My understanding of the dynamic interaction of theatrical representation and an evolving bourgeois self in the early modern period has been shaped by Agnew, *Worlds Apart*; Francis Barker, *The Tremu-
lous Private Body: Essays on Subjection* (London: Methuen, 1984); Catherine Belsey, *The Subject of Tragedy*
(New York: Methuen, 1985); and Greenblatt, *Renaissance Self-Fashioning*.
[43] Lawrence Stone, *The Crisis of the Aristocracy, 1558–1641* (Oxford: Clarendon Press, 1965), 35; see also
Stone's "Social Mobility in England, 1500–1700," *Past and Present* 33–35 (1966): 17–55.

behaviors were merely assumed, the increasingly flexible social situation in turn provided topics and audiences (*subjects* in both senses of the word) for the maturing institution.

A focus on the performing *object*, however, complicates these widely shared insights about the interaction of theatrical and social practice in early modern England. As I will continue to observe, the puppet figures, both as observation and trope, in a wide variety of early modern discourse, including the plays of the public theater, where it embodies at once a hierarchical vision of authorship and the corresponding social hierarchies of gender and class. This process is necessarily conditioned by the extensive cultural history I have been sketching. Onto the basic, irresistibly obvious opposition between the puppet and the player, the physical object and the corporeal body, some of the many other "dichotomous distinctions" that characterize what Pierre Bourdieu calls "the logic of practice" are projected. As a material object, a passive vehicle or vessel available for a mastering authorial form, the puppet is associated with the flesh in its conventional opposition to the "spirit," and with performance itself in its opposition (newly constructed in this period) to the dramatic text. By an extension of the same hierarchical habit of thought, the puppet is figurally linked to a range of social and sexual subordination—the woman, the child, the servant, the "upstart" or social climber, each of whom appears to take analogous positions in hierarchies at once ontological and cultural.[44] The puppet is thus inscribed in early modern culture as a figure in both senses—merely material and merely metaphoric. In its own objective materiality the puppet illuminates more generally the role of *objects* in the formation of middle-class identity, the multifarious ways in which things (or people) were construed as distinctive signs of social status: as tools or symbols, the "particulars of cultural wealth and show."[45] As metaphor, even more broadly, the puppet links materiality, servitude, and multiple forms of ontological and cultural lowness in a tacit system whose only logic is the logic of domination itself.

I will now try to sketch the outlines of this complex cultural landscape by

[44] Among the recent studies that have influenced my understanding of the interconnection of class and gender distinctions in Renaissance discourse and theater are Dympna Callaghan, *Woman and Gender in Renaissance Tragedy* (Atlantic Highlands, N.J.: Humanities Press, 1989); Karen Newman, *Fashioning Femininity and English Renaissance Drama* (Chicago: University of Chicago Press, 1991); Mary Beth Rose, *The Expense of Spirit: Love and Sexuality in Renaissance Drama* (Ithaca: Cornell University Press, 1988); and Frank Whigham, *Ambition and Privilege: The Social Tropes of Elizabethan Courtesy Theory* (Berkeley: University of California Press, 1984).

[45] Patricia Fumerton, *Cultural Aesthetics: Renaissance Literature and the Practice of Social Ornament* (Chicago: University of Chicago Press, 1991), 1.

focusing closely on the intricate genealogies and multiple meanings of three words used to denote puppets or performing objects, and by considering allusions to and appropriations of puppet theater in plays and pamphlets produced during that intense half century preceding the closing of the London theaters in 1642. The pattern of associations is grounded, like so many other aspects of Western discourse and social practice, in a fundamental subordination of the female to the male. Even the linguistic genealogy of the word *puppet*, as it descends to its early modern usage, itself embodies a sequence of shifting but persistent associations of femininity.[46] The word derives, as I observed briefly in the previous chapter, from *pupa*, the feminine version of the classical Latin word for "little child," which also had the meaning "doll." *Pupa* thus seems to manifest at once a psychosexual expectation of gender behavior (little girls play with dolls) and a more general semantic impulse of diminution (the small made smaller). The word also embodies a metonymic or paradigmatic displacement of meaning between life and the image of life, between the living child and the material figure of the child transfigured for the purposes of play. Furthermore, the Latin *pupa* itself derives from the Indo-European root *pou*, "little," which figures in other English words such as *pupil, puppy, puberty, pauper,* and *poverty*—a semantic map of social and corporeal subordination.[47]

The word's primal sense of diminution seems, then, to manifest itself in a historical series of hierarchical meanings. The Latin *pupa* descends into its various English cognates through the Middle French word *poupe*, which primarily meant "doll" (a children's plaything), but which is also defined in seventeenth-century French dictionaries as "tette" or "mamelle" or, in one case, "bout de sein."[48] I will later discuss an apparent Shakespearean play on words between *puppet* and *pap*, a term whose common meaning as "nipple, teat, breast giving suck," is also a linguistic displacement from an earlier

[46] Here again I have consulted, in addition to the *Oxford English Dictionary*, Robert K. Barnhart, ed., *The Barnhart Dictionary of Etymology* (New York: H. W. Wilson, 1988); Joseph Shipley, *The Origins of English Words: A Discursive Dictionary of Indo-European Roots* (Baltimore: Johns Hopkins University Press, 1984); and Walter W. Skeat, ed., *An Etymological Dictionary of the English Language*, 2d ed. (Oxford: Clarendon Press, 1924).

[47] Shipley, *The Origins of English Words*, 326–27.

[48] Frederic Godefroy, *Dictionnaire de l'ancienne langue française* (Paris, 1888), cites *poupe* as "bout de sein," citing the *Thresor des trois langues* (1617). The etymological progress from the baby to the breast seems also to reflect the infantile displacement described in the psychoanalytic idea of the part-object. The infant, it is speculated, sometimes attributes to the breast the attributes of the mother and hence adapts the mere *corporeal* object as, in the broader sense, his object in the sense of goal, aim, "object" of desire. See J. Laplanche and J.-B. Pontalis, *The Language of Psycho-Analysis*, trans. Donald Nicholson-Smith (New York: Norton, 1973), 301–2.

sense, "baby food," which is thought to derive from an onomatopoetic attempt to reproduce "the sound made by an infant in opening and shutting the lips."[49] The original Latin word *pupa* has also been adopted unchanged into English as a biological term for the intermediate stage in the life cycle of certain insects: the "chrysalis" or "nymph" between the caterpillar and the butterfly. *Nymph* and *nympha* are also recorded in the seventeenth century as scientific (and occasionally poetic) terms for the labia minora (*OED*, s.v. "nymph" 4, "nympha" 2). The pervasive, overdetermined etymological link between the performing object and the female body suggests that conventional philosophic and scientific vision of the latter, consolidated in authoritative medical texts from Aristotle to Galen to the scholastics and beyond, as an inverted, imperfect, or incomplete version of the male body, a puppetlike vessel providing passive material for the active masculine form.[50]

Feminine associations continue to cling to the word *puppet* as it descends into English through a series of French and English words including *poupard* ("chubby baby," a term of affection) and *poupette* ("little doll"). The modern French *poupée* means "doll," and the English word *puppet* also originally referred either to a children's plaything or to a performing object in the strict theatrical sense. Thus, the metonymic or paradigmatic displacement manifest in the Latin word (from little girl to doll) has been symmetrically displaced by an inverse double meaning (from child's plaything to performing object). The English words *puppet, poppet,* and various cognates, from the late Middle Ages to the Renaissance, could also be used as colloquial terms of condescending affection used to a child or a pretty girl—one recalls, for example, Chaucer's Alison, who was "so gay a popelote and swich a wench."[51]

---

[49] See the *Oxford English Dictionary*, s.v. "pap." Subsequent citations will be given parenthetically in the text.

[50] In sex, writes Aristotle, "the female always provides the material, the male that which fashions it, for this is the power we say they each possess. . . . While the body is from the female, it is the soul that is from the male." *On the Generation of Animals* 2.4.738b.20–25. Aquinas argues, similarly, that in sex, "the entire active operation is on the part of the male and the passive on the part of the female. . . . In the arts the inferior art gives a disposition to the matter to which the higher art gives the form . . . so also the generative power of the female prepares the matter, which is then fashioned by the active power of the male." Quoted in Vern L. Bullough, "Medieval Medical and Scientific Views of Women," *Viator* 4 (1973): 485–503. For commentary on this discursive construction in European culture, see R. Howard Bloch, *Medieval Misogyny and the Invention of Western Romantic Love* (Chicago: University of Chicago Press, 1991), 26–27; Stephen Greenblatt, "Fiction and Friction," in *Shakespearean Negotiations: The Circulation of Social Energy in Renaissance England* (Berkeley: University of California Press, 1988), 79–81; and Thomas Laqueur, *Making Sex: Body and Gender from the Greeks to Freud* (Cambridge: Harvard University Press, 1990), 4–5, 29–30, and passim.

[51] *The Canterbury Tales*, l. 3254, cited from *The Works of Geoffrey Chaucer*, ed. F. N. Robinson (Boston:

These linked meanings evoke a descending hierarchy of generation and incarnation: the woman's procreative body; the child that body bears and sustains; the child's plaything; and, taking its place at both the top and the bottom of that hierarchy, so to speak, Woman conceptualized and reified as herself an object (or plaything) of male desire.

As these examples further suggest, the association of the puppet not just with corporeality in general but specifically with the female body manifests an obvious cultural tendency to objectify the latter. Even the word *doll* similarly emerges as a diminutive of the female name Dorothy, and is first recorded by the *OED* in its slang sense as "a female pet, a mistress" in 1560, more than a century before its first appearance (in 1700) in the sense of "an image of a human being . . . used as a plaything." The latter sense in the sixteenth and seventeenth centuries was usually conveyed instead by *puppet* or simply by *babby* or *baby*.

The word *doll*, however, could also have the connotation "prostitute"—as in the names of two familiar dramatic characters, Doll Tearsheet and Doll Common. This secondary sense must be assumed to have contributed to the continuing slang usage of the term as applied (usually in a sexual context) to a woman. Just as "doll" is a diminutive of the name Dorothy applied by arbitrary convention to a woman of loose virtue, so "moll" is a diminutive of the name Mary sometimes similarly applied.[52] In this case the contrast between the original proper name and its diminutive itself precisely embodies the all too familiar cultural opposition of the madonna and the whore, woman as spirit and woman as flesh. Even today, in certain modes of male discourse women can still be referred to as "baby," "doll," "baby doll," or even "doll baby," usages that manage to objectify the woman's body and to diminish it, as it were from two directions at once. The linguistic link between the female body and the puppet insistently and illogically conflates figuration and performance (culture) with the purely material and corporeal (nature), even as it subordinates both on a hypothetical hierarchy of representation. One might even venture to suggest (recalling, for example, the Protestant wordplay on "puppetry" and "popery" cited in the previous chapter) that the linguistic chain of *pupa, pap, puppet,* and *pope* embodies

Riverside-Houghton Mifflin, 1957).

[52] In Thomas Middleton and Thomas Dekker's play *The Roaring Girl*, ed. Paul A. Mulholland (Manchester: Manchester University Press, 1987), Sir Alexander claims that there are "more whores of that name than of any ten other" (2.2.160). In Middleton's *Chaste Maid in Cheapside* we hear similarly of corrupt promoters who give presents to "their Molls and Dolls" (2.2.73). The sense survives in vestigial form in modern slang (i.e., a gangster's "moll").

and is inscribed within the mutually transparent hierarchies of representation and authority: descending from a spiritual and authoritative Father to the maternal body, from the child to the doll, from the divine logos to the infant's inarticulate cry.

I am suggesting, in short, that the puppet—whose cultural and discursive meanings stretch from the primary, the corporeal, and the "natural" to the secondary, the mimetic, and the deceptive—resembles the cultural image of Woman as, similarly, both natural and artificial, associated with the body in its binary opposition to the spirit and yet also with dress, cosmetics, and social dissimulation.[53] By the late sixteenth century, as I began to suggest in the previous chapter, the word *puppet* had become invested with pervasive social anxieties about gender and class, two categories newly available to a transgressive flexibility and similarly contingent on practices of dress and deportment. Accordingly, the word *puppet* began to be commonly used like *mammet* or *marmoset*, as another term of reproach and contempt for women or, alternatively, for social climbers and effeminate males. The new colloquial senses of the word obviously relied in part on an implicit analogy between the literal doll or performing object and the supposedly deceptive appearance and behavior of these social types. Philip Stubbes, in *The Anatomie of Abuses* (1583), excoriates women for their use of makeup and elaborate attire, and at one point concludes that "when they have all these goodly robes uppon them, women seem to be . . . not naturall women, but artificiall Women, not Women of flesh & blod, but rather puppits, or mawmets of rags & clowtes compact together."[54] Stubbes's text, of course, also makes clear an implicit and explicit analogy between the behavior of contemporary women and the alleged social (and ontological) subversiveness of contemporary drama— both of which, in Stubbes's view, were conducive to a society in which one could no longer know "who is a gentleman, who is not" (C2v), or distinguish "an honorable, or worshipfull Woman, from them of the meaner sorte" (F7r).

[53] On the binary conception of Woman, see Caroline Walker Bynum, " '. . . And Woman His Humanity': Female Imagery in the Religious Writing of the Late Middle Ages," in *Gender and Religion: On the Complexity of Symbols*, ed. Caroline Walker Bynum, Stevan Harrell, and Paula Richman (Boston: Beacon Press, 1986). On the image of cosmetics in the drama and society of early modern England, see Frances E. Dolan, "Taking the Pencil Out of God's Hand: Art, Nature, and the Face-Painting Debate in Early Modern England," *PMLA* 108.2 (1993): 224–39; Annette Drew-Bear, "Face-Painting in Renaissance Tragedy," *Renaissance Drama* 12 (1981): 71–93; and Laurie A. Finke, "Painting Women: Images of Femininity in Jacobean Tragedy," *Theatre Journal* 36 (1984): 357–70.

[54] Philip Stubbes, *The Anatomie of Abuses* (London, 1583), F6r. Subsequent citations are given parenthetically by signature in the text.

By the turn of the seventeenth century, satirists were still drawing what had evidently become a conventional analogy between the performing object and the specter of social mobility, the latter construed as itself a form of pernicious imitation, a kind of parody or debased representation of traditional values and roles. In the seventh satire of his *Scourge of Villany* (1598), John Marston attacks a number of duplicitous social types, referring to them collectively at the end of the poem as "puppets, painted Images."[55] The titular character of George Chapman's *Gentleman Usher* (1602) describes courtiers who are "so politike and prowd / They skorne to give good lookes to worthy men," and claims he would "skorne such puppet lords" (3.2.69–77). Thus, the so-called painted puppet—an object conveying the illusion of life through histrionic embodiment of a particularly literal kind—becomes a figural correlate for the dissimulations of dress and behavior. Within the same web of association, however, these apparent issues of class are constantly resexualized: the metaphor of the puppet circles back both to suggest the proverbial dissimulation of the harlot and whore and to connect social mobility in general with effeminacy and homoerotic attraction. Joseph Swetnam, in *The Arraignment of Lewd, idle, froward, and unconstant women* (1615), for example, first compares women to "Idols in Spain which are bravely gilt outwardly and yet nothing but lead within them," and then describes them as "painting themselves, and frizzing their hairs, and prying in their glass like Apes to prank up themselves in their gaudies, like Puppets."[56] Even more strikingly, in his poem "Ingling Pyander," from *Micro-cynicon*, Middleton tells the story of a hermaphrodite boy who dresses as a girl and works as a prostitute in London. At the end the rueful narrator warns the reader:

> Trust not a painted puppet, as I've done . . .
> The streets are full of juggling parasites
> With the true shape of virgins' counterfeits.
> (8:133)

[55] John Marston, *The Scourge of Villany*, ed. G. B. Harrison (New York: E. P. Dutton, 1925), 75. Subsequent citations are given parenthetically in the text.

[56] Cited from *Half Humankind: Contexts and Texts of the Controversy about Women in England, 1540–1640*, ed. Katharine Usher Henderson and Barbara F. McManus (Urbana: University of Illinois Press, 1985), 195, 205. Strictly speaking, the operative meaning of *puppet* in Swetnam and Stubbes may be "doll" as opposed to "performing object"; but even so the satirical point depends on a metaphoric analogy between the "painted" doll and the living woman (cf. the modern slang expression "living doll"). On the Jacobean pamphlet controversy initiated by Swetnam, see the introduction to *Half Humankind*, 16–20, and Linda Woodbridge, *Woman and the English Renaissance: Literature and the Nature of Womankind, 1540–1620* (Urbana: University of Illinois Press, 1986), 81–103.

The "ingle," whose literal maleness has been transformed with complete verisimilitude into an alluring image of femininity, evokes the image of the merely material puppet (the body) invested with histrionic "life" (the soul). Thus, the very word *puppet*, like the metaphoric suggestiveness of performing objects in general, seems to embody a constellation of interrelated cultural meanings. The other term used to refer to puppet shows in this period—*motion*—further suggests how and why the performing object figures so frequently in early modern discourse. In the *Bartholomew Faire* pamphlet cited earlier in this chapter, the anonymous writer begins his rhetorical journey into the fairgrounds with an intricate sequence of puns: "Let us now make a progresse into Smith-field, which is the heart of the faire, where in my heart, I think there are more *motions* in a day, to be seene, than are in a terme, in Westminister Hall to be heard. But whilst you take notice of the severall *motions* there, take this caution along with you, let one eye watch narrowly that no one's hand make a *motion* into your pocket, which is the next way to *move* you to impatience" (emphasis added). In this ingenious passage, the writer envisions "motions" as at once haunting his own "heart," performing at the fair, heard at the law courts, and reaching toward his pocket. This complex pun is made possible by a basic ambiguity in the word *motion*, which in this period retained its presumably primal sense of physical movement but also conveyed a series of quasi-figural meanings: (1) "an inward prompting or impulse; an instigation or incitement from within"; (2) "a proposition or proposal formally made in a deliberative assembly," and hence, by extension, "an application made to a court or judge by a party to an action or his counsel to obtain some rule or order of court"; and finally (3) "a puppet show" (see *OED*, s.v. "motion," 9, 8, 8b, 13).

The word *puppet* could refer, as I have frequently observed, both to a doll and to a histrionic vehicle of performance, the latter distinguished from the former precisely by those external mechanical gestures or "motions" that manifest its (illusory) internal "motions." Early modern scientific discourse conceived of human behavior, in not dissimilar terms, as essentially mechanistic: the internal activity of the "sensitive soul" (as distinct from the "vegetative" and "rational" souls) was believed to be the precedent and efficient causes of an animate being's external actions.[57] John Bulwer's *Chironomia* (1644), for example, describes and illustrates a system of sign language grounded in the conventional early modern idea that "the hand . . . by ges-

[57] See Lawrence Babb, *The Elizabethan Malady: A Study of Melancholia in English Literature* (East Lansing: Michigan State University Press, 1951), 4.

ture makes the inward *motions* of the minde most evident."[58] Throughout the early modern period, not only rhetorical *pronunciatio* and theatrical "playing" but all forms of human communication and behavior were understood to involve a combination of gesture and speech—a matching, so to speak, of the motion with the (e)motion.[59] As Ben Jonson argues in *Discoveries*: "Doe wee not see, if the mind languish, the members are dull? Looke upon an effeminate person: his very gate confesseth him. If a man be fiery, his *motion* is so: if angry, 'tis troubled and violent" (8:592–53; emphasis added). Here Jonson uses the word to express the external manifestation of the internal nature or personality; as he describes it, the latter constitutes the self-evident and self-present "truth," the higher ontological reality, whereas the former is merely its guise, appearance, or index ("If a man *be* fiery, his motion is so"). The word *motion* constantly slips between the two sides of the physio-psychological opposition which it also predicates, linking biology and behavior, rhetoric and theater, within a transparent system of correspondences.

Such a system inevitably also had a theological dimension: the same word that refers to the subject's own inner impulses could also refer to "a working of God in the soul" (*OED*, s.v. "motion," 4b). This sense of the word, too, links the invisible inner life with those external gestures that manifest it in the visible world. Earlier in the *Bartholomew Faire* pamphlet, for example, the author recounts the story of a Puritan who (like Jonson's Zeal-of-the-Land Busy, the comic Puritan of *Bartholomew Faire*) attacks the religious images on sale at the fair, remarking that "the good *motions* of the spirit had brought him to town" (emphasis added). This sense of the word also conflates the invisible inner life with those external gestures that manifest it in the visible world. Sir Thomas Browne, in *Religio Medici*, is thus almost making a pun when he asserts that he loves "to use the civility of my knee, my hat, and hand, with all those outward and sensible *motions* which may express or promote my invisible devotion."[60] So conceived, humanity is, as in

[58] Quoted by A. G. H. Bachrach in "The Great Chain of Acting," *Neophilologus* 33 (1949): 168–69 (emphasis added). On the connection between Bulwer's theories and early modern ideas about acting, see Joseph R. Roach, *The Player's Passion: Studies in the Science of Acting* (Newark: University of Delaware Press, 1985), 33–39.

[59] On early modern acting styles, see Bachrach, "The Great Chain of Acting"; Alfred Harbage, "Elizabethan Actors," *PMLA* 54 (1939): 685–708; B. L. Joseph, *Elizabethan Acting*, 2d ed. (London: Oxford University Press, 1964); Roach, *The Player's Passion*, 23–57; and William B. Worthen, *The Idea of the Actor: Drama and the Ethics of Performance* (Princeton: Princeton University Press, 1984), 10–69.

[60] Thomas Browne, *Religio Medici*, pt. 1, sec. 3 (emphasis added), in *The Works of Sir Thomas Browne*, ed. Geoffrey Keynes, 6 vols. (1928–31; rpt. Chicago: University of Chicago Press, 1964), 1:12–13.

Plato's parable from the *Laws*, a kind of puppetlike material body mastered both from within and from without, moved by its own inner "motions" and yet also capable of being filled by the breath, spirit, or inspiration that descends from some transcendent, divine sphere.

The ambiguity of the word *motion*—linking the inner impulse with the external gesture, individual action with collective authority—further suggests how and why early modern writers could project social anxieties about dress, deportment, and class mobility onto the idea of the puppet. The same ambiguity also indicates, again, how social notions of power and authority and conventional cultural images of subordination seem to derive from and reflect theological or ontological dualities of matter and spirit, the corporeal and the animate. To complete this web of association I must pursue a third and final linguistic genealogy and analyze one more word that will further suggest the discursive involvement of the puppet in the cultural construction of class. This time I begin with Shakespeare's *Merry Wives of Windsor*, in which both "Jack" Falstaff and his page Robin are compared, on separate occasions, to a "Jack-a-Lent,"which E. K. Chambers defines as "a puppet, set up on Ash Wednesday and decorated with fish-emblems of the penitential season, used as a target for missiles during the six weeks of Lent, and finally destroyed in triumph on Palm Monday."[61]

By extension, Shakespeare's metaphor of the Jack-a-Lent, in its dramatic context, puts into figural play a series of binary oppositions beginning with the animate and inanimate, the gigantic and the miniature. Both in *2 Henry IV* and in *The Merry Wives*, Falstaff appears on stage side by side with a page whose childish diminution provides an obvious visual contrast to the knight's enormous bulk. As Falstaff himself puts it at the beginning of the former play: "I do here walk before thee like a sow that hath overwhelm'd all her litter but one. If the Prince put thee into my service for any other reason than to set me off, why then I have no judgment. Thou whoreson mandrake, thou art fitter to be worn in my cap than to wait at my heels. I was never mann'd with an agot till now" (*2 Henry IV* 1.2.12–17). As the biological im-

[61] E. K. Chambers, *The English Folk-Play* (New York: Haskwell House, 1966), 157. See also Brand, *Observations on the Popular Antiquities of Great Britain*, 1:101; T. F. Thiselton Dyer, *Folk-Lore of Shakespeare* (1883; rpt. New York: Dover, 1966), 281; and see the citations in G. L. Apperson, *English Proverbs and Proverbial Phrases: A Historical Dictionary* (London: J. M. Dent, 1929), 329; and F. P. Wilson, *The Oxford Dictionary of English Proverbs* (Oxford: Clarendon Press, 1970). On the carnivalesque connotations of the "Jack-a-Lent," see Neil Rhodes, *Elizabethan Grotesque* (London: Routledge & Kegan Paul, 1980), 103, 122–61; Burke, *Popular Culture in Early Modern Europe*, 185; and Frederick B. Jonassen, "The Meaning of Falstaff's Allusion to the Jack-a-Lent in *The Merry Wives of Windsor*," *Studies in Philology* 88.1 (1991): 46–68.

age of the sow and her litter succeeds quickly to that of the "agot" (a kind of portrait miniature or cameo), Falstaff seems to strike an implicit analogy between the diminutive and the artificial. Falstaff is also quite literally Robin's "master"; but he complains here that he has been "mann'd" (provided for) with a servant who is *not* a man. Thus, Shakespeare's rhetoric and his stage picture collectively evoke an apparently transparent series of oppositions:

large	small
man	boy
animate	inanimate
master	servant
presence	representation

At the conceptual level where the hierarchy of representation merges with the related hierarchy of social subordination, the servant (who is literally *mastered* by "authority") is, by the momentum of this associative structure, construed as figurally *inanimate* (passive matter available for authoritative form). This discursive association of servitude and lifeless materiality, despite its obvious illogic, may also be said to underlie (and in part produce) the dehumanizing conditions which have typically characterized the real economic exploitation of class by class.

The same network of associations I have drawn from Shakespeare's text is also manifest, more broadly, in the the word *jack* itself. A familiar form of the proper name John, "Jack" had become by the fourteenth century what the *Oxford English Dictionary* calls "a generic proper name for any representative of the common people." This basic semantic sense of class distinction eventually converged with particular expectations of class-based behavior, and by the sixteenth century the name had acquired the more specifically pejorative sense of a "low bred or ill-mannered fellow" (*OED*, s.v. "jack," 2). In *The Taming of the Shrew*, for example, Katherine complains sarcastically that, in allowing Petruchio to become a suitor for her hand, her father has shown

> a tender fatherly regard,
> To wish me wed to one half lunatic,
> A madcap ruffian and a swearing Jack.
> (2.1.286–88)

Here Katherine intends to charge Petruchio not only with vulgarity but also with a carnivalesque social license. Correspondingly, a kind of clown who performed at early modern fairs, often as a showman who introduced or followed a puppet show, was commonly known as a "Jack Pudding."[62] The word *jack* also had, throughout the seventeenth century, the connotation "rogue" or "knave." The so-called Black Jack, "whose liquor oftentimes breeds household wars,"[63] was a tavern bully; and by the end of the century *jack* is first recorded as referring to the "knave" in a suit of playing cards. A "Jack-in-the-box" was a kind of con-man or cheat who "deceived tradesmen by substituting empty boxes for others full of money."[64] The confluence of transgressive, theatrical, and carnivalesque associations may be glimpsed in a passage from Thomas Dekker and John Ford's *Spanish Gipsy* (1623), in which a group of pretend Gypsies celebrate the vagabond life in song while performing a kind of induction ceremony for a noble convert to their band.

> Brave Don, cast your eyes
> On our gipsy fashions . . .
> We no camels have to show
> Nor elephant with growt head . . .
> No blind bears
> Shedding tears
> For a collier's whipping;
> Apes nor dogs
> Quick as frogs
> Over cudgels skipping.
> Jack in boxes, nor decoys
> Puppets, nor such poor things,
> Nor are we those roaring boys
> That cozen fools with gilt rings;

[62] On the Jack Pudding or "merry-Andrew," see Morley, *Memoirs of Bartholomew Fair* (297, 335); Sybil Rosenfeld, *Strolling Players and Drama in the Provinces, 1660–1765* (1939; rpt. New York: Octagon, 1970), 7; and Speaight, *History of the English Puppet Theatre*, 152.

[63] I cite the prefatorial poem from John Taylor's comic pamphlet *Jack A Lent: His beginning and entertainment* (1625), which also provides a lengthy catalogue of other idiomatic expressions based on the "jack." See *Works of John Taylor the Water Poet Comprised in the Folio Edition of 1630*, Spenser Society no. 3 (1869; rpt. New York: Ben Franklin, 1967), 1:123.

[64] See "jack in the box" in Robert Nares, *A Glossary of Words . . . in the Works of English Authors* (London: Routledge, 1905); cf. the entries in Apperson, *English Proverbs and Proverbial Phrases*, and Wilson, *Oxford Dictionary of English Proverbs*. Thomas Dekker describes, in his *Cryer of Lanthorne* pamphlet (1612), how a "*Jacke in a Boxe*" steals money from a goldsmith's stall (*Non-Dramatic Works*, 3:286–87).

For an ocean,
Nor such motion
As the city Nineveh.

(4.1.88–114)

Here, the histrionic exhibition of monsters, performing animals, and puppets or "motions" are placed into the same social space as the "Jack-in-the-box,"
the Gypsy, the street bully or "roaring boy," and social marginality in general.
At the same time, however, the connotations of social lowness embodied
in the word *jack* were also susceptible to convenient inversion. A "Jack
Dandy" was an effeminate fop, and a "Jack in office" was an arrogant or
insolent official—senses that simply invert the word's more common meaning even as the social climber himself is seen to subvert the class hierarchy.
The ninth satire of Marston's *Scourge of Villany* (1598), for further example,
asks derisively:

Yee Mimick slaves, what are you percht so hie?
Downe Jack an Apes from thy fain'd royalitie . . .
Oh world of fooles, when all mens judgment's set
And rests upon some mumping Marmoset!

(92–93)

Marston's rhetoric obviously links servitude with imitation ("mimick slaves,"
"fain'd royaltie"), calls on the conventional social associations of the "ape" or
"marmoset," and also invokes one more compound phrase from this seem-
ingly inexhaustible etymology. A "Jack an Apes" apparently referred first to a
literal performing monkey or "baboon"; but by the end of the sixteenth century the expression had taken on the class-based meaning of "a ridiculous
upstart" (*OED*, s.v. "jackanapes," 2c). As one glimpses in Marston's usage,
this phrase diminishes its target in terms at once representational and social
(by reference to a kind of effeminate exaggeration of gesture and a sauciness
or impertinence of manner) and also by invoking a mode of literal performance whose carnivalesque lowness embodies the social status from which
the upstart jackanapes seeks to escape.

It is interesting to note, however, that Bishop Ridley, one of the celebrated
Marian martyrs of the English Reformation, is reported by John Foxe to have
contemptuously referred to the sacramental Host of the Catholic Mass as
"Jacke of the box." Here the semantic sense of deception (which allows
"Jack" to apply at once to a huckster or lower-class rogue and to a bourgeois

aspirant to high social rank) circles back to reveal an underlying theological resonance similar to that of the performing object in general. Ridley's epithet repeats a rhetorical strategy I previously observed in which Catholic ritual was figurally reinterpreted as a kind of puppetry that animates the dead Host with apparent life: thus the "Jack" is both the presence said to dwell in the sacramental wafer *and* the priest who indulges in a kind of histrionic trickery.[65] An analogously supernatural meaning of the word is reflected in a particular form of English folk belief. Stephano, in *The Tempest*, having been led through a horse pond by Prospero's spirits, complains to Caliban: "Your fairy, which you say is a harmless fairy, has done little better than play'd the Jack with us" (4.1.196–98). Stephano is referring to the "Jack-a-lantern" or "will-of-the-wisp," the ignis fatuus with which Robin Goodfellow and other fairy creatures were believed to deceive travelers by leading them from their way. These multiple interrelated senses inscribe an implicit hierarchy of meaning in which literal magic dwindles into legerdemain (from Jack-a-lantern to Jack Pudding), in which class distinction is both affirmed and overturned (from Black Jacks to jackanapes), and on which, in general, some form of primal belief or presence constantly moves toward representations of itself. This semantic process continues within the popular culture of our own day. "Jack-o'-lantern" now refers, in America, to a Halloween decoration carved from a pumpkin in the shape of a human face: an iconic representation, intended for children's play, of the original threatening figure of folklore. This, by the way, is also an instance of a process I will eventually note more generally in terms of puppet theater itself, in which distinctions of class (here exemplified by folk belief) are displaced onto the child, a cultural descent already adumbrated in the hierarchical structure of associations I have been sketching here.

Let me pursue just one more branch of this intricate etymology which once again refers to literal performing objects. In the late fifteenth century the word *jack* is also recorded in the sense of "a small mechanical figure of a man which strikes the bell on the outside of a clock" (*OED*, s.v. "jack," 6). A celebrated example of the clock jack from about 1480 survives at Southwold Church, Suffolk, and there were similar figures on the old St. Paul's Cathedral in London.[66] This specific meaning of *jack* once again converges

---

[65] An anonymous anti-Catholic pamphlet from the 1680s, *The Pope's Harbinger*, suggests that, in the sacrament of the Mass, "the *Priest* as *Jack-pudden* makes the *Parade* to the *Show*." Cited in Morley, *Memoirs of Bartholomew Fair*, 281.

[66] Thomas Dekker in *The Gull's Hornbook* describes "the strangeness of the motions" and "the sauciness of the Jacks" on St. Paul's (Dekker, *Non-Dramatic Works*, 2:236). The first phrase confirms how these

with the word's other connotations of social marginality. In *Lanthorne and Candle-Light*, one of his many pamphlets detailing the practices of rogues, vagabonds, and con men, Dekker refers to "another Fraternitie of wandring Pilgrims who merrily call themselves *Jackes of the Clocke-house*" (3:248). These "jacks," Dekker explains in detail, pretend to dedicate a book to a rural squire and receive a sum of money in return, repeating the process over and over again with the same book and different dedicatees. The literal transfer of mechanical causality by which the clock jack appears to strike the hour by its own motion and agency is here transformed, significantly, into a metaphor for the transmission of literary authority by means of the printed text.

By the late sixteenth century, according to the *OED*, a "jack" begins, by extension, to denote a whole variety of devices "which in some way take the place of a lad or man, or save human labours," for example, a turnspit, a sawhorse, a "jackknife," a "bootjack," and so forth. In these examples two of the word's common semantic senses coalesce. The literal clock jack, for example, is an icon of a "common" man, a kind of "servant" whose apparent labor, actually performed by hidden clockwork motion, is a histrionic illusion or trick. The turnspit or "jack" had fastened to its handle a tiny figure of a man who appeared to turn it.[67] On the one hand, the word's semantic sense of servitude has outlasted its iconicity: even today, for example, one refers to an electrical outlet or a device for raising an automobile off its axle as a "jack." On the other hand, the etymology also seems to foreground the very process of iconic figuration. The mechanical man from the famous puppet show of the Resurrection at Witney, which I discussed in the previous chapter, went down in collective memory as "Jack Snacker"; and the "jack-in-the-box," once denoting a specific cultural practice, eventually became a children's toy, a puppetlike figure enclosed in a literal box.[68]

---

mechanical figures were seen as essentially analogous to theatrical puppets or "motions." The second seems to allude, by contrast, to what John Taylor refers to (in *Jack A Lent*) as "Jack Sauce," another proverbial compound that refers to a "saucy" or impudent person, often a child or a social inferior. On the clock jack, see also Mary Hillier, *Automata and Mechanical Toys* (London: Bloomsbury Books, 1976), 18–20.

[67] The turnspit or "jack" figures in an interesting passage from George Chapman, *The Gentleman Usher* (1602), in which one character calls the "little man in shred" who "stands at the winder / And seems to put all things in act about him" (3.2.12–33) becomes a metaphor for the transfer of authority. Cited from *The Plays of George Chapman: The Comedies*, ed. Allan Holaday (Urbana: University of Illinois Press, 1970). Cf. how John Heminge and Henry Condel, in their preface "To the great Variety of Readers" in the First Folio Shakespeare (1621), enjoin potential readers to "buy" the book even if they judge it harshly, because "censure" alone "will not drive a Trade, or make the Jacke go."

[68] The "jack-in-the-box" would much later become for Henri Bergson a paradigm of the laughable, the latter itself construed as an inevitable phenomenological response to the mechanization of the animate

This dizzying multiplicity of meaning thus leads us back once more to the same conclusion: early modern discourse associates social subordination with materiality, with diminution, and with the idea of histrionic embodiment. These etymologies and preliminary examples thus seem to manifest a pervasive social anxiety, itself focused and intensified by all modes of performance, that both gender and class might be "a kind of persistent impersonation that passes as the real."[69] I am extending this familiar point by noting the evident connection between the construction of social difference and the appropriation of the performing object in early modern discourse. The empty corporeality and historic passivity of the performing object—the same characteristics foregrounded in player-puppets by the theological model of theater—become the figural equivalents of social subordination. Both women and social-climbing men are like "painted puppets" when they attempt to transgress the "natural" bounds of gender or class; yet they are also the "objects" of male desire or communal authority, available to be filled and mastered by masculine form or the expectations of a conservative social order, even as the player-puppet is filled by authorial inspiration.

Thus, in the drama itself a common figural association between women, servants, social mobility, and performing objects typically also evokes a kind of spiraling involution of image within image, play within play. In one of Shakespeare's earliest comedies, even as he was beginning to experiment with what would become his familiar comic devices of disguise, cross-dressing, role playing, and the like, he uses puppet theater as a characteristically ambiguous metaphor for the emotional tug-of-war between male and female. In *Two Gentlemen from Verona* Valentine's page, Speed, observes his master court Silvia and comments on the scene in several asides:

> *Valentine.* Peace, here she comes.
> *Speed.* [*Aside.*] O excellent motion! O exceeding puppet! Now will he interpret to her.
> *Valentine.* Madam and mistress, a thousand good morrows.
> *Speed.* [*Aside.*] O, give ye good ev'n! here's a million of manners.
> *Silvia.* Sir Valentine and servant, to you two thousand.
> *Speed.* [*Aside.*] He should give her interest, and she gives it him.
> *Valentine.* As you enjoin'd me, I have writ your letter

---

body. See my discussion of Bergson in Chapter 4.

[69] The quoted phrase is from Judith Butler, *Gender Trouble: Feminism and the Subversion of Identity* (New York: Routledge, 1990), viii.

Unto the secret, nameless friend of yours.

(2.1.94–105)

In the dramatic context Speed's opening metaphor evokes a series of mutually inverse meanings. The "interpreter" of a puppet show was, as I have observed, the puppet master, the figurative "author" whose voice and intentions the puppets speak and enact. Thus, Speed suggests that Valentine, the
master, "interprets" to Silvia, the puppet; male desire is thus figurally equivalent to a kind of metaphoric authorship. In fact, however, the real situation
of the scene is exactly opposite. Silvia had previously asked Valentine to write
a love letter for her to some "secret, nameless friend" who is really Valentine
himself. In this scene, after Silvia pointedly leaves the letter with Valentine,
Speed quickly realizes: "My master sues to her; and she hath taught her
suitor, / He being her pupil, to become her tutor" (137–38).[70] So Sylvia is
really manipulating Valentine by giving him the illusion of mastery. This is
the primary, "romantic" irony of the scene: a comic give-and-take of mutual
submission. At the same time, however, the staging of the scene almost inevitably suggests that the witty and cynical Speed, addressing himself directly
to the audience and providing a running commentary, is himself the metaphoric "interpreter" of these puppetlike lovers. After all, as Valentine had
told Proteus in the first scene of the play, "Love is your master, for he masters
you" (1.1.39). Here, as in his other romantic comedies, Shakespeare suggests
that love is at once a performed role or act, a "pageant truly played" (*As You
Like It* 3.4.53), and a kind of mastering of the self by an overwhelming impulse that kills "the flock of all affections else" and fills "liver, brain and
heart, / These sovereign thrones . . . with one self king" (*Twelfth Night*
1.1.34–38). But even this secondary metaphor (Speed as the interpreter of the
puppet/lovers), which is already one level "outside" the primary metaphoric
situation (lovers who manipulate each other), simultaneously suggests its
own reversal. For would not the diminutive child actor who played the page
visually evoke those entwined linguistic associations of "apishness," parody,
and diminution manifest in the word and the idea of the puppet?

The whole scene, that is, seems finally to overturn the oppositions of master and mastered, puppet and interpreter, "true" emotion versus assumed
role, which it clearly also evokes, and which serve as the ground and moti-

[70] The word *pupil*, meaning either a young student or the small opening in the eye, is yet one
more cognate of *puppet*, manifesting the persistent semantic sense of diminution that characterizes the
etymology.

vation of the original puppet metaphor. Shakespeare seems similarly to exploit the figural ambiguity (and etymological complexity) of the puppet in a difficult passage from *Hamlet*, which has, I believe, never been adequately explained. Provoked by the prince's incessant commentary on the action of the play within the play, Ophelia begins what will become an intricate exchange of bawdy wit:

> *Ophelia.* You are as good as a chorus, my lord.
> *Hamlet.* I could interpret between you and your love, if I could see the puppets dallying.
> *Ophelia.* You are keen, my lord, you are keen.
> *Hamlet.* It would cost you a groaning to take off mine edge.
> *Ophelia.* Still better, and worse.
> *Hamlet.* So you mistake your husbands.
>
> (3.2.245–52)

Most modern commentators on the second line merely explain the reference to the "interpreter" of puppet theater and acknowledge that the lines also convey a bawdy jest.[71] But what, precisely, is that jest? How does Hamlet's metaphor, which clearly alludes to the conditions and conventions of puppet theater, make sense either as sexual flirtation or in the larger context of the scene and the play? As some commentators have suggested, though only implicitly, Hamlet's metaphor evokes the etymological and histrionic associations of the word *puppet* with the (female) body. The variorum, for example, cites E. H. Seymour's paraphrase, "If I could observe the agitations of your bosom," a gloss that seems to call on the false etymological connection between *puppet* and *pap* and that corresponding semantic connection between the breast, the baby, and the doll.[72] Seymour's interpretation invites comparison with the linguistic peregrination in the notes of the New Cambridge *Hamlet*, where Philip Edwards claims that the spelling "poopies" in the first quarto suggests a pun on "poop" or "rump" in its slang sense of "the female genitals," and therefore "the genital organs of either sex."[73] If these crudely physical glosses are correct, then Hamlet means that Ophelia and some hy-

[71] For example, see G. Blakemore Evans's note in *The Riverside Shakespeare*, or Harold Jenkins's in the Arden Shakespeare edition (New York: Methuen, 1982).

[72] William Shakespeare, *Hamlet: A New Variorum Edition*, ed. Horace Howard Furness (Philadelphia: J. P. Lippincott, 1877), 256.

[73] William Shakespeare, *Hamlet, Prince of Denmark*, ed. Philip Edwards (Cambridge: Cambridge University Press, 1985), note to 3.2.223–24.

pothetical other lover are like two puppets, who in the sexual act are emptied of spirit and objectified as mere bodies, mere "parts." Hamlet is saying, then, that if he might "grossly gape on" and "behold her topp'd" (*Othello* 3.3.395–96), the sexual performance would embody its own obvious meaning and interpretation. Elsewhere, of course, Hamlet frequently questions whether Ophelia is "honest" and suggests she is a "painted" woman; and as such, she is also a "puppet" in its sense of "whore" or "deceiver," someone who, like all women, will "mis-take" her husband.

But the variorum also cites Robert Nares's claim that Hamlet's phrase "is synonymous with the babies in the eyes," which the same author explains in his *Glossary of Shakespearean English* as "the miniature reflection of himself which a person sees in the pupil of another's eye," a phrase associated with the intimacies of love. Nares, in his turn, must be implicitly calling on the etymological connection between *puppet* and *pupil*, the latter word (in its sense of the small hole in the eye) calling on the former's persistent etymological sense of diminution. Here, however, the suggested sexual relationship is visual and spiritual, a diminution that magnifies by exquisite self-reflection in the Other's gaze. The metaphor thus interpreted seems inevitably to suggest that Hamlet himself is both puppet and puppet master, both lover and interpreter of love. But perhaps Hamlet intends to suggest instead that the two puppets are Ophelia and her own (e)motion; thus, love is a performance (as Shakespeare's comedies often suggest) in which the lovers themselves are always both participants and spectators. Hamlet might then be using the puppet to suggest, in that perennial male fashion, that Ophelia's polite "no, my Lord" (3.2.113) really means "yes," and that she just doesn't know what she really wants. Thus, the edge of Hamlet's displayed wit (the mind) stands for, as it expresses, the displaced desire (the body) that it would cost Ophelia "a groaning" to take off.

In the larger context of the scene and play, Hamlet and Ophelia can also quite literally see "the puppets dallying": they are watching players who are at this moment "puppets" in both its primary and secondary senses, both acting in a play and also participating in Hamlet's metadramatic device to "catch the conscience of the King." So the puppet metaphor also embodies in miniature the sense of metadrama and "infinite regress" which critics have often discovered in the play.[74] Main plot and subplot, Gertrude and

[74] See, for example, Maurice Charney, "Analogy and Infinite Regress in *Hamlet*," in *Psychoanalytic Approaches to Literature and Film*, ed. Maurice Charney and Joseph Reppen (Rutherford, N.J.: Fairleigh Dickinson University Press, 1987), 156–67; Malcolm Evans, *Signifying Nothing: Truth's True Contents in*

Ophelia, Hamlet as son and Hamlet as lover are for a moment simultaneously recast as plays within the play in which the prince can envision himself as author instead of as the figural puppet of either cosmic forces or the family drama. Hamlet's puppet metaphor thus evokes the power relations of representation itself, even as it also imposes on Ophelia that familiar double bind in which Woman is associated at once with nature and with art, with the body in its overwhelming power and with the mind in its binary detachment from the body. The two processes (representation itself and the social construction of Woman) are revealed as related by their simultaneous reflection in the image of the puppet, which similarly alternates between mere matter and the illusion of agency, between the top and the bottom of the hypothetical hierarchy of representation.

These examples from Shakespeare suggest a recurrent figural comparison between the female body and the puppet which tends to naturalize the subordination of the female in a hierarchical system enfolding both social distinction and an ontological opposition of being and representation. Similar habits of thought could allow the performing object to become, in other plays from the public theater, a figural correlate for class and social authority. The young writers attracted to the London theater around the turn of the seventeenth century frequently observed and commented on the broad social changes that, modern historians largely agree, were transforming the socio-economic structures of traditional English society: the consolidation of estates through rack-renting and enclosure, the consequent upheaval of cottagers and copyholders, the rise of a bourgeois merchant class, and the growth of aspirations toward an urbane gentility among the rural gentry. The playwrights dramatized these complex cultural developments with an astonishingly keen sense of the interconnection of social life and its representations, even as they also tended to adapt a particular kind of conservative, sentimental judgment toward the events they depicted. It was perhaps precisely this combination—the way in which a growing sophistication about histrionic effect collided with assumptions about social distinction and a nascent vision of theatrical authorship—that made the image of the puppet so useful to these playwrights.

I continue with a brief example from John Marston's *Histriomastix*

Shakespeare's Text (Athens: University of Georgia Press, 1986), 129–32; and Terence Hawkes, "Telmah," in *Shakespeare and the Question of Theory*, ed. Patricia Parker and Geoffrey Hartman (London: Methuen, 1985), esp. 313–17.

(1599?), which obviously combines a conservative vision of theatrical author-ship with an explicit allegory of social change. Much like Greene in his *Groat's Worth of Wit*, Marston attacks the new generation of poets writing for the public stage, lamenting, in the voice of one Chrisoganus, an "age" in which

> every Scriveners boy shall dippe
> Prophaning quills into Thessaliaes Spring,
> When every artist prentice that hath read
> The pleasant pantry of conceipts, shall dare,
> To write as confident as *Hercules*.
> When every Ballad-monger boldly writes:
> And wind froth of bottle-ale doth fill
> Their purest organ of invention.[75]

Note the quasi-materialist way in which Marston describes how mere "wind froth of bottle-ale" substitutes for the true breath of authorial inspiration. The larger design of the play similarly depicts how Pride temporarily seduces England away from the benevolent reign of Plenty, a process manifest in the decline of feudal hospitality, a familiar topos of the period. The lords Mar-vortius and Philarchus, whose houses formerly were "open to the poore" (257), are taught by Pride to "scorne the abject and the base" (270). Slightly later they also discharge their manservants in favor of boy pages more befit-ting the elegant new life-style of a postfeudal nobility. The servants com-plain, and are chastised by their replacements:

> *Page.* Be Patient fellow, seest thou not my Lord?
> *1. ser.* What an I see him? puppet prating ape?
> *2. ser.* We are no stocks, but we can feele disgrace.
> *3. ser.* Nor tonglesse blocks, but since we feele, weele speake. . . .
> *2. ser.* For service, this is savage recompence.
> Your fathers bought lands and maintained men!
> You sell your lands, and scarce keepe rascall boyes,
> Who Ape-like jet, in garded coates; are whipt
> For mocking men!
>
> (3.1)

[75] *The Plays of John Marston*, ed. H. Harvey Wood (Edinburgh: Oliver and Boyd, 1939), 274. Subse-quent citations are given parenthetically by page number in the text, in the absence of line numbers in this edition.

The first servant's bitter epithet, applied primarily to the diminutive page, seems also applied, by the force of grammar and the theatrical context, to the lord himself. The chaotic syntax of the passage conjures up a social situation in which oppositions of relative size, power, and agency ironically contradict one another: lordly status manifests itself in the maintenance of mere boys who apishly mock the men they figuratively and literally displace. Conversely, the servants—nameless emblems of a feudal order supposedly based on loyalty and tradition—explicitly refuse to be the puppetlike stocks and blocks which, except for this passing theatrical moment, the actual power relations here dramatized compel them to be. Thus, a momentary revelation of real social power (the commodification and objectification of the human) coexists with a nostalgic, conservative vision that construes protocapitalist social mobility as itself a process of objectification, a matter of style and costume. The implicit or explicit images of puppetlike figures (servants or masters) suggest both subjugation and affectation, both the real power relations of an increasingly market-based economy and a merely satiric vision of deportment and dress.

As I have suggested, the figural efficacy of the puppet within this network of associations is particularly striking in the works of Ben Jonson, who continued to reveal his fascination with the performing object in the comedies of his middle career. In Jonson's works the puppet figures at once within the construction of an elite mode of dramatic art (distinguished from mere popular entertainment), and in a satiric project that demonizes every kind of social (or sexual) mobility. In *Volpone* (1606), at the climax of the subplot, when Peregrin humiliates the social-climbing Sir Politic Would-Be by tricking him into hiding inside a tortoiseshell, his confederates, two English merchants, exult:

> *Merchant 1.* 'Twere a rare motion, to be seene in Fleet-street!
> Merchant 2. I, i'the terme.
> Merchant 1. Or Smithfield, in the faire.
>
> (5.4.77–79)

This moment is a kind of summation of Jonsonian "humour" comedy: the puppetlike comic gull, mastered by his own compulsions no less than by the manipulating tricksters, is constrained to exhibit and exhaust the full repertoire of his "humourous" behavior. The metaphor of the puppet also at once links and separates the comic action of Jonson's own play and the popular entertainment whose parodic texture and subordinate social location (the street or fair) is the ground of the metaphor's appropriateness within the dramatic context. In the prologue to the same play, Jonson had trumpeted his artistic divorce from popular entertainment, promising that, in his play,

> no egges are broken;
> Nor quaking custards with fierce teeth affrighted
> Where your rout are so delighted.
>
> (20–22)

Yet both the main and subordinate plots of the play center, as do all of Jonson's best-known comic plots, on the relentless manipulation of puppetlike gulls; and Jonson's casual metaphor concedes a subtle analogy between this recurrent comic situation and the puppet performance it figurally resembles. Such an analogy, however, also declares the distance between Jonson's own drama and the merely performative "motion" by recontextualizing the latter within multiple frames of histrionic representation. Peregrine's trick might "descend" to the puppet show as it has in fact "ascended" into the larger design of Jonson's magisterial play.

Similarly, in *Epicoene* (1609) Jonson once again evokes the image of the puppet at a climactic moment of his own play's comic action. At the first of two turning points in the main plot, when Morose realizes his new bride is not the silent woman he had believed her to be, she asks him: "Why, did you thinke you had married a statue? or a motion, onely? one of the French puppets, with the eyes turn'd with a wire?" (3.4.36–38). In the theatrical moment, the comic effect seems to stem from the sudden reversal of puppetmaster and puppet, the manipulator and the manipulated—a triumphant reassertion of vitality in the face of social paralysis, subjugation, and silence. But Epicoene is also a "puppet" in the common figural sense of the period—as Sir Dauphine's "ingle," the veritable boy painted and made effeminate by his role in Dauphine's (and Jonson's) plot. Jonson's irony thus overflows its apparent figural expression, just as the play's ending overturns the audience's expectations in a metadramatic revelation of the literal mechanisms of the stage (the boy actor playing a boy actor).

Similarly, at the end of *The Alchemist* Lovewit returns home unexpectedly and, seeing evidence of strange goings-on at his house, initially assumes his butler Jeremy has been exhibiting "Babions, or Puppets . . . or the new Motion / Of the Knights courser, covering the Parsons mare" (5.1.14–24). Subtle, Face, and Doll, whose relentless manipulation of a whole cast of humorous gulls constitutes the play for its literal audience, are both figural puppet masters and literal denizens of the carnivalesque underground of ape trainers and puppeteers. As such they personify at once the implacable cruelty and relentlessly exercised power that characterize Jonsonian "humour" comedy and an ultimate social powerlessness as *characters* that is figurally equivalent to their status as performers in the Jonsonian vision of theater. This paradoxical combination corresponds to Jonson's own authorial position as I described it in the previous section: suspended between his imperious theoretical claims of literary privilege and the practical constraints of a theater that was still inextricably entwined with so-called popular modes of culture.

All these passages, along with many others from approximately the same period, show the traces of a habit of thought that links the puppet, the woman, the servant, and the effeminate social climber within a master system of representation and being which also privileges the author over the actor, and the masculine, mastering "spirit" over the supposedly passive, feminized flesh. This intricate cultural and philosophical system also underlies the more specific process by which popular performance is implicitly defined as such even as it is appropriated within the texts of a relatively more literary form of drama. The same social anxieties that the puppet seems so frequently to figure forth were, after all, always applicable to the poets' own precarious social positions. The performing object thus seems to be a trope whose meaning constantly threatens to overflow its announced formal limits. Indeed, the astonishing figural and metadramatic power of the performing object tends almost inevitably to contradict, precisely as such, the low social and cultural status that underlies its metaphoric significance. Transplanted from the tiny box stages on Fleet Street and Holborn Bridge or the booths of Bartholomew Fair, the puppet is forced to bear the discursive burden not only of the theological theater but also of the social and sexual hierarchies it resembles.

"The Mouth of 'hem All":
The Tempest and *Bartholomew Faire*

They are Actors, Sir, and as good as any, none disprais'd, for dumb showes: indeed, I am the mouth of 'hem all!
—Ben Jonson, *Bartholomew Faire*

Ben Jonson's *Bartholomew Faire* is, of course, the period's most obvious example of the process of cultural appropriation which I have considered throughout this chapter. Jonson explicitly and self-consciously appropriates the voices and practices of carnival, and concludes by importing a fully realized puppet show into his play. My discussion here juxtaposes *Bartholomew Faire* with Shakespeare's *Tempest*, a play that similarly, if more subtly, exploits popular culture in general and the puppet in particular. The two plays, written and performed within a few years of each other in the second decade of the seventeenth century, have often been compared—for example, by Alvin Kernan, who declares the works to be representative of the two playwrights' "characteristic visions of the world."[76] Observing a more specific connection between the plays, I see them as works that declare their own "literary" status, at least in part, by their pointed allusions to the puppet—which the playwrights thus construct as a paradigm both of popular culture and of performance itself. Each play envisions (its own) authorship within a hypothetical structure of representation that, once again, is profoundly linked to the specific modes of social subordination they otherwise affirm.

At a climactic and familiar moment of *The Tempest*, King Alonso and the rest of the shipwrecked Italian noblemen confront a sudden vision:

> *Enter several strange Shapes, bringing in a banket; and dance about it with gentle actions of salutations; and inviting the King, etc., to eat, they depart.*
> *Alonso.* Give us kind keepers, heaven! what were these?
> *Sebastian.* A living drollery.
>
> (3.3.19–21)

Most editors of this passage gloss "drollery" to mean a puppet show, and conclude that Sebastian is seeing these mysterious dancing waiters as puppets that have come to life. I agree with this reading, and suggest that Shakespeare appropriates the performing object, here and elsewhere in *The Tempest*, as a metaphor relevant to both of the two most common interpretations of the play, which has often been seen either as an allegory of theatrical authorship or as a text "imbricated within the discourse of colonialism," a crucial document in the construction of a colonial Other.[77] Sebastian's comparison of the

---

[76] Alvin Kernan, "The Great Fair of the World and the Ocean Island: *Bartholomew Faire* and *The Tempest*," in vol. 3 of *The Revels History of Drama in English*, ed. Lois Potter (London: Methuen, 1975), 457.

[77] Frank Kermode briefly surveys the nineteenth-century view of *The Tempest* as Shakespeare's lyrical farewell to his art in the introduction to his Arden edition of the play (Cambridge: Harvard University Press, 1954), lxxi-ii. More recently Leah Marcus has argued that "*The Tempest* enacts a fantasy of near-total

"strange shapes" to "a living drollery" is a curious one, however, for it makes better sense from the audience's point of view than from his. By this time the audience is well aware that the various spiritual beings on the island are one kind of figural puppet, the tools of Prospero's intricately theatrical "plot"; and they may suspect that Sebastian and the other human characters are also Prospero's puppets on a different level, manipulated against their will toward some impending final reconciliation. But Sebastian himself knows none of this. Nor would the "strange shapes" of the spirits seem necessarily to suggest by their size or appearance a comparison to the literal puppets of Shakespeare's day. In fact, the metaphor emphasizes, precisely in its apparent incongruity to the context, a particular vision of authorship and authority otherwise manifest in the play as a whole.

This becomes clear as one considers Shakespeare's term "drollery," which proves to be yet one more word embodying an intricate constellation of social, theological, and theatrical meaning. Half a century ago M. A. Shaaber suggested, marshaling a variety of other texts as evidence, that the phrase means not "living puppets" but rather "an animated grotesque picture," since parodic drawings, figures, or pictures were also called drolleries.[78] The Dutch were apparently known as creators of this type of grotesque image, a connection that perhaps recalls the work of painters such as Bosch and Brueghel. Thomas Dekker, in *The Bellman of London* (1608), describes a roomful of beggars and vagabonds who "shewed . . . like a dutch peece of *Drollery*: for they sat at table as if they had been so many Anticks: a Painters prentice could not draw worse faces than they themselves made, . . . no, nor a painter himselfe vary picture into more strange and more ill-favord gestures" (3:87). A puppet show, then, was presumably sometimes called a drollery by reference to its similarly grotesque qualities: its typically farcical and parodic content and the inevitable diminution and physical deformity of its artificial players. A puppet and a "droll" or "drollery" in Shaaber's sense are thus two manifestations of a similar cultural impulse; and by about the time of *The Tempest* and well into the eighteenth century, the latter words also referred to

authorial power and control in which What the Author Intends comes close to infallible execution." Leah Marcus, *Puzzling Shakespeare: Local Reading and Its Discontents* (Berkeley: University of California Press, 1988), 49. The phrase quoted in my text is from Francis Barker and Peter Hulme, "Nymphs and Reapers Heavily Vanish: The Discursive Con-Texts of *The Tempest*," in *Alternative Shakespeares*, ed. John Drakakis (London: Routledge, 1985), 204; see also Paul Brown, " 'This Thing of Darkness I Acknowledge Mine': *The Tempest* and the Discourse of Colonialism," in *Political Shakespeare: New Essays in Cultural Materialism*, ed. Jonathan Dollimore and Alan Sinfield (Ithaca: Cornell University Press, 1985), 48–76.

[78] M. A. Shaaber, " 'A Living Drollery' (Tempest III, iii, 21)," *Modern Language Notes* 60 (1945): 391. Cf. *OED* s.v. "drollery," 2a and 2b.

short farcical plays like those performed at market fairs by actors and puppets alike.[79]

At the same time, the kind of carved figurines that in early modern England were associated with the Dutch could evoke the same kind of theological associations I have previously observed with "mammets," "marmosets," and puppets. John Foxe's *Book of Martyrs*, for example, recounts the story of a woman, identified only as "Prest's Wife," who, "entering into St. Peter's church, beheld there a cunning Dutchman, how he made new noses to certain fine images that were disfigured in king Edward's time: 'What a mad man art thou,' said she, 'To make them new noses, which within a few days shall all lose their heads!' The Dutchman accused her, and laid it hard to her charge."[80] Some years later, in *Antonio and Mellida* (1599), John Marston illustrates the general convergence of inanimate puppet and parodic figure within the context of the familiar early modern belief in a theological and ontological hierarchy or "chain of being":

> Philosophy maintains that nature's wise
> And forms no useless or unperfect thing.
> Did nature make the earth, or the earth nature?
> For earthly dirt makes all things, makes the man,
> Moulds me up honour and, like a cunning Dutchman
> Paints me a puppet even with seeming breath
> And gives a sot appearance of a soul.
>
> (3.1.27–33)

The image of the "drollery," like that of the puppet, evokes a semantic hierarchy in which radically different but related senses coexist: grotesque deformity, the magical efficacy or idolatrous deception of the religious image, and a theological vision of divine spirit descending into "earthly dirt" (the third sense turning back to the first in the theological association of corporeality and materiality).

I complete this particular web of connection by briefly considering another rather different cultural source that also underlies the passage about the "living drollery." The play's involvement with the discourses of colonialism

---

[79] On the theatrical "droll" during the Commonwealth and later, see Hyder E. Rollins, "A Contribution to the History of the English Commonwealth Drama," *Studies in Philology* 18 (July 1921): 302; and Sybil Rosenfeld, *The Theatre of the London Fairs in the Eighteenth Century* (Cambridge: Cambridge University Press, 1960), 2–3, 135–49.

[80] John Foxe, *The Acts and Monuments*, ed. Stephen Reed Cattley, 8 vols. (London, 1837–41), 8:500.

has been much discussed in recent years, but as far back as 1914 Rachel M. Kelsey suggested that the vision of the "strange shapes" was influenced by an account of an Indian dance performed before Captain John Smith, from William Strachey's pamphlet on "the proceedings of the English Colonie in Virginia," a text later reprinted in *Purchas His Pilgrimes*.[81] As the pamphlet describes it, Captain Smith was sitting before a fire at the camp of the celebrated Indian King Powhatan, when

> sudddenly amongst the woods was heard such a hideous noise and shriking, that they betooke them to their armes, supposing Powhatan with all his power came to surprise them; but the beholders . . . satisfied the Captaine there was no such matter, being presently presented with this anticke, thirty yong women came naked out of the woods . . . their bodies all painted, some white, some red, some blacke, some party colour, but every one different. . . . These Fiends with most hellish cries and shouts rushing from amongst the trees, cast themselves in a ring about the fire, singing and dancing with excellent ill variety, oft falling into their infernall passions, and then solemnely againe to sing and dance. Having spent neere an houre in this Maskarado, as they entred, in like manner they departed.[82]

This passage obviously portrays the Indian dance as wild, savage, and "natural," on the one hand, and painted, theatrical, and artificial, on the other, an "anticke" or "Maskarado" that, moreover, displaces for the moment the potential threat of Indian warriors. "Antic" or "antique" referred originally to a kind of grotesque image (like a gargoyle); and, by extension, was associated with the same kinds of carnivalesque, paratheatrical performance among which one would include the puppet, the "droll," and the performing ape. In Greene's *Groat's Worth of Wit*, for example, the popular playwrights were dismissed in the same sentence as "puppets . . . that speake from our mouths" and "*Anticks* garnisht in our colours"; and the anonymous author of the Bartholomew Fair pamphlet which I have previously cited describes "a rogue like a wild woodman, or in an *antick* shape, [who] desire[s] your com-

---

[81] Rachel M. Kelsey, "Indian Dances in 'The Tempest,' " *Journal of English and Germanic Philology* 13 (1914): 98–104. Strachey is, of course, also the author of *The True Repertory of the Wrack*, one of two accounts of Sir Thomas Gates's shipwreck in Bermuda which have generally been recognized as sources of *The Tempest*.

[82] William Strachey, "The Proceedings of the English Colony in Virginia . . . enlarged out of the Writings of Capt. John Smith . . . ," in *Hakluytus Posthumus or Purchas His Pilgrimes*, 20 vols. (Glasgow: James MacLehose and Sons, 1906), 18:496.

pany to view his motion." In the Strachey pamphlet and elsewhere, that is, the colonial Other is conceptualized in the terms of the same semantic and cultural hierarchy in which the social, sexual, and cultural distinctions of early modern England were also being placed. Thus, Shakespeare in the passage about the "living drollery" may have been alluding at once to the spectacle of New World strangeness and to the native grotesquerie of the puppet show.

Now, as I observed in the beginning of this discussion, the "strange shapes" who appear before Sebastian and the others are, in a simple figural sense, Prospero's "puppets," the tools of his master plan, and yet also, in some ultimate theatrical sense, Shakespeare's. Gonzalo goes on to describe the "strange shapes" in more detail:

> *Gonzalo.*   If at Naples
> I should report this now, would they believe me?
> If I should say I saw such islanders
> (For certes, these are people of the island),
> Who though they are of monstrous shape, yet note
> Their manners are more gentle, kind than of
> Our human generation you shall find
> Many, nay almost any.
> *Prospero [Aside].* Honest Lord,
> Thou hast said well; for some of you there present
> Are worse than devils.
>
> (3.3.27–35).

Gonzalo here invokes the paradox of the "noble savage" (which Shakespeare himself had presumably taken from Montaigne) in a passage that implicitly links this idea with the histrionic paradox of a *living* drollery, a puppet or image brought magically to life. The idea of a puppet who becomes literally alive evokes the wonder of an illusion breaking its bounds, a creation breaking free from its creator. A living puppet would subvert the representational hierarchy of the theological theater, that hypothetical vision of authorship in whose construction *The Tempest* otherwise participates in its implicit and oft-noted conflation of divine providence, Prospero's magic, and the playwright's own art.

In this scene, however, the "strange shapes" are still, almost literally, mere performing objects: they are a "living" drollery (if "spirits" may be said to live), and yet they wholly and merely embody the "motions" and intentions of Prospero. As Caliban had earlier affirmed of them,

they'll nor pinch,
Fright me with urchin-shows, pitch me i'th'mire,
Nor lead me, like a fire-brand, in the dark
Out of my way, unless he bid 'em.

(2.2.4–7)

This puppetlike servitude of the spirits, like that of Caliban himself, transcends the ontological subversion evoked momentarily in this scene, by which an apparent representation returns to the fullness of presence. Just so, the announced gentility of these "islanders," which Prospero ironically confirms by contrasting it with the devilish behavior of Sebastian and Antonio, is subsumed within the cultural alterity announced by the opening image of the puppet, and continued in the ensuing references to "monstrous" islanders and deformed "mountaineers" (3.3.31, 43). As, in Strachey's pamphlet, the potential threat of the Indian dancers recedes first into the comfortable strangeness of the merely theatrical, and then into the absolute safety of narrative itself, so the physical monstrosity and genuine wonder of the living puppets recedes first into the sentimental fantasy of the noble savage, then into the mastering gaze of Prospero (at once an onstage spectator and surrogate playwright), and finally into the vicarious, suspended disbelief of the real spectatorial point of view. Thus, Shakespeare titillates his audience with the spectacle of the exotic while assuaging their anxiety about the cultural, geographic, or racial Other; and he does so in a scene that simultaneously serves, like the play as a whole, as a metadramatic meditation on theatrical representation and its effects.

The image of the puppet not only operates within both frames of reference but also illuminates their interconnection. Insofar as Prospero is read as a type or emblem of the author/creator, then the "strange shapes" who do his bidding are puppets, so to speak, in two distinct but related senses. When Prospero, in perhaps the most celebrated speech of the play, prepares to abjure his "rough magic" even as he invokes the myriad spirits over which that magic has held sway, he includes among them

demi-puppets that
By moonshine do the green sour ringlets make
Whereof the ewe not bites.

(5.1.36–38)

Here again, "demi-puppets" may seem a curious phrase with which to describe these elfin supernatural beings; and most editors gloss it, with Frank

Kermode, as referring to "the doll-like size of the elves." Shakespeare's passage also alludes, as has long been recognized, to a speech spoken by Medea in Ovid's *Metamorphoses* (7.197–209). But neither the word nor the image of the puppet appears in Ovid's Latin or in the English translation by Arthur Golding which Shakespeare probably knew. Shakespeare's choice of word thus reinforces the implicit reference to witchcraft (by echoing the popular belief in demonic familiars often referred to as "puppets") even as it further links Prospero's literal magic to the histrionic illusion of the performing object. The prefix "demi" apparently operates as a qualifier—in the sense of "quasi." But such grammatical qualification renders the whole phrase ambiguous. It is one thing to call Mark Antony the "demi Atlas of this earth" (*Antony and Cleopatra* 1.5.23), since here the prefix merely qualifies an extravagant bit of rhetorical praise.[83] But since the metaphoric idea of a puppet already conveys passivity and servitude, the "demi" here reverses itself to operate as a kind of intensifier, conveying the idea, perhaps, of a puppet not quite under Prospero's control. As such the phrase also converges with the "living drollery" to suggest a puppet escaping from its representational subservience.

Similarly, a few scenes earlier, as Prospero prepares to demonstrate his magical "art" for Ferdinand and Miranda, he enjoins Ariel to

> bring the rabble
> (O'er whom I give thee pow'r) here to this place.
> Incite them to quick *motion.*
> (4.1.37–39; emphasis added)

As these lines seem subtly to suggest, the spirit-players of Prospero's ensuing wedding masque are almost literally puppets—passive histrionic vehicles who perform a kind of "motion." In this scene Shakespeare seems to be deliberately playing with the conventional structure of the representational hierarchy by inverting the puppet's association with corporeality, "earthly dirt," and the grotesque body. These player-puppets are not, as it were, all *body*— mere corporeal containers available for a mastering authorial inspiration— but, conversely, "all spirit[s]" (4.1.148–49). Or, to put it another way, they are literal players who represent spirits who represent players who represent spirits (the goddesses Ceres, Iris, and Juno), and who also resemble the courtly amateurs who played gods and demigods in the "real" masques of King

---

[83] In the Arden edition of *The Tempest*, Kermode suggests this parallel in his note to the passage.

James's court, where *The Tempest*, too, was once performed. But then these bewilderingly secondary or tertiary theatrical signs "enact" what Prospero calls "my present fancies" (4.1.121–22), a vision of performance unmediated by either time or the text, a performance of absolute self-presence that overcomes the inevitable gap between author and actor, between conception and interpretation. In one sense, then, the masque may be seen as an elaborate vision of the theological theater, in which the real author/creator, Shakespeare, stands at the apex of a dizzying abyssal structure of play within play within play.

Even this spectacular metadramatic tour de force, however, implicitly qualifies the power of representation by subordinating it to the ideological issues of the play. For Prospero's metaphoric authorial power is still but a tool for the paternal and political authority he also represents, and whose affirmation or reestablishment is the business of the masque and the play as a whole. In the masque, Prospero's "puppets" playact a pageant of sexual prohibition explicitly intended to preserve Miranda's "virgin knot," the fragile foundation on which Prospero's larger dynastic and political goals depend. Obviously enough, that virginity is threatened far less by Ferdinand's possible sexual impatience in the theatrical present than it was, once upon a time, by Caliban's attempted rape. Thus, Shakespeare (or Prospero) writes into the masque a version of the "living drollery" which can be seen to figure forth Caliban's literal rebellion against Prospero's authority and the inevitable defeat of that rebellion. The goddess Iris describes how Cupid, the childlike god of love,

> has broke his arrows,
> Swears he will shoot no more, but play with sparrows,
> And be a boy right out.
>
> (4.1.99–101)

Reversing the conventional idealizing motion of the masque in a projected grammatical future of as yet unrealized intention, this version of Eros accepts what sounds like the castrating necessity of the same Law on whose sovereignty, sexual and political, the play's father/author otherwise insists. Cupid here is a representation who aspires, or condescends, to the fullness of natural presence—descending from spirit to flesh, from the iconic to the mundane, from one kind of "play" to another. But Prospero's puppets will never finish their magical performance, precisely because the mind that controls them is also "troubled" by the inescapable deformity of the "earthly" Caliban, that other puppetlike slave whose body Prospero incessantly manipulates with pinches, aches, and cramps (e.g., 1.2.321–71; 2.2.4–14). Caliban is thus both a "living drollery" and a "demi-puppet," a figure who "must obey" Prospero's "control" (1.2.372–73) and yet who persists to the last in his irredeemable selfhood. Correspondingly, Caliban is also both the play's central "popular" attraction (as Jonson confirms in a passage I will presently cite) and its obvious central figure of aboriginal strangeness and cultural alterity. The play's metadramatic bravura and its exploration of otherness are thus inextricably linked in the same image (the living puppet) whose figural meaning instantiates the representational and social hierarchies which it appears, ever so briefly, to destabilize.

If the puppet remains an implicit figural presence in *The Tempest*, in *Bartholomew Faire*, by contrast, Jonson literally appropriates puppet theater by directly importing it into his play. In this, as in so much else, *Bartholomew Faire* seems to sum up all of its author's theatrical, moral, and philosophical obsessions.[84] Jonson attempts in this play to transcend and transform popular performance by embracing it with a self-conscious irony; and he reaffirms his lifelong commitment to the sovereignty of authorship by suggesting its connection to other forms of social authority. In the elaborately metadramatic induction to the play, the stagekeeper's nostalgic reminiscences about improvisational forms of Elizabethan popular performance are interrupted by a "Booke-holder," or prompter, and a "Scrivener," who proceed to read a mock "contract" between Jonson and his audience. In both cases these are figures of literary and legal authority, and at the same time *representatives* of the literally absent author who through them attempts to govern the theatrical site from a distance.[85] The comic contract lays down the conditions for proper spectatorship and for Jonson's own compromise with performance as his audiences liked it. In it the puppets who will eventually appear in the play are named as the key term in that compromise: "If there be never a *Servant-*

---

[84] *Bartholomew Faire*, asserts Richard Dutton, is "designed to stand as the keystone of [Jonson's] writing to that point." Richard Dutton, *Ben Jonson: To the First Folio* (Cambridge: Cambridge University Press, 1983), 157. It is "the ultimate version," writes Alvin Kernan, "of the play Jonson wrote again and again." Alvin Kernan, "The Plays and the Playwrights," in Potter, *Revels History of Drama in English*, 3:463. On Jonson's delicate compromise between popular and elite forms of performance in this play, see also John Gordon Sweeney, *Jonson and the Psychology of Public Theater* (Princeton: Princeton University Press, 1985), 160; and Jonathan Haynes, "Festivity and the Dramatic Economy of Jonson's *Bartholomew Faire*," *ELH* 51 (Winter 1984): 645–68.

[85] Cf. Jacques Derrida, *Writing and Difference*, trans. Alan Bass (Chicago: University of Chicago Press, 1978), 235.

monster i'the *Fayre*, who can helpe it? he sayes; nor a nest of *Antiques?* The Author . . . is loth to make Nature afraid in his Playes, like those that beget Tales, Tempests, and such like Drolleries . . . yet if the Puppets will please any body, they shall be entreated to come in" (Ind. 118–34). This passage not only links puppets, "drolleries," and "antiques" (antics), but also places Shakespeare's late romances within this spectrum of the popular. It also conveys a self-conscious and perhaps slightly disingenuous heartiness that contrasts markedly with previous Jonsonian rejections of popular culture and does not quite conceal the underlying tone of contempt.

In traditional thematic terms, however, the play that follows this induction has often seemed among Jonson's clearest and most single-minded. Jonson neither taunts the audience with the gap between their moral and theatrical sympathies (as in the shockingly punitive ending of *Volpone*), nor manipulates the "epistemic" status of his plot by withholding crucial information from the audience (as in *Epicoene*).[86] Instead, as critics generally concur, Jonson uses the play's carnivalesque setting in an obvious parable of moral imperfection and forgiveness, exposing and humiliating but finally reconciling the play's three embodiments of moral, religious, and political authority: Humphrey Wasp, tutor and governor; Zeal-of-the-Land Busy, Puritan railer against the "idolatries" of the fair; and Justice Over-Do, magistrate of the fair's special court of Pie Powder and aspiring reformer of its alleged "enormities." Even as he overturns various examples of false authority in his comic plot, however, Jonson pointedly defers, in another of his characteristic framing devices, to the veritable authority of the offstage world. "Your Majesty is welcome to a fair," Jonson begins a prologue written for the play's performance at court; and in a concluding epilogue declares correspondingly:

> Your Majesty has seen the play, and you
> Can best allow it from your ear and view.
> You know the scope of writers, and what store
> Of leave is given them, if they take not more,
> And turn it into license: you can tell
> If we have us'd that leave you gave us well:
> . . . .

---

[86] I take the term "epistemic" in this sense (referring to the relative level of knowledge of the true state of affairs in a dramatic plot) from Thomas G. Pavel, *The Poetics of Plot: The Case of English Renaissance Drama* (Minneapolis: University of Minnesota Press, 1985); see, for example, 48–49, 60, 68, and passim.

This is your power to judge, great sir.

(epi. 1–9)

The temporary social inversions enacted within the play are obviously circumscribed by a larger authority reaffirmed in its absolute inviolability both within and without the theater.[87]

I want to suggest, by extension, that the actual puppet show repeats, along the axis of the hierarchy of representation, something like the same strategy: an overturning and eventual reaffirmation of authorship and authority. Within the play the puppet show is literally authored by John Littlewit, another "humour" character whose behavior is held out to us as a ludicrous parody of authorial propriety in both senses of the word:

> *Sharkwell.* What, doe you not know the *Author*, fellow *Filcher?* you must take no money of him; he must come in *gratis.* Mr. *Littlewit* is a voluntary; he is the *Author.*
> *John.* Peace, speake not too lowd, I would not have any notice taken, that I am the *Author*, till wee see how it passes.

(5.3.20–24)

Correspondingly, the showman or "interpreter" of the puppets, Lantern Leatherhead, has sometimes been read as one more of Jonson's many satiric images of Inigo Jones, whose extravagant designs for the Jacobean court masques are thus conflated with the lowest common denominator of performative spectacle.[88] Leatherhead (whose onomastic name itself collapses the representational distance between puppet and puppeteer)[89] at one point reminisces about his histrionic career in a passage that seems deliberately to echo the induction: "O, the *Motions*, that I, *Lanthorne Leatherhead* have given light to, i' my time, since my Master *Pod* dyed! *Jerusalem* was a stately thing; and so was *Ninive*, and the citty of *Norwich*, and *Sodom* and *Gomorrah*; with the rising o' the prentises; and pulling downe the bawdy houses there, upon *Shrove-Tuesday*, but the *Gunpowder-plot*, there was a get-penny! I have presented that to an eighteene, or twenty pence audience, nine times in

---

[87] Cf. Wayne, "Drama and Society in the Age of Jonson," 118.

[88] See Hereford and Simpson, *Ben Jonson*, 2:146–48, for a summary of the evidence for this identification.

[89] On Jonson's frequent use of "onomastic" or denotative names, see Anne Barton, *Ben Jonson, Dramatist* (Cambridge: Cambridge University Press, 1984), 170–93; and idem, *The Names of Comedy* (Toronto: University of Toronto Press, 1990).

an afternoone" (5.1.6–14). Leatherhead's frankly commercial attitude to his "art" is at once a parody of and essentially indistinguishable from Jonson's opening agreement that each member of the audience may "judge his six pen'orth, his twelve pen'orth, so to his eighteene pence, 2. shillings, halfe a crowne, to the value of his place" (Ind. 87–89). That theatrical taste might be susceptible to such financial quantification is, in one sense, the ground of Jonson's ambivalence about the practical theater; but in another sense such implicit correspondence between social class and literary judgment would, if true, confirm the transparency of the social and representational hierarchies. Here again Jonson seems to satirize his own craft as little better than mere puppetry, even as this satiric point itself depends on a hierarchical system distinguishing between player and puppet, between high and low modes of performance.

If the puppet show is thus in part a diminutive parody of authorship, so it is also, as critics have frequently observed, a kind of concentrated, miniature version of the play as a whole.[90] The puppet Dionysius, for example, appears "in a Scriveners furr'd gowne" (5.4.362), as if to echo the scrivener who appears in the induction. The other puppets "quarrel and fall together by the ears" (5.4.335) in a manner that explicitly echoes the "game of vapours" played by Quarlous, Wasp and others in a previous scene, in which "every man . . . oppose[s] the last man that spoke: whether it concern'd him or no" (4.4.27). The puppets Damon and Pythias, competing ludicrously for the puppet Hero, echo Quarlous and Win-Wife, who compete for the love of Grace Wellborn. The unmistakable parallels between the puppet play and the real play are both thematic and metadramatic. On the one hand, Jonson suggests that the various social types dramatized in his play are all humorous "puppets," enslaved to their own compulsions and hence vulnerable to the bawds, conmen and cutpurses of the fair.[91] On the other hand, puppets have already been foregrounded as a paradigmatic instance of low, carnivalesque entertainment; and even as Jonson indulges both his onstage and offstage audience with them, he pointedly suggests that their enjoyment is itself one more example of "humourous" social behavior.

Accordingly, Bartholomew Cokes (whom Barish appropriately calls "the

[90] See, for example, G. R. Hibbard, introduction to *Bartholmew Fair* (*sic*) (London: Ernst Benn, 1977), xxvii; Alexander Leggatt, *Ben Jonson: His Vision and His Art* (London: Methuen, 1981), 18; and Watson, *Ben Jonson's Parodic Strategy*, 142.

[91] The thematic idea of character-as-puppet has been observed by numerous critics. See, for example, Jonas Barish, *Ben Jonson and the Language of Prose Comedy* (Cambridge: Harvard University Press, 1960), 237; Hibbard, *Bartholmew Fair*, xxx; and Watson, *Ben Jonson's Parodic Strategy*, 155.

archetypal puppet among men"),[92] shows his typical "humourous" enjoyment of the puppets and even an apparent inability to distinguish between them and human actors, not only aesthetically but also in absolute mimetic terms. At one point Jonson's marginal stage direction suggests that Cokes "handles" the puppets in what is presumably a sexually suggestive way (5.4.7–9). During the puppet show itself Cokes frequently interrupts, as if to suggest his naive confusion of performance and reality, his inability to read the semiotic "codes" of puppet theater:

> *Puppet Pythias.* Downe with him, Damon.
> *Puppet Damon.* Pinke his guts, Pythias.
> *Leatherhead.* What, so malicious?
> Will ye murder me, Masters both, i' mine own house?
> . . . .
> *Cokes.* How is't friend, ha' they hurt thee?
> *Leatherhead.* O no!
> Between you and I Sir, we doe but make show.
> . . . .
> *Cokes.* Well, we have seen't, and thou hast felt it, whatsoever thou sayest.
>
> (5.3.261–86)

In portraying Cokes's naïveté as spectator, however, Jonson is also demonstrating how multiple layers of improvisational performance are finally subsumed within the fixed boundaries of a master theatrical text. The puppets' attacks on Leatherhead, which apparently interrupt the narrative of the puppet play, are themselves interrupted by Cokes; but the latter then provokes an apparently spontaneous reply from Leatherhead which nevertheless completes Cokes's previous line so as to suggest the doggerel meter and rhyme of the puppet show "text": "How is't friend, ha' they hurt thee?/ O no! / Between you and I Sir, we doe but make show." Cokes becomes, so to speak, a participant in a hypothetical, mediate level of performance just in between the puppet play and Jonson's play. His theatrical naïveté either collapses the hierarchy of representation by confusing secondary and primary (as when he seems to assume that puppet bodies are anatomically correct) or implicitly confirms that hierarchy by insisting on the pure material reality of the puppet (as when he asserts that a blow on the head is always real, however it is

---

[92] Barish, *Ben Jonson and the Language of Prose Comedy*, 238.

"interpreted").[93] Throughout this scene, in other words, Jonson seems to suggest that puppets are a diminutive and secondary version of "real" performance; but they are also, precisely as such, a paradigmatic instance of a representational process here reconstrued as a progressive descent of meaning and "truth" into a histrionic multiplicity of play within play.

Just so, Jonson himself reinscribes this ephemeral and improvisational mode of popular performance within the coherent unity of his own play, and even seems to uphold puppetry as an incongruous affirmation of histrionic (and social) freedom. When the Puritan Zeal-of-the-Land Busy interrupts the puppet show and proceeds to dispute with the puppet Dionysius (fabled tyrant of ancient Syracuse reborn as a Jacobean scrivener and schoolmaster), his defeat seems to affirm the performative impulse as an imperfect but morally superior alternative to Puritan hypocrisy: "I know no fitter match, than a Puppet to commit with an Hypocrite!" (5.5.50). But this apparent "victory" of performance embodies another terminal confusion of truth and image, text and performance. An actor plays a puppet master (Lantern Leatherhead), who speaks the voice of a puppet, who represents a historical figure degraded to the level of the mundane, and who then "breaks" this character to speak as "himself" in defending theater and confuting Busy. But whose voice wins the debate? That of Dionysius the puppet and character? That of the hypothetical puppet-player somehow "outside" his role? That of Lantern Leatherhead? That of Ben Jonson? This puppet-player seems enjoined quite specifically to speak more than has been set down for him; and the authorial voice here speaks at once *of* and *against* itself, in a scene that seems to affirm not only performance in both its high and low manifestations but even that histrionic improvisation that Jonson so carefully silences in the induction. All this, however, is itself merely an illusion. The whole scene of improvised debate within puppet show within play also constitutes (and is constituted by) the text of *Bartholomew Faire*.

Finally, of course, the puppet wins the disputation by answering Busy's familiar Puritan charge that "the Male, among you, putteth on the apparell of the Female, and the Female of the Male" simply by taking up his garment to reveal the mere wood and cloth of the puppet's body, or perhaps the smooth flesh of the puppeteer's forearm.[94] The puppets, Dionysius concludes triumphantly, "have neyther Male nor Female amongst us"

[93] For an analysis of this scene in semiotic terms, see Jiri Veltrusky, "Puppetry and Acting," *Semiotica* 47.1–4 (1983): 72–73, 106.

[94] The latter possibility was first suggested to me by my colleague Lawrence Breiner.

(5.5.99–106). I have previously suggested that in early modern discourse puppets frequently evoke figural associations of femininity or effeminacy, which are linked to the theological or ontological lowness of the inanimate and correspondingly inscribed in a master cultural system of social subordination. Such associations provide a problematic context for this scene's more obvious affirmation of theatrical illusion. The puppet body, in its undifferentiated materiality, is somehow both "below" and "above" the multiplicity of gender in an imagined hierarchy of objective being: it possesses both a formlessness that precedes anatomy and an ontological unity that transcends sex. Nevertheless, within the histrionic sphere that body becomes a sort of tabula rasa on which the complex cultural patterns of sexuality and gender are endlessly (re)written and read:

> *Puppet Leander.* A pox of your maners, kisse my hole here, and smell.
> *Leatherhead.* Kisse your hole, and smell? there's manners indeed.
>
> (5.4.134–35)

> *Puppet Pythias.* You whore-masterly Slave, you . . .
> *Puppet Damon.* Whore-master i'thy face,
> Thou hast lien with her thy selfe, I'll prove't i'this place.
>
> (5.4.235–38)

Dionysius' victorious assertion of his anatomical failure obviously gives the lie to the scatological discourse of his fellow puppets. As Jonson's modern editors point out, however, the puppet also echoes Saint Paul's theological affirmation that, in the sphere of ultimate reality, "there is neither male nor female: for ye are all one in Christ Jesus" (Galatians 3:28).[95] Thus, in this celebrated theatrical moment the absence of flesh speaks for the Flesh, the absence of freedom speaks for theatrical license, and pure material artifice becomes the final testimony of the Spirit. An ultimately secondary and attenuated signifier, a multilevel sign of a sign of a sign (puppet as character; puppet as mere matter), merges with divine unity, the assumed source and origin of all signification. On the one hand, formlessness; on the other, Form itself. "Nay, I'le prove," claims Dionysius, in a last thrust at the defeated Busy, "that I speak by inspiration, as well as he" (5.5.111). His pun conflates the practical conditions of puppet performance (the inanimate object filled

---

[95] On this allusion, see also Debora K. Shuger, "Hypocrites and Puppets in *Bartholomew Faire*," *Modern Philology* 82 (1984): 70–73.

with histrionic "motion" in both senses) with the behavior and discourse of the Puritan, just as the character of Busy itself already conflates the Jonsonian concept of a self-mastering "humour" with the Puritan discourse of divine inspiration (the elect individual as a conduit for the "motions of the spirit").[96] Dionysius' pun sparks a kind of short circuit in the hierarchy of representation that momentarily threatens its structure. The theatrical sign strains toward either pole of that hierarchy, signifying at once that transcendent spiritual Word whose assumed presence sets in motion the descending chain of representation and the "seeming breath" of the performing artifact. Still, even this moment of strange theatrical vertigo finally reinvokes the Jonsonian system of representation with an implacable logic; for the puppet is also quite literally "in-spired" by the voice of Lantern Leatherhead (and of Ben Jonson), "the mouth of 'hem all" (5.3.79), and Dionysius's triumphant "self"-assertion contradicts itself by and in the conditions of its utterance.

Thus, the puppet show of *Bartholomew Faire* becomes Jonson's most fully realized vision of the theological theater, a theater here demonstrated as powerful enough to subsume even the most degraded and degrading form of performance within a master text whose unity subsumes the signs it (reluctantly) sets in motion. Just as the king frames the whole play, secure in his entwined literary and political authority, so the author pervades the mere performance from his position of inviolable externality: a sovereign voice whose presence transcends (and also requires) its own absence, a voice that reaffirms its own mastery in the apparent act of relinquishing it. That Jonson's own text is also now the most complete historical source of information on early modern puppets, and thus virtually the only site from which their parodic, carnivalesque voice still speaks, is merely the final cultural consequence of Jonson's deliberately appropriate strategy.

Nearly twenty years later Jonson would conclude what was probably his last complete work, *A Tale of a Tub* (1633?), with one more example of a puppet show within a play.[97] This play provides an appropriate coda for this chapter because it illustrates how the process of cultural appropriation in its

[96] Busy, we are told earlier in the play, "sayes a grace as long as his breath lasts him" (1.2.67); he claims to be "mov'd in spirit, to bee here, this day, in this *Faire*," to rail against its "Images" and "Idols" (87–97); and, just before his ludicrous disputation with the puppet, he asks once again for the "spirit" to "fill me, fill me, that is, make me full" (5.5.45).

[97] Hereford and Simpson consider this Jonson's *earliest* surviving play, claiming that he merely revised and added to it slightly at the time it was entered into the Stationer's Register in 1633 (*Ben Jonson*, 3:3). I follow Anne Barton's contrary conclusion that the play "makes sense only when read—in its entirety—as a Caroline work," and have also been influenced by Barton's view of this play as an instance of "Caroline nostalgia." See Barton, *Ben Jonson, Dramatist*, 321–23; and cf. Riggs, *Ben Jonson*, 334–36.

totality can never be delimited or controlled, even by an author as imperious and self-confident as Jonson. At the end of this rather curious play, Jonson's characters sit down to watch a "motion" staged by the "architect" In-and-In Medley, another obvious satiric image of Inigo Jones. Medley's "motion" involves some kind of crude clockwork automaton, whose precise workings remain obscure to modern commentators. As Jonson and Medley describe the device, a candle is placed into a "Tub" that is then "capt with paper" so that "the very vapour of the Candle" would "drive all the motions of our matter about / As we present them" (5.7.30–36). The "motions" themselves were either flat cutout figures that the heat of the candle moved around the circular rim of the upright tub, or shadow figures moving across the "fine oild paper" stretched across its top.[98] Whereas the puppet show of *Bartholomew Faire* roughly parallels the larger plot, here the five "motions" precisely re-enact the five acts of the preceding play. The device itself also suggests puns on both Squire Tub, the motion's "author" (5.7.22–23), and on the title of Jonson's play, a proverbial phrase that refers to a foolish trifle, a "cock and bull story." The "motion" and the play alike are thus both literally and figurally tales of a Squire Tub who is, as he puts it, the "Subjectum Fabulae," the subject or protagonist of the "play" within and the play without. After recapping the whole story, the fifth and final "motion" brings the cycle of representation full circle, re-representing the onstage audience themselves in the present moment, when, as Medley puts it, "I, In-and-In, / Present you with a show" (5.10.87–88).

For the Carolingian theatergoer, as for the modern scholar, the motion of *A Tale of a Tub* also inevitably echoes the puppet show of *Bartholomew Faire*, reaching back to the prime of Jonson's career even as the whole play, with its country bumpkins and rural comedy, seems to echo an Elizabethan theatrical mode of some half a century earlier. In a variety of ways, Jonson seems deliberately to invoke a kind of abyssal chain of play within play, a chain that simultaneously descends into a fictional world that here re-views itself and ascends into the widening circle of early modern theater history, within which Ben Jonson's authorial career approaches its conclusion. In one sense, as in *Bartholomew Faire*, Jonson's metadramatic strategy both reaffirms and questions his own characteristic privileging of text over performance. In-and-In's mechanism may, as Anne Barton points out, mock the elaborate *machina versatilis* which Inigo Jones had used to change the scenery in his extravagant courtly masques; but at the same time, as Barton also suggests, this rural

---

[98] See Speaight, *History of the English Puppet Theatre*, 66.

spectacle becomes a celebration of performance as an occasion for social reconciliation, a vision of a community united in self-representation.[99] These primitive puppets, however, must also be assumed to have evoked no trace of representational rebellion, no combative attacks on their manipulator or parodic satire of the audience and characters they depict. They enact a miniature version of the master play with its life transmuted into literal two dimensionality or ghostlike shadows, a mere vestige of histrionic illusion.

Whereas Jonson had once asserted an absolute sovereignty of authorial control by setting in motion puppets who appear to subvert that control, here he does something like the reverse: he concedes a kind of independent life to his characters, but only by diminishing them into crude icons of themselves. In the fictional world Squire Tub achieves in his motion precisely that control over events which the play's comic plot denies to him; but, like the literal author, he does so in a medium whose mimetic inadequacy degrades its objects so as to idealize them. Nevertheless, the conditions of Jonson's own performance re-reversed precisely the situation he had tried to enact, in which an author reaffirms his singular voice by affirming his community with his audience. For *A Tale of a Tub* failed dreadfully on the Carolingian stage, with spectators to whom its curious puppet show must have seemed a bewildering intervention of some alien cultural code rather than a gracious concession to their taste for popular entertainment. Thus, here at the end of Jonson's long career, the imagined power relations of a theological theater dissolve, as they often must, into the actual conditions of a commercial stage, in which the drama's laws the drama's patrons give, and in which authorial mastery is always and merely a representation of itself.

[99] Barton, *Ben Jonson, Dramatist*, 333–35.

Three

The Violence of Appropriation:
From the Interregnum
to the Nineteenth Century

In the two centuries following the closing of the London theaters by Parliament in 1642, English puppetry would thrive, as perhaps never before or since, on both sides of the division between popular and elite culture.[1] The terms of such an opposition, drawn in the previous age, condition the social history of the puppet in this extended period. Immediately after 1642 the literal and figural diminution of puppetry and the relative simplicity of its practical requirements usually allowed it to evade the general Puritan supression of theater. By the early years of the eighteenth century, however, the same cultural lowness would be reinterpreted as an appealing preciosity for a bourgeois audience at once hungry for amusement and occasionally jaded by the conventions of the legitimate drama. "Never before or since," writes George Speaight of this period, "have the puppets played quite so effective and so well publicized a part in fashionable Society."[2] Toward the end of the eighteenth century, the process of cultural definition comes, as it were, full circle as a relatively more popular form of puppetry emerges whose apparent

---

[1] A thriving tradition of puppetry in London and in English provincial towns and fairs during the late seventeenth and eighteenth centuries is documented in Peter Burke, "Popular Culture in Seventeenth-Century London," in *Popular Culture in Seventeenth-Century England,* ed. Barry Reay (New York: St. Martin's, 1985), 40; R. W. Malcolmson, *Popular Recreations in English Society, 1700–1850* (Cambridge: Cambridge University Press, 1973), 20–21; Sybil Rosenfeld, *The Theatre of the London Fairs in the Eighteenth Century* (Cambridge: Cambridge University Press, 1960), 52, 63, 97, 153, and passim; and George Speaight, *The History of the English Puppet Theatre,* 2d ed. (London: Robert Hale, 1990), 73–175.

[2] Speaight, *History of the English Puppet Theatre,* 92.

cultural lowness and social marginality would be celebrated precisely *as* the authentic voice of the popular.

In this chapter I describe more specifically some of the many ways in which the bourgeois discourses and practices of the Enlightenment appropriated the puppet, even while constructing it and defining it as culturally "low." Although I proceed again in roughly chronological fashion, I will discover neither a coherent linear history nor even a consistent evolution, but rather a dynamic and shifting process of cultural interchange. I frequently consider theaters whose conditions belie their self-announced cultural status and texts that participate, whatever their other goals, in the construction of an urbane bourgeois reader who might learn to recognize the various distinctions—between high and low, popular and literary—both personified and bridged by the puppet itself. As usual, I will glimpse the actual social history of puppet theater primarily through its indirect reflection in texts that also defined it as Other, and in which such relentless cultural definition and self-definition merges with a larger process of cultural and social subordination. Thus, my task is again complicated by the constant semantic overlap between specifically literary or theatrical modes of subordination—the puppet as a model of theatrical authorship, histrionic passivity, or cultural lowness—and the political and theological metaphors to which such subordination reciprocally contributes.

The first section of the chapter broadly compares the conditions of the human and puppet stages in this period, suggesting that the idea of a performing *object* continued to shape and illuminate notions of theatrical authorship and hierarchies of cultural distinction. In the second section I turn back chronologically to describe how pamphleteers and periodical essayists in the Interregnum and beyond used the puppet, during an era of pervasive debate about sovereignty and the body politic, as a complex metaphor of social or theological authority. The third section focuses on two writers and performers, Henry Fielding and Charlotte Charke, who inhabit the frontier between elite and popular culture, and who resorted to puppetry at different moments in their entwined theatrical careers. The fourth and final section describes how the most celebrated of all English puppet shows, Punch and Judy, developed as an enduring form of working-class street theater at the end of the eighteenth century, only to be reappropriated as a target of bourgeois nostalgia. Throughout the extended period covered in this chapter, the categories of high and low, elite and popular were at once constructed and dislocated to serve the needs of writers, performers, and audiences in different cultural contexts. Whether as "fashionable" entertainment, discursive figuration of power, or bourgeois symbol of cultural otherness, the puppet was continually reappropriated from a hypothetical Bakhtinian world of folklore and festivity and used in a process of social and cultural subordination in which the puppet's own definition as "popular" is a paradigmatic example.

"Managers of Human Mechanism": From "Popular" Puppetry to the "Legitimate" Stage

> *Mr. Gibbon.* But surely [Mr. Garrick] feels the passion at the moment
> he is representing it.
> *Dr. Johnson.* About as much as Punch feels.
> —Two dialogues by Sir Joshua Reynolds

The puppet performers of the late seventeenth and early eighteenth centuries seem to have employed roughly the same biblical, historical, and conventional theatrical stories that had been performed by the "motion men" of the preceding period. The Blasphemy Act of 1604, which prohibited the dramatic portrayal of biblical subjects, had the presumably unintentional effect of relegating such stories to the puppet stage.[3] Edmund Gayton in 1654 laments precisely this situation by versifying a section of Cervantes's *Don Quixote*, in which

> The Canon and the Curate find out waies;
> To make Romances good, and write good plaies,
> Such as may edifie; such I have seen
> Of holy subjects, and with Psalmes between
> The Acts of *Dives* and of *Lazarus;*
> Of *Hester* good, and great *Ahasheverus:*
> Which now, through Poets vanity and sloth
> Are seen in puppet plaies, or painted cloth.[4]

John Locke, writing to a friend during a visit to the Continent in 1664, described a similar scene:

[3] On the Blasphemy Act, see Patrick Collinson, *The Birthpangs of Protestant England: Religious and Cultural Change in the Sixteenth and Seventeenth Century* (New York: St. Martin's, 1988), 113–14.

[4] Edmund Gayton, *Pleasant Notes upon Don Quixote* (London, 1654), 270. Gayton's passage paraphrases and adds to the discussion in *Don Quixote*, pt. 1, chap. 48.

Near the high altar in the principal church at Cleeves, was a little altar for the service of Christmas Day. The scene was a stable, wherein was an Ox, an Ass, a Cradle, the Virgin, the Babe, Joseph, shepherds and angels, dramatis personae. Had they but given them motion it had been a perfect Puppet Play, and might have deserved pence a piece; for they were of the same size and make that our English puppets are; and, I am confident, these shepherds and this Joseph are kin to that Judith and Holofernes which I had seen at Bartholomew Faire.[5]

Both passages illustrate in miniature the general dynamic of cultural appropriation I have been considering throughout and will continue to observe in this chapter. In the first Gayton implicitly superimposes his own disparaging judgment on the naive moralizing project of the curate and canon. In the second Locke echoes that earlier mode of English Protestant discourse which envisions Catholic ritual as mere puppetry, while replacing its theological valence with the cool gaze of ethnographic curiosity. One mode of subordination succeeds another, repositioning an observed cultural practice within a new discursive context, and calling for a readjusted judgment from the intended reader or audience.

In historical terms both descriptions also suggest that puppet theater still catered to a popular English taste for Bible stories despite the temporary ascension of an iconoclastic and antitheatrical Protestantism. The story of the Creation and Fall of Man was an enduringly popular subject for puppet theater at least until the eighteenth century. In 1643, while making a much larger theological and political argument about the freedom of the human will in his *Areopagitica*, John Milton would dismiss those "that complain of divin Providence for suffering Adam to transgresse," and insist that God gave Adam "freedom to choose" because "he had been else a meer artificiall Adam, such an Adam as he is in the motions."[6] In this celebrated metaphor the puppet figures not only passivity and servitude but also cultural subordination (the "Adam of the motions" versus the Adam realized in theology, Scripture, and eventually in Milton's epic). By the end of the seventeenth century, Thomas D'Urfey was still mentioning puppet plays about "the woman of Babylon, the Devil and the Pope," "*Dives and Lazarus*," and "the *World's Creation*"; and several playbills from Bartholomew Fair in the early

[5] Henry Morley, *Memoirs of Bartholomew Fair* (London, 1859), 241–42.
[6] *The Works of John Milton*, ed. James Holly Hanford and Waldo Hillary Dunn, 18 vols. (New York: Columbia University Press, 1931–38), 4:319.

eighteenth century advertise a puppet play of "The creation of the World."[7] The puppeteer Martin Powell, a well-known performer in London and Bath between about 1709 and 1720 who will be frequently mentioned in this chapter, had his own version of this conventional story. An anonymous pamphleteer of 1717 described this

> famous Show,
> Compos'd of Puppets in a beauteous Row.
> Here noted *Powel* his fam'd art display'd,
> A new Creation this Mechanick made.
>
> . . . .
>
> Here Beasts and Fowls of various kinds are seen,
> All Species which on Earth hath ever been;
> They artful move, and to the Sight appear
> As terrible as tho' alive they were.
> By nimble hands the Babies dance and play,
> And wires unseen now turn them ev'ry way:
> With mimick Voice the fam'd Performer speaks
> Thro *Powel's* mouth a Puppet loudly squeaks.
> Here Heaven and Hell with Art presented are;
> An *Harloquin* performs with wond'rous care
> And *Punchinello* he compleats the Rear.[8]

Even here a poet himself at the margins of bourgeous culture still cannot resist pointing to the ironic incongruity between the content and the conditions of a puppet show which at once mechanizes the natural order and places a mere "Mechanick" in the role of the divine, an "unseen" presence speaking the multiplicity of creation through the singular "in-spiration" of his mouth and "art."

The passage is also one of many cited by historians of theater who have traced in detail the emergence of the puppet Punchinello, or Punch, who seems to have been brought to England during the Restoration period by itinerant Italian puppeteers. I will not dwell here on the much-discussed question of Punch's ethnographic origins but will simply observe that Punch

---

[7] Thomas D'Urfey, *Wit and Drollery,* cited in Morley, *Memoirs of Bartholomew Fair,* 288. For the Bartholomew Fair playbills, see John Ashton, *Social Life in the Reign of Queen Anne* (New York: Scribner's, 1925), 193–95; Morley, *Memoirs of Bartholomew Fair,* 354–55; and Robert Leach, *The Punch and Judy Show: History, Tradition, and Meaning* (Athens: University of Georgia Press, 1985), 22.
[8] *Bartholomew Fair: An Heroi-Comical Poem* (London, 1717), 16–17.

becomes, almost immediately after he is first recorded in the 1660s, the most familiar character of the English puppet stage. Pepys frequently mentions seeing performances by Punchinello in the first decade after the Restoration. As his and other contemporary records confirm, Punch was used as a kind of carnivalesque interpolator within the conventional stories of earlier puppet drama, a sort of celebrity "actor" whose character and presence remained constant from play to play, and who would pretend to disrupt a narrative within which he was in fact the chief attraction. Swift in 1728 vividly describes the effect of this characteristic technique:

> Why *Tim*, you have a Taste I know,
> And often see a Puppet-show.
> Observe, the Audience is in Pain,
> While *Punch* is hid behind the Scene,
> But when they hear his rusty Voice,
> With what Impatience they rejoice.
> And then they value not two Straws,
> How *Solomon* decides the Cause,
> Which the true Mother, which *Pretender*,
> Nor listen to the Witch of *Endor*,
> Sho'ld *Faustus*, with the Devil behind him,
> Enter the Stage they never mind him,
> If Punch, to spur their fancy, shews
> In at the door his monstrous Nose.

Martin Powell seems sometimes to have performed puppet shows that parodied Italian opera, using Punch, as Swift puts it, to "interrupt all serious Matter."[9] I will have more to say about Punch later in this chapter; for the moment I merely note that this characteristic rhythm of appropriation and parody suggests that in the eighteenth century, puppet theater itself continued to be "popular" in only a partial and problematic sense. Even as it was being reappropriated within relatively more elite forms of discourse and theater, the puppet was already involved in a complex process of cultural transmission and transmutation.

Within the discourse and practice of the human stage, the puppet could also

[9] Jonathan Swift, "Mad Mullinix and Timothy," ll. 91–104, 144, in *The Poems of Jonathan Swift*, ed. Harold Williams, 2d ed. (Oxford: Clarendon Press, 1958), 776.

serve, much as it had done during the Renaissance, as a symmetrically contradictory metaphor, that is, as both a personification of the low popular culture from which the legitimate drama still struggled to separate itself, and the quintessential figure of a theological theater dominated by a sovereign author/creator. Theories of acting and drama from the Restoration on, which Joseph Roach has surveyed in detail, were profoundly conditioned by the mechanist theories of Enlightenment science and philosophy.[10] Hobbes's influential political theory, for example, emerges from a basic assertion that "life is but a *motion* of limbs," and envisions the body politic, in a quasi-theatrical metaphor, as composed of multiple actors through whom the authority of a sovereign author speaks.[11] Descartes's mechanistic theories may similarly have been conditioned by his memories of the intricate automata in the royal gardens of Saint-Germain-en-Laye, and Boyle's famous metaphor of the clockwork universe envisions humanity as, so to speak, the "jacks" on the famous Strasbourg clock.[12] Within a philosophic climate in which all animate beings were increasingly construed as forms of automata invested with an indwelling spirit, the literal actor could easily be seen as a kind of performing object whose external motions or gestures were the absolute indices of his inner (e)motions.

In legal and financial terms, the practical status of players could also suggest, after as before the Restoration, this familiar figural comparison of player to puppet.[13] Socially the players' status remained precarious: still declared by statute to be "Rogues and Vagrants," many players were virtually bound to one particular theatrical company, and were commonly considered "hired menials" even by writers who otherwise defended the cultural status of the

[10] Joseph R. Roach, *The Player's Passion: Studies in the Science of Acting* (Newark: University of Delaware Press, 1985), 58–93.

[11] Thomas Hobbes, *Leviathan*, ed. C. B. MacPherson (New York: Viking Penguin, 1986); the quotation is from the introduction (81, emphasis added); see also chap. 16 (217–19).

[12] Roach, *The Player's Passion*, 62; Marie Boas Hall, *Robert Boyle on Natural Philosophy: An Essay with Selections from His Writings* (Bloomington: Indiana University Press, 1965).

[13] On eighteenth-century acting, see the *Critical Introductions* to the relevant volumes of *The London Stage*: Emmett L. Avery, *1700–1729*, cxxv–xxxviii; Arthur H. Scouten, *1729–1747*, cxxi–xxxv; and George Winchester Stone, Jr., xc–c (Carbondale: Southern Illinois University Press, 1968); Alan S. Downer, "Nature to Advantage Dressed: Eighteenth-Century Acting," *PMLA* 58.4 (1943): 1002–37; Philip H. Highfill, Jr., "Performers and Performing," in *The London Theatre World, 1660–1800*, ed. Robert D. Hume (Carbondale: Southern Illinois University Press, 1980), 143–80; George Taylor, "'The Just Delineation of the Passions': Theories of Acting in the Age of Garrick," in *The Eighteenth-Century Stage*, ed. Kenneth Richards and Peter Thomson (London: Methuen, 1972), 51–72; and William Worthen, *The Idea of the Actor: Drama and the Ethics of Performance* (Princeton: Princeton University Press, 1984), 70–130.

theater as institution.[14] Correspondingly, an increasing subordination of performance to text manifests itself in the institution of the prompter and in references by eighteenth-century theorists and critics to the memorization of parts.[15] Thus, when one of Fielding's characters asserts, in the 1730s, that "the theaters are puppet shows"; when Samuel Johnson, in the 1740s, compares David Garrick to Punch; or when Samuel Foote, in the 1770s, refers to a "raw country girl" at the theater who thought that "all the players were puppets," they are calling on a familiar and widespread cultural trope.[16]

In many respects, however, the conditions of performance in this period also tended to contradict the neat hierarchies through which theorists continued to envision the process of representation. Most obviously, whereas in the preceding age authorship and acting tended to diverge (Shakespeare and Jonson, for example, gave up acting when they became established as poets), in the eighteenth century the two roles were entwined. Actor-managers such as John Rich, or the celebrated theatrical triumvirate of Colley Cibber, Robert Wilks, and Barton Booth, assumed either a virtual or actual authorial position within the hierarchy of the eighteenth-century stage. Despite the endless mockery to which they were subjected by voices of the literary establishment such as Pope (who, of course, enshrined Cibber as the King of the Dunces in *The Dunciad*), the actor-managers controlled in practice not just the theatrical repertory and the conditions of playing but also the performed text. Even the legal restrictions mentioned earlier may be seen in some sense to attribute to players precisely that individual agency and discursive authority which they were denied in theory. Particularly in the years leading up to the Licensing Act of 1737, individual actors were still subject to arrest and were sometimes held personally responsible for the words they had uttered on the

[14] Avery, *The London Stage, 1700–1729*, 121; Scouten, *The London Stage, 1729–1747*, 126; John Loftis, *Steele at Drury Lane* (Berkeley: University of California Press, 1952), 22.

[15] The critic and journalist Aaron Hill, for example, insists in *The Prompter*, May 23, 1735, that "the words of a Play shou'd be perfect on the memory" of the actor, a histrionic technique conducive to viewing the play as "the work of a great master," and which should, correspondingly, be encouraged by "the people of best judgment and condition." Aaron Hill and William Popple, *The Prompter*, ed. William W. Appleton and Kalman A. Burnim (New York: Benjamin Blom, 1966), 67–69. Fifteen years later the theorist John Hill similarly insisted, in a treatise on the art of acting, that players must be "rotten perfect" in their lines; quoted in Taylor, "The Just Delineation of the Passions," 68.

[16] Henry Fielding, *The Author's Farce*, ed. Charles B. Woods (Lincoln: University of Nebraska Press, 1966), 1.5.27–34. All further citations are from this edition and are given parenthetically by act, scene, and line (or in the case of the lengthy and continuous third act, simply by act and line number) in the text. Samuel Johnson, *Johnsonian Miscellanies*, ed. George Birkbeck Hill, 2 vols. (New York, 1897), 2:248. Samuel Foote, "Samuel Foote's Primitive Puppet-Shew Featuring Piety in Pattens: A Critical Edition," ed. Samuel N. Bogorad and Robert Gale Noyes, *Theatre Survey* 14.1a (1973): 20.

stage.[17] Moreover, the comic players of eighteenth-century drama evidently continued to subvert the authority of the text by means of improvisations that, as one journal complained in 1709, could make it "impossible to see the Poet for the Player."[18] Such improvisations could in turn incite further political repression. In one of the most famous theatrical incidents of the century, according to a contemporary account,

> at the performance of Love Runs all Dangers . . . one of the Commedians took the Liberty to throw out some Reflections upon the Prime Minister and the Excise, which were not designed by the Author; Lord Walpole, being in the House, went behind the Scenes, and demanded of the Prompter, whether such Words were in the Play, and he answering they were not, his Lordship immediately corrected the Commedian with his own Hands very severly [sic].[19]

Here, Walpole's bypassing of the official chain of political power is, so to speak, symmetrically opposite but analogous to the player's subversion of the textual authority of author and play.

A few other preliminary examples may suggest some of the characteristics of the cultural landscape considered in the rest of this chapter. In 1712 Sir Thomas Burnet and George Duckett, two minor political functionaries and occasional writers, produced a book-length satire of Robert Harley, first duke of Oxford, the Tory minister who had dominated the government during the last few years of Queen Anne's reign. Their book, *A Second Tale of a Tub: or, The History of Robert Powel the Puppet-Show Man*, attempts to evoke a satiric analogy between the powerful Tory politician and the puppeteer who, as the two writers put it, "has worthily acquired the Reputation of one of the most dextrous Managers of human Mechanism"[20] Throughout most of their crude and disorganized narrative, the writers fail to sustain the satiric metaphor announced in the title and the introduction; but in the final

---

[17] This happened, for example, in the summer of 1731, when *The Fall of Mortimer* (a play judged subversive by the Walpole ministry) was performed by Fielding's company at the little theater in the Haymarket. See Scouten, *The London Stage, 1729–1747*, 49; and Martin C. Battestin, *Henry Fielding: A Life* (London: Routledge, 1989), 121.

[18] Quoted in Avery, *The London Stage, 1700–1729*, 125.

[19] *Appelbee's*, March 31, 1733; describing a performance at the New Haymarket on March 22, 1733; quoted in Scouten, *The London Stage, 1729–1747*, 167.

[20] Sir Thomas Burnet and George Duckett, *A Second Tale of a Tub: or, The History of Robert Powell the Puppet-Show Man* (London, 1715), xxvi. Subsequent citations are given parenthetically in the text.

pages they conclude with a verse epilogue supposedly in the voice of the puppeteer:

> I'm come to beg your Favour to our Stage,
> The lively Emblem of the present Age.
> For as my Puppets, when you hear them squeak,
> Are but the *Wooden Tubes* thro' which I speak:
> So many now a-days strut and look vain
> With the productions of another Brain.
> . . . .
> You can't imagine, Sirs, what Art can do;
> 'Twill make a *Wooden Head*, a Wise one too.
> So have I often in a Play-house seen
> The pompous Figure of a *Buskin Queen*,
> Start from her Throne, and make a solemn Speech,
> Which hidden Downs stood prompting at her Breech.
> The Gazing Crowd ne'er smelt the subtle Joke,
> But thought poor Moppet of her self had spoke.
>
> (220–21)

Here again, the political metaphor rests on that conventional model of theatrical representation which envisions both players and puppets as mere conduits "thro' which" an authoring voice manifests itself in illusory motion and speech. This vision of authorship, however, both converges with and diverges from the political situation satirized in the text, in which a "Minister of State" manipulates the real monarch from behind the scenes. In the structure of the satiric metaphor, Harley/"Powel" is the puppet master or "author," while Queen Anne is a mere "Moppet"—that is, according to Johnson's dictionary, a "puppet made of rags, as a mop is made."

Burnet and Duckett thus conceive both representation and politics in the familiar hierarchical way, as structures in which authorship or authority descends from some authoritative figure into a puppetlike vehicle or mouthpiece. Applied to either politics or performance, however, this theoretical model reveals its inadequacy to the real conditions. In the government the minister becomes the real source of the authority he is alleged to serve. In the theater the manipulating agent seems to be not the literal playwright but rather the *prompter*. As the writers implicitly suggest by their curiously scatalogical image of John Downs (the famous prompter of the Theatre Royal at Drury Lane) at the "Breech" of the "Buskin Queen," the function of prompter both confirms and destabilizes the hierarchical model of the theological theater. On the one hand, as a kind of priest or agent who mediates between the author/creator and the player-puppet, the theatrical prompter serves as "the hidden but indispensible center of representative structure."[21] At the same time, however, the prompter also serves as a constant, living proof that the histrionic distance from poet to player is never simple or unproblematic. Earlier in the text itself, for example, Burnet and Duckett describe how "Powel" worked for a time as a prompter,

> which he was very dextrous at, even to the Astonishment of the famous Mr. Downs; for as that Gentleman prompted honestly, and put the Poet's own Words and Sense into the Mouth of the Actor, to the Credit of both; so our *Hero*, having a Genius too *Mercurial* to be bounded by the dull Rules of the Stage, or tied down by the Establish'd Laws of *Parnassus*, would very often prompt out of his own Head, and to the great Surprize of the Audience, he would make a Theatrical King or Queen talk like a downright *Zany*. (216)

This passage, like the epilogue, assumes that theatrical players are merely passive vehicles of authorial intention, figural puppets who "strut and look vain / With the productions of another Brain." But the discursive strategy that transforms this theoretical situation into a political metaphor also betrays the incongruity between the literal conditions of politics or theater and the broadly similar hierarchies in which both were envisioned.

About twelve years later William Hogarth, in his engraving "A Just View of the British Stage, or Three Heads Are Better Than None" (1724), illustrates a common critique of the contemporary theater (see Figure 3). Hogarth depicts the three managers of the Theatre Royal—Cibber, Wilks, and Booth—rehearsing "a new Farce" to compete with the successful pantomime version of Dr. Faustus that had recently been performed by John Rich, the manager and star performer at the rival theater at Lincoln's Inn Fields, who performed as a mime under the stage name "Lun."[22] Each of the three managers also holds a miniature, stringed figure. In the case of Booth and

---

[21] Jacques Derrida, "The Theater of Cruelty and the Closure of Representation," in *Writing and Difference*, trans. Alan Bass (Chicago: University of Chicago Press, 1978), 235–36.

[22] No. 1761 in F. G. Stephens and M. D. George, eds. *Catalogue of Political and Personal Satires Preserved in the Department of Prints and Drawings of the British Museum*, 11 vols. (London: British Museum Publications, 1978); plate 48 in *Hogarth's Graphic Works*, ed. Ronald Paulson, 2 vols. (New Haven: Yale University Press, 1965).

Figure 3. Cibber, Wilks, and Booth manipulate puppet-actors, while the ghost of Ben Jonson rises from a stage trapdoor. Detail of William Hogarth, "A Just View of the British Stage, or Three Heads Are Better Than None" (1724). Reproduced by permission of the Huntington Library, San Marino, California.

Cibber, as the caption confirms, these figures represent the actors of the proposed new farce, suggesting the tyrannical control exerted by the triumvirate over the actors and writers they employed. This, too, was a familiar point in the discourse of the period. Wilks, by contrast, holds a marionette whose humped back and protruding nose clearly indentify him as Punch. Above the managers a Latin motto proclaims "Vivitur Ingenio," "We live by the spirit," a famous Renaissance epigraph which in this context takes on an ironic new meaning. In the background the ghost of Ben Jonson rises, a murdered, ghostly father, from a stage trapdoor.

The hierarchical assumptions embodied in Hogarth's iconography—

about literary history, canon, genre, and histrionic technique—reappear with tedious regularity in a wide variety of eighteenth-century discourse. As the engraving suggests, by midcentury the puppet could serve as a visual emblem not just for the process of performance itself, but also for a broad spectrum of paratheatrical entertainment seen as invading and polluting a theater that had finally achieved the legitimacy to which Jonson had so painfully aspired over a century earlier. Hogarth's print also illustrates how a hierarchical vision of theater—in which some central power "inspires" or manipulates puppetlike players—persisted within a theatrical institution dominated by actor-managers and encompassing a whole range of nonverbal performers. In the first decades of the eighteenth century, Richard Steele and Joseph Addison were already decrying, in the pages of *The Tatler* and *The Spectator*, the carnivalesque variety entertainments presented on the London stage by John Rich's father, Christopher—who, as Steele writes, "brought in upon us, to get in his Money, Ladder-dancers, Rope-dancers, Juglers, and Mountebanks, to strut in the Place of *Shakespear's* Heroes, and *Johnson's* Humourists."[23] Alexander Pope, in the first version of *The Dunciad* (1728), similarly complains that the "Smithfield Muses"—that is, the "Shews, Machines, and Dramatical Entertainments" of Bartholomew Fair—have been "brought to the Theatres of Covent-Garden, Lincoln-inn Fields, and the Hay-Market, to be the reigning Pleasures of the Court and Town."[24] As such passages suggest, the legitimate literary theater of Shakespeare and Jonson is also a theological theater, which privileges the author over the actor and is itself privileged over forms of performance grounded in sonority (the opera) or the acrobatic body (rope dancers and mimes, puppets and performing objects). Another satirical engraving from about 1729, for example, depicts Harlequin and Punch driving Apollo from the stage while books labeled "Shakespear" and "Johnson" lie on the ground around them (see Figure 4). "Shakespeare, Rowe, Johnson, now are quite undone / These are thy Tryumphs, thy Exploits O Lun!" proclaims the caption.[25] In a wide range of discourse across this extended period, the idea of the puppet would be inseparable from a vision of theatrical authorship complicated by issues of canon and tradition

---

[23] *The Tatler*, ed. Donald F. Bond, 3 vols. (Oxford: Clarendon Press, 1987), no. 12, May 7, 1709. All further citations are from this edition and are given parenthetically by date and number in the text.

[24] Alexander Pope, *The Dunciad* (1728) in *The Poems of Alexander Pope*, ed. John Butt (New Haven: Yale University Press, 1963), 1.2 and note; cf. the couplet, asserting that theatrical "Dullness" has been "rais'd from booths, to Theatre, to Court" (1728 version, 3.301; 1743 version, 3.299).

[25] No. 1838 in Stephens and George, *Catalogue of Satires*.

Shakespear, Rowe, Johnson, now are quite undone
These are thy Tryumphs, thy Exploits O Lun!

Figure 4. Harlequin and Punch drive Apollo from the stage. "Shakespeare, Rowe, Johnson, now are quite undone / These are thy Tryumphs, thy Exploits O Lun!" Anonymous satirical engraving (1729). Reproduced by permission of the British Museum.

and accompanying hierarchical assumptions about class, gender, and political sovereignty.

"The Sacred and Politique Puppet-Play": Puritans, Power, and the Performing Object

> I told you before . . . that there was a strict resemblance between the states political and theatrical; there is a ministry in the latter as well as the former . . . and if one considers the plays that come from one part, and the writings from the other, one would be apt to think the same authors were retained in both.
> —Henry Fielding, *The Historical Register for the Year 1736*

As far back as 1614 Jonson's Zeal-of-the-Land Busy railed against the puppet as a "heathenish *Idoll*" (*Bartholomew Faire* 5.5.5) in what Jonson intended as a grotesque parody of real Puritan objections to the theater. Part of the satiric point, of course, is the incongruity between the fictional rhetoric and the presumed harmlessness or triviality of its target. As I have suggested, however, it was precisely this literal and figural diminutiveness that often allowed puppet theater to evade the Puritan suppression of theatrical activity after 1642. In the extended period that begins with the Interregnum, the various political and religious crises of the seventeenth century invested the puppet with a new dimension of discursive meaning. In the Renaissance, as I have suggested, the idea of the performing object evoked a broad spectrum of social subordination on which the puppet's own lowness combined with its histrionic power to suggest trangressive forms of gender or class behavior. To be sure, this discursive process also evoked the existing social hierarchies of power and authority, although what is, in modern parlance the basic figural meaning *puppet*—in the sense of a person or thing that is the "tool" or "puppet" of another—is curiously rare in Renaissance discourse. This simpler political meaning seems to have crystallized during the Interregnum, when the performing object not only became a practical stand-in for the human stage but also lent itself to newly specific figurations of power. In this new age—during which the English overturned authority, contemplated the leveling of social distinctions, and silenced or controlled the theater—the puppet was once again appropriated in discourses that pursued various political goals while also constructing a shared hierarchy of cultural value.

In 1643, about a year after the closing of the London theaters by order of Parliament, a small pamphet was published to express, in the words of its title, *The Actors Remonstrance . . . for the Silencing of Their Profession.* In this now famous document the anonymous author complains of a particular cultural confusion brought about by the order. Although human actors had been banished "from their severall Play-houses," he observes, "other publike recreations of farre more harmfull consequence [were] permitted, still to stand *in statu quo primu.*"[26] Specifically, the writer goes on,

> puppit-plays, which are not so much valuable as the very musique betweene each Act at ours, are still up with uncontrolled allowance, witnesse the famous motion of *Bell* and the *Dragon,* so frequently visited at *Holbourne-bridge;* these passed Christmas Holidayes, whither Citizens of all sorts repaire with far more detriment to themselves than ever did to Playes, Comedies and Tragedies being the lively representations of mens actions, in which, vice is always sharply glanced at, and punished, and vertue rewarded and encouraged; the most exact and naturall eloquence of our English language expressed and daily amplified. (5)

The writer thus grounds his argument in an implicit cultural hierarchy by distinguishing between two different forms of performance, one high (the bearer of moral value and linguistic eloquence) and the other low (a popular attraction "famous," as the writer puts it, with "Citizens of all sorts").

The unmistakably ironic tone of the pamphlet complicates its explicit comparison of drama and puppetry. The anonymous author spends most of his time listing and describing in detail a long series of moral abuses of which he concedes the players were formerly guilty but which he claims they have recently reformed. Such abuses, the author suggests, were both representational and social. "Wee have purged our Stages," he argues, "from all obscene and scurrilous jests; such as might either be guilty of corrupting the manners, or defaming the persons of any men of note in the City or Kingdom" (2). The players would now refrain, he promises, from "the inveigling in young Gentlemen, Merchants Factors, and Prentizes to spend their patrimonies and Masters estates upon us and our Harlots in Tavernes" (4). Nevertheless, the author still includes among those now financially inconve-

---

[26] *The Actors Remonstrance and Complaint for the Silencing of Their Profession* (London, 1643), 4. Subsequent citations are given parenthetically in the text.

nienced by the closing of the theaters not only "such as were sharers" in the theatrical enterprise, "their friends, young gentlemen, that used to feast and frolick with them at Tavernes," but even "their verie Mistresses, those Buxsome and Bountifull Ladies, that usually were enamoured on the persons of the younger sort of Actors, for the good cloathes they wore upon the stage, beleeving them really to be the persons they did only represent" (6). At the end, the author promises again that, if permitted to resume their professional activity, the players would no longer admit "into our sixpenny-roomes those unwholesome inticing Harlots" (8).

Thus, when the author contrasts "the motions of Puppets" to "the lively representations of mens actions" on the human stage, he implicitly exposes a disjunction between the representational and social hierarchies. Does the presumed lowness of puppetry in the hierarchy of generic and aesthetic distinction make it more or less pernicious to the moral health of the commonwealth than the legitimate drama against which it is measured? In effect, the author attacks the authorities for suppressing representation from the top down instead of from the bottom up. This text thus subtly problematizes the system of moral, social, and aesthetic distinction that went hand in hand with real political power and the prohibition whose exercise had provoked the author's complaint. At the same time, in its repeated references to "harlots" and "mistresses" (the very social types sometimes referred to in earlier decades as "painted puppets"), the text sets up a subtle equation of trangressive sexuality and the "low" performing object. While ostensibly attempting to divide the theater's *content* (in which "vice is always sharply glanced at, and punished, and vertue rewarded and encouraged") from its *conditions* (the licentious sexual freedom made possible by the seductive pleasure of performance), the text implicitly satirizes the moral critique of representation which it explicitly acknowledges. After all, just what is this "detriment" that citizens supposedly suffer from attending the puppet show on Holborn Bridge? Is it, so to speak, merely a question of aesthetic distinction and taste, in which the audience itself is somehow lowered by exposure to puppets whose literal and figural diminution is suggested by contrast with a human stage where "naturall eloquence" is "expressed and daily *amplified*"?

In one incident a few years later puppets did briefly provoke the serious concern of the Puritan authorities in London. In July 1647 the two houses of Parliament revived the ordinance of 1642 that had prohibited stage plays during the "publike Calamities" of the Civil War; and later that summer John Warner, Lord Mayor of London, attempted to suppress the puppet performers at the fair in Smithfield.[27] The incident provoked a popular broadside, *The Dagonizing of Bartholomew Fayre*, a text that inverts the more sophisticated irony of *The Actors Remonstrance* of five years earlier.[28] Here the joke lies in the incongruity between the power of the urban authorities and its trivial, diminutive target:

> On August's foure and twentieth Eve,
> The Cities Soveraigne and the Shrieve
> To Smithfield came if you'l beleeve
> to see th'ungodly flagges.
> . . . .
> Entring through Duck-lane at the Crowne,
> The soveraigne Cit began to frowne,
> As if 't abated his renowne
> the paint did so o'retop him.
> Down with these Dagons then, quoth he,
> They outbrave my dayes Regality.
> . . . .
> I'le have no puppet-playes, quoth he,
> The harmlesse-mirth displeaseth me.

Even while mocking the Lord Mayor, in effect, for breaking a butterfly upon a wheel, the broadside also makes clear that what had happened at Bartholomew Fair was an exercise of power for its own sake. The text suggests that the Lord Mayor was simply reasserting his "Soveraigne" authority, his "renowne" and "Regality," against manifestations of carnivalesque license that might otherwise "o'retop" and "outbrave" him. Here again, the text implicitly evokes a disjunction between the antitheatrical prejudice (so recently manifested in practical political action) and that quasi-Platonic hierarchy of representation in which the former is partly grounded. The ballad suggests, in its own crude way, that to turn the force of actual political repression on mere illusion is to attribute to the latter a ludicrous effect on reality:

[27] Other, more severe ordinances against stage plays were passed in October of the same year and in the early months of 1648. See Samuel R. Gardiner, *History of the Great Civil War, 1642–1649* (London, 1893), 4:68–69, and Hyder E. Rollins, "A Contribution to the History of the English Commonwealth Drama," *Studies in Philology* 18.3 (1921): 281–83, 284–89.

[28] *The Dagonizing of Bartholomew Fayre caused through the Lord Majors Command, for the battering down the vanities of the Gentiles, comprehended in Flag and Pole, appertayning to Puppet-play*, August 23, 1647.

Another wight (in woful wise)
Besought the mayor, his pupetries
That he would not Babell-onize,
    surely they were not whorish.
Oh do'nt my bratts Jsabellize,
They ne'er did Meretritialize
Betwixt your Lordships Ladies thighes.

One is also struck here by an overdetermined conjunction of contradictory associations of class and gender. A carnivalesque male sexuality that might threaten the chastity of the Lordship's lady is at once attributed and denied to the puppets, even as it is expressed in the feminine categories of whore, Jezebel, and meretrix. Similarly, the text "dagonizes" or carnivalizes the Lord Mayor's actions, but can do so only from a perspective that implicitly concedes the carnivalesque as a category within a system of cultural subordination here curiously at odds with the larger system of political authority.

Both this ballad and *The Actors Remonstrance* are texts located at the frontier separating elite from popular culture. Themselves ephemeral and anonymous, with no clearly defined author or audience, they are nevertheless distanced by the written word and the printed page from the street theater and literal carnival they describe. Both texts use and confuse the discursive conventions of generic and social distinction, claiming for the puppet a salutary powerlessness *as* illusion and a pervasive histrionic power, and construing the puppet as at once "harmless mirth" and a seductive pleasure to which "Citizens of all sorts repaire." In both, similarly, the carnivalesque quality of puppet theater as explicitly described reemerges as a discursive strategy in the texts themselves. Moreover, both texts use this particular mode of popular culture (as Jonson had done in *Bartholomew Faire*) to attack the Puritan impulse toward a tangible political regulation of drama and society. Just as rural folk customs such as the Maypole and Sunday sports were thrust into the political limelight during the revolutionary decades and defended by conservative political thinkers otherwise committed to maintaining the social hierarchy, so the puppet was forced to become, as it were, the standard bearer of theater itself, whose prohibition was a particularly visible manifestation of Puritan power for the urbane Londoner.[29] In January 1650, for example, following the execution of King Charles I, and in the wake of several severe

---

[29] On the politics of recreation, see Leah Marcus, *The Politics of Mirth: Jonson, Herrick, Milton, Marvell, and the Defense of Old Holiday Pastimes* (Chicago: University of Chicago Press, 1986).

ordinances against stage plays that had been passed by Parliament, the authorities raided and closed an unauthorized performance at the Red Bull, a theater that had survived since Elizabethan times. The derisive account of this incident in a Royalist newsbook, the *Mercurius Pragmaticus*, similarly adopts a theatrical metaphor to deride the political suppression of drama, declaring to Parliament:

> If you be destitute of something to do, you may go hang your selves for a pastime to the people; I believe you would have more spectators than the *Players* in *St. John's street*, yes and Lords and Ladies too would laugh more to see the *Juncto* and State hang, then any Play in the world Acted.
>
> But your own Play-houses at *Westminister, Whitehall, Darby House, Somerset House,* &c. are the only Stages where Players must come, and who those players must be, I'le tell you; all in Parliament Robes. . . .
>
> Me thinks the Supreme Poppet-players of State should have somthing else in their minds then suppressing Playes.[30]

Here again, the author defends theater only by assuming its essential triviality relative to politics, an assumption that reinforces the satiric metaphor comparing the Parliamentarians to players and their leaders to puppeteers. Another Royalist newsbook from 1653 laments, much as the anonymous author of *The Actors Remonstrance* had done about ten years earlier, that only low entertainments such as puppet plays and rope dancing were permitted to continue. "It were much to be desired," the account declares, "that such fools-bables were flung by, and that the poor Comedians . . . were permitted to represent some modest and harmless *Pastorals*."[31]

Throughout the Interregnum, Royalist and Presbyterian writers confronting the threat of radical Puritan politics used the puppet in a sort of rearguard attack, transforming it into a metaphor for political power and, eventually, for Puritanism itself. Lucy Hutchinson observed retrospectively of her fellow Puritans that, in the decade just before the Civil War, "not only . . . every stage, and every table" but also "every puppet-play, belched forth profane scoffs upon them."[32] A Presbyterian political pamphlet from 1648, *An Agitator Anotomiz'd, or the Character of an Agitator*, similarly manifests what

---

[30] Rollins, "Contribution to the History of the English Commonwealth Drama," 300–301.
[31] Ibid., 310.
[32] Lucy Hutchinson, *Memoirs of Colonel Hutchinson* (London, 1905), 81–82.

would be a continuing figural association between Puritans and performing objects.[33] In the summer of 1647 the New Model Army, following its decisive victory in the first phase of the Civil War, organized itself into representative councils whose members came to be known as "agitators," and from whose ranks some of the leaders of the so-called Leveller movement would spring.[34] For the rest of the year Oliver Cromwell maintained an equivocal position between the demands of agitators and the more conservative Presbyterian-dominated Parliament.

In the pamphlet, written from the Presbyterian point of view, the anony-mous writer opens by describing the agitator derisively as "one that hath voted himself a ruler in Israel and is in order thereunto a representative of the lamp triumphant, a devout member of the Militant house of Commons, the peoples viceroyes, and though he a Parliament man of the *Plebean* house, rhime better than any of *Sternholds* Psalms, yet is he no more to him than a *Barthlomew-baby* is to my Lady *Waller*" (A2r). Despite the chaotic syntax and a confusing succession of metaphors, this rhetoric evokes what finally becomes a complex discursive structure linking political, theatrical, and theological representation precisely so as to call such linking into question. Rather than a "representative of the lamp triumphant" on earth, the agitator is declared instead to be a hypocrite who has taken up a theological discourse (exemplified by Sternhold's famous sixteenth-century edition of the Psalms) just as Lady Waller might pick up a doll or "Barthlomew-baby" at the fair. In an implicit four-part figural structure of class and discursive distinction, the "Plebean" agitator who presumes to emulate the biblical text corresponds, with reverse symmetry, to the noble lady who condescends to acquire a car-nival trinket. The disparaging comparison also calls on two conventional associations of the puppet: a sense of commodification (the doll as salable object) and a sense of iconic illusion (the doll as a merely material represen-tation of a living child). Both meanings converge in the satiric accusation that the agitator uses the sacred text as a kind of prop in an act of histrionic political deception. Moreover, a rhetoric of class also implicitly serves as a

---

[33] *An Agitator Anotomiz'd, or the Character of an Agitator* (London, 1648). Subsequent citations are given parenthetically by signature in the text.

[34] See William Haller and Godfrey Davies, eds., *The Leveller Tracts, 1647–1653* (New York: Columbia University Press, 1944), 9; Sir John Davies, *The Early Stuarts, 1603–1660* (Oxford: Clarendon Press, 1959), 146–47; and Fenner Brockway, *Britain's First Socialists: The Levellers, Agitators and Diggers of the English Revolution* (London: Quartet Books, 1980). On the rocky relations between the Levellers and Cromwell, see Gardiner, *History of the Great Civil War*, 3:266, 4:116–17.

rhetoric of cultural taste, since Sternhold was frequently taken as a type of the bad, "popular" poet.[35] The anonymous author goes on to envision a similar form of manipulation in which the agitator becomes himself a "Bartholomew-baby" or puppet manipulated by General Cromwell. The agitators, says the writer dismissively, "would have made . . . a very fit purpose for a broken Citizen that had a designe to undoe the Puppet-players at *Bartholomew Faire*" (A3r). Indeed, "many thinke his Excellency is pleased to follow the Custome of the Romane Emperors, who to solemnize great triumphs presented shewes unto the people, and most commonly of things that best relished with them. And by this rabble of Agitators to act the Parliament of England in a serious Camp-Stage-play since the people have so much idoliz'd them heretofore: this is the most sacred and politique puppet-play" (A3v). In this fascinating passage the agitators are depicted as Cromwell's "puppets," first in what would become the conventional figural sense (that is, they are tools who serve his purpose); second, because the Parliament in which they serve is merely a "sacred and politique puppet-play," a spectacle for the people's delight; and finally, because the agitators have "heretofore" been the people's "idols," a deceptive image of uncertain political efficacy. The last sense, evoking the ancient association of puppets with religious images, has a peculiar resonance within the situation more generally satirized by the writer, in which theology has, in his view, illegitimately invaded politics. The Puritan/puppet is subordinated alike within the hierarchies of histrionic representation and cultural distinction.

After the Restoration the puppet would continue to provide a figural space where political, theological, and theatrical issues overlap. Specifically, the puppet was now enlisted in the critique of Puritan "fanatics" or "enthusiasts" and their belief in "the motions of the spirit," that is, the direct divine inspiration of the elect individual. Ben Jonson had already employed this figural strategy when he derisively compared the Puritan Busy, who claims to be "mov'd in spirit," to the puppet who literally "speak[s] by inspiration, as well as he" (*Bartholomew Faire* 5.5.111). This satiric point reemerges in a variety of more serious philosophical and theological discourse after the Restoration. Writing in the late 1660s, Samuel Butler defines a fanatic as "a Puppet Saint, that moves he knows not how, [whose] Ignorance is the dull leaden Weight

[35] John Dryden, in "The Second Part of Absalom and Achitophel," refers to "Poor Slaves in metre, dull and adle-pated, / Who Rhime below ev'n *David*'s Psalms translated" (ll. 403–4), in *The Works of John Dryden*, ed. Edward Niles Hooker, H. T. Swedenberg, et al. (Berkeley: University of California Press, 1955-), 2:74.

that puts all his Parts in Motion."[36] Butler in effect calls on the combined theological and political valence accumulated by the metaphor of the puppet in the decades between Jonson and the Restoration and places that metaphor in a secular, psychological context befitting the changed ideological climate of the Royalist ascendancy and the early Enlightenment. His rhetoric foregrounds the discursive categories of inner and outer, flesh and spirit, portraying the "puppet saint" as a kind of clockwork automaton moved by the "leaden weight" of ignorance instead of a divine "spirit" that should predominate within a hierarchy at once ontological and representational. Butler's dismissive comparison of the fanatic to a puppet may thus be usefully compared to his definition of a player, in the same text, to "a Motion made by clockwork," who is as such " but a puppet in great, which the poet squeaks to, and puts into what posture he pleases; and though his calling be but ministerial to his author, yet he assumes a magistry over him, because he sets him on work, and he becomes subordinate accordingly" (301). This passage seems both to employ and to destabilize the conventional vision of histrionic "in-spiration," envisioning the player as a "puppet in great," wholly mastered by the authorial voice, and yet also taking into account something of the theater's real conditions, in which authors too were, after all, mere employees of the theatrical enterprise. Revealing in its own texture how these familiar discursive formulations are susceptible to virtually unlimited use, Butler's political vision of theater refers by reciprocal implication to the "fanatic,"whose self-mastering "motion" was itself but a type of the organized Puritan political power of the previous age.

A few decades later John Locke would draw a similar but more complex distinction in the chapter of the *Essay Concerning Human Understanding* on "enthusiasts." Here the image of the puppet has been submerged within a language that resists figuration; but Locke, like Butler, argues that an enthusiast is motivated by internal impulses or "motions" which he takes for an external divine inspiration. Although they "feel the hand of God moving them within," Locke writes, enthusiasts are in fact merely being "forwardly obedient to the impulses they receive from themselves," acting in accordance with "a natural *motion*."[37]

By the time of Shaftesbury's "Letter Concerning Enthusiasm" (1707), the rhetorical comparison of the fanatic to the puppet returns in a text otherwise

---

[36] Samuel Butler, *Characters*, ed. Charles W. Daves (Cleveland: Press of Case Western Reserve University, 1970), 128. Subsequent citations are given parenthetically in the text.

[37] John Locke, *An Essay Concerning Human Understanding*, ed. Alexander Campbell Fraser, 2 vols. (1894; rpt. New York: Dover, 1959), 4.19.7–8; emphasis added.

framed by an intensely hierarchical awareness of literary and social taste. In the leisurely opening peroration to John, Lord Sommers, Shaftesbury discusses the classical convention whereby "poets, at the entrance of their work . . . address themselves to some muse"; and he suggests that "this imitation . . . must at some time or other have stuck a little with your lordship, who is used to examine things by a better standard than that of fashion or the common taste."[38] In fact, however, Shaftesbury argues that "the imagination of such a presence must exalt a genius," for "a common actor of the stage will inform us how much a full audience of the better sort exalts him above the common pitch. And you, my lord, who are the noblest actor, and of the noblest part assigned to any mortal on his earthly stage, when you are acting for liberty and mankind; does not the public presence, that of your friends, and the well-wishers to your cause, add something to your thought and genius?" (8). A few pages later, in what seems an equally leisurely apology for the "ridicule" with which he intends to treat enthusiasts in his own text, Shaftesbury stipulates that no one "of the least justness of thought [can] endure a ridicule wrong placed. The vulgar, indeed, may swallow any sordid jest, any mere drollery or buffoonery; but it must be a finer and truer wit which takes with the men of sense and breeding" (10). Finally, he goes on to argue that "good-humour [is] the best security against enthusiasm" (17). He then in effect provides an instance of what he means by ironically contrasting the fate of the French Protestants, who were openly persecuted all the way to martyrdom, with the English treatment of their home-grown enthusiasts:

> But how barbarous still, and more than heathenishly cruel, are we tolerating Englishmen! For, not contented to deny these prophesying enthusiasts the honour of a persecution, we have delivered them over to the cruellest contempt in the world. I am told, for certain, that they are at this very time the subject of a choice droll or puppet-show at Bart'lemy Fair. There, doubtless, their strange voices and involuntary agitations are admirably well acted, by the motion of wires and inspiration of pipes. For the bodies of the prophets, in their state of prophecy, being not in their own power, but (as they say themselves) mere passive organs, actuated by an exterior force, have nothing natural, or resembling real life, in any of their sounds or motions; so that how

---

[38] Anthony Ashley Cooper, Third Earl of Shaftesbury, *Characteristics of Men, Manners, Opinions, Times*, ed. John M. Robertson (Indianapolis: Bobbs-Merrill, 1964), 5–6. Subsequent citations are given parenthetically in the text.

awkwardly soever a puppet-show may imitate other actions, it must needs represent this passion to the life. (21)

Here the satiric comparison of Puritan and player transcends the conventional accusation of hypocrisy. The enthusiast is again construed as puppet-like in his passive receptiveness to the "exterior force" of divine inspiration; but in this case the grotesque awkwardness of puppet performance—which otherwise defines it as culturally low—becomes the source of an ironic verisimilitude. Puppets, not in spite of but *in* their wooden awkwardness, their grotesque iconicity, can represent the Puritan "to the life."

This association between the religious enthusiast and the performing object was evidently so useful to the former's opponents that, about three years after Shaftesbury's image of Puritans as puppets at the fair, the puppeteer Martin Powell was actually commissioned by the government to satirize a group of French Protestant fanatics. According to the later account of Lord Chesterfield, when these so-called "French prophets . . . used to assemble in Moorfields" to exert their claimed "gift of prophecy," the Ministry "were . . . wise enough not to disturb these madmen, and only ordered one Powell, who was the master of a famous puppet-show, to make Punch turn prophet, which he did so well, that it soon put an end to the prophets and their prophecies.[39] Some fifty years later, in William Hogarth's unpublished satirical print "Enthusiasm Delineated" (ca. 1761), a Methodist preacher resembling George Whitfield stands in his pulpit, a Harlequin costume visible beneath his gown, holding in either hand a puppet representing, respectively, God with angels and the devil with a gridiron (see Figure 5). Puppet versions of Adam and Eve, Peter and Paul, and Moses and Aaron hang from the pulpit, as if ready for imminent use, while members of the congregation clasp other puppetlike figures in idolatrous devotion.[40] Hogarth thus seems to suggest that the enthusiast, himself no better than a carnival clown, nevertheless presumes to manipulate at once his listeners and the dramatis personae of divine history in a grotesque parody (and potential subversion) of the theological hierarchy of being.

As these last few examples confirm, a satiric and philosophic critique of

[39] Letter to the Bishop of Waterford, January 26, 1766, cited in Speaight, *History of the English Puppet Theatre*, 101; see also *Dictionary of National Biography*, s.v. "Martin Powell."

[40] No. 2425 in Stephens and George, *Catalogue of Satires*; plate 231 in Paulson, *Hogarth's Graphic Works*. Hogarth evidently decided that the unpublished print could be interpreted as a satire on religion generally; in the revised published print "Credulity, Superstition, and Fanaticism" (1762), the preacher holds a puppet representing a witch on a broomstick.

Figure 5. A Methodist minister and his congregation with their puppets. William Hogarth, "Enthusiasm Delineated," unpublished print (ca. 1761). Reproduced by permission of the British Museum.

religious enthusiasm continued to appropriate the notion of the puppet well into the eighteenth century. The fanatics' belief in direct individual inspiration was belittled by virtue of its conceptual resemblance to the literal conditions of puppetry, even as the latter evoked the theological model of authorship and representation. This figural process as a whole also participated in the ongoing process by which its own implicit cultural categories of the elite and the popular were defined and confirmed. Whether in the crudest of political diatribes or in Shaftesbury's elegant prose, one discovers a generally similar note of cultural condescension and nostalgia: the puppet is "defended," so to speak, against political suppression, and its parodic power is conceded, even celebrated, but only as part of a larger cultural strategy that reconfirms the puppet's subordinate position within a nascent bourgeois system of distinction.

So far I have been considering how relatively conservative writers—Royalists confronting Puritan political insurgency, Presbyterians opposing agitators and Levellers—appropriated the puppet as a metaphor for political power or histrionic license. I conclude this section by considering how the relatively more liberal writers of the Whig bourgeoisie in the early years of the eighteenth century used the puppet as a figure and instance of cultural subordination. In the examples that follow, the latent theological and political valence of the puppet as metaphor persists in new discursive contexts, but issues of taste and aesthetic distinction have now been made explicit. Even when using the puppet, in the familiar manner, as a metaphor of politics, writers such as Addison and Steele seem equally concerned with their "totalizing project of moral education" and the consequent construction of an appropriate bourgeois readership.[41] In a period in which new discursive forms such as the novel and the periodical essay produced a corresponding new reading public, the observation and description of a particular mode of quasi-popular culture goes hand in hand with a larger project of social and cultural distinction, illustrating how, in Bourdieu's words, "the enterprise of cultural appropriation" becomes one of the "qualifications" for the "rights and duties" of bourgeois life.[42]

---

[41] The quoted phrase is from Peter Stallybrass and Allon White, *The Politics and Poetics of Transgression* (Ithaca: Cornell University Press, 1986), 83. On this general point, see David Marshall, *The Figure of Theater: Shaftesbury, Defoe, Adam Smith, and George Eliot* (New York: Columbia University Press, 1986), 9.

[42] Pierre Bourdieu, *Distinction: A Social Critique of the Judgment of Taste*, trans. Richard Nice (Cambridge: Harvard University Press, 1984), 23.

About 1699 the young Joseph Addison, while a fellow of Magdalen College, Oxford, published several mock-heroic Latin poems including one titled "Machinae Gesticulante, or The Puppet Show," a poem that embodies a complex, multilevel dynamic of cultural appropriation. Most obviously the poem is a literate version of and a response to a mode of performance explicitly declared to be low and popular, characteristics with which the text's own pompous Latinity is designed to contrast:

> Admiranda cano levium spectacula rerum,
> Exiguam gentem, et vacuum sine mente popellum.

> (I sing the admirable spectacle of trivial things,
> The tiny race, the empty, mindless puppet.)[43]

Addison here adapts the neoclassical convention of the mock-heroic to a subject whose literal size corresponds to its assumed triviality. In a double movement of magnification and diminution, the text's rhetorical strategy reverses the theatrical strategy of the puppet show, in which all human actions are depicted in a miniature popular theater ("quicquid agunt homines . . . Ludit in exiguo plebecula parva theatro").

But then, Addison's account continues, a "homuncio rauca," an aggressive little man, intrudes into a performance that otherwise represents the conventional heroic subjects of the stage ("concursus, bella, triumphos"). As one contemporary translation of Addison's Latin puts it:

> But one there is, that lords it over all,
> Whom we or Punch, or Punchanello call,
> A noisy wretch, like boatswains always hoarse,
> In language scurrilous, in manners coarse
>
> . . . .
>
> His belly turgid of enormous size,
> Behind his back a bulk of mountain lies.
>
> . . . .
>
> E'en when some serious action is displayed,

---

[43] Here I cite my own prose translation of the Latin text in *The Works of the Right Honourable Joseph Addison*, ed. Richard Hurd (London: Clarendon Press, 1873), 249–51. I will subsequently cite the partial English translation in Speaight, *History of the English Puppet Theatre* (88–90), which conflates several eighteenth-century translations of Addison's text.

And solemn pomps in long procession made,
He uncontrollable, of humour rude,
Must with unseasonable mirth intrude.
Scornful he grins upon their tragic rage,
And disconcerts the fable of the stage.
Sometimes the graceless wight, with saucy air,
Makes rude approaches to the painted fair,
The nymph retires, he scorns to be withstood,
And forces kisses on th'unwilling wood.

Again, the puppet's literal diminution corresponds to his evident social lowness. The puppet Punch and the authorial voice of the poem face each other
from their respective levels of class and culture, each performing his respective gestures of invasion or appropriation. Among other things, Addison's
poem thus confirms the elusiveness of cultural definition itself. Just where
is the "popular" in this multilingual and multiply parodic text? Punch
himself—with his disconcerting, carnivalesque voice, his grotesque physical-
ity, his disruptions of authority and convention—seems the very embodiment of the Bakhtinian festive impulse. Yet his intrusion into other narrative
contexts, as described in this poem and elsewhere, corresponds to the puppet's assumed status as a cultural interpolator, a "sophisticated" Italian import to some imagined "native" tradition of puppetry. Moreover, one simply
cannot see either Punch or the rest of the "pigmy race" except as filtered
through an authorial voice that in every conceivable discursive way declares
its own distance from the object of its elite attentions. Addison would eventually discover in the practical conditions of the puppet show, as playwrights
of a previous age had before him, an exemplum of a hierarchical, theological
theater:

Now sing we, whence the Puppet actors came,
What hidden power supplies the hollow frame,
What cunning agent o'er the scenes presides,
What hand such vigour to their limbs supplies.
. . . .
And now, directed by a hand unseen,
The finished puppet struts before the scene,
Exalts a treble voice and eunuch tone,
And squeaks his part in accents not his own.

The vision of an omnipotent histrionic power locates itself first in the puppet, then in its "master," and finally, by implication, in the authorial voice of the poem. The process by which Punch's carnivalesque energy is defused within the total discursive context also corresponds to a curious iconographic incongruity which I will have reason to mention again later: the disparity between Punch's grotesque masculine sexuality (his "rude approaches" to the "painted fair") and his "treble voice and eunuch tone." Just so, Addison's revision of the literal popular performer as a mysterious "hidden power" who "presides" over the scene supplements the process of cultural subordination that takes place both in the described performance and in the poem.

In the ensuing decades Addison's fellow essayist Richard Steele would repeatedly refer to puppet theater in the pages of *The Tatler* and *The Spectator*. To juxtapose some of Steele's references to the puppeteer Martin Powell with his other references to contemporary theater and politics is to illuminate how this discourse participates in an implicit project of cultural and social distinction, and in the construction of a bourgeois subject capable of apprehending the literary judgments and stylistic nuances of the journals themselves. In one of the first issues of *The Tatler* (no. 8, April 28, 1709), for example, Steele's famous narrative voice, Isaac Bickerstaff, transcribes the comments of one "Eugenio" about Edward Ravenscroft's popular farce *The London Cuckolds* (1681), which had been performed at Drury Lane two days earlier: "Of all Men living, said he, I pity Players, (who must be Men of good Understanding to be capable of being such) that they are oblig'd to repeat and assume proper Gestures for representing Things, of which their Reason must be asham'd, and which they must disdain their Audience for approving." Eugenio contrasts the presumed selfhood of the actor to what he also presumes is the actor's passivity within the process of representation. The literal performer becomes the mere vehicle for a meaning that flows through him into spectators whose acceptance of it he disdains. In Eugenio's view this assumed hierarchical structure of representation applies to mere farce and to legitimate drama alike, to both low and high forms of performance.

Eugenio goes on to locate his argument in the familiar neoclassical doctrine of *emulation*, the idea—whose roots go back as far as Plato—that a viewer of any artistic representation tends to imitate it in his own being. If historians and painters can induce virtuous behavior by representing it, "what may not be perform'd by an excellent Poet? when the Character he draws is presented by the Person, the Manner, the Look, and the *Motion* of an accomplish'd Player" (emphasis added). Accordingly, Eugenio concludes that "the Amendment of these low Gratifications is only to be made by

People of Condition, by encouraging the Presentation of the Noble Characters drawn by *Shakespear* and others." This would make the theater "the most agreeable and easie Method of making a Polite and Moral Gentry, which would end in rendring the rest of the people regular in their Behavior." Emulation in the audience and the "apt use" of the puppetlike passivity of the actor combine to *reproduce* a corresponding social hierarchy.

This assumed interrelation of performance and politics provides the conceptual foundation for the essayists' appropriation of the puppet, whether as mere social observation or as political metaphor. Steele first specifically mentions the puppeteer Martin Powell in a letter purportedly written from Bath (*Tatler*, no. 16, May 17, 1709), which describes how "two ambitious Ladies," Florimell and Prudentia, compete for the favor of fashionable society by bespeaking, respectively, a production of *The Rival Queens* by Nathaniel Lee and Powell's puppet show *The Creation of the World*. The fictional letter writer describes at some length how the puppets succeeded in engrossing the attention of the resort town:

> On *Thursday* Morning, the Poppet-Drummer, *Adam*, and *Eve*, and several others who liv'd before the Flood, pass'd through the Streets on Horseback, to invite us all to the Pastime, and the Representation of such Things as we all knew to be true; and Mr. Mayor was so Wise as to prefer these innocent People the Poppets, who, he said, were to represent Christians, before the wicked Players, who were to show *Alexander*, an Heathen Philosopher. . . . All the World crowded to *Prudentia's* House, because it was giv'n out, no body could get in. When we came to *Noah's* Flood in the Show, *Punch* and his Wife were introduc'd dancing in the Ark. An honest plain Friend of *Florimel's*, but a Critick withal, rose up in the midst of the Representation, and made many very good Exceptions to the *Drama* itself, and told us, That it was against all Morality, as well as Rules of the Stage, that *Punch* should be in Jest in the Deluge, or indeed that he should appear at all. This was certainly a just Remark, and I thought to second him; but he was hiss'd by *Prudentia's* party. . . . Old Mrs. *Petulant* desir'd both her Daughters to mind the Moral; then whisper'd Mrs. Mayoress, *This is very proper for young People to see*. *Punch* at the End of the Play made Madame *Prudentia* a Compliment, and was very civil to the whole Company, making Bows till his Buttons touch'd the Ground.

The passage is both an instance of and a commentary on the "two-way traffic" between elite and popular forms of culture which it describes. Powell's performance, not unlike Steele's account of it, evokes a complex cultural tension between its "fashionable" aspirations and the impulse of parody, between the resurgent carnivalesque (Punch's intrusion) and the fleeting attention of a bourgeois audience who make elaborate (and erroneous) moral rationalizations for their acceptance of an entertainment they otherwise might dismiss. Punch himself becomes, as it were, both a tool and an actor in an intricate game of social and literary distinction, transmuted from crude showman to "civil" gentleman so as to mirror (and mock) the social aspirations of his audience. Steele intends the various comic nuances of the scene—the mayor's identification of Alexander as a "heathen philosopher," the critic's interpolation of a moral and critical judgment not unmixed with social prejudice, Mrs. Petulant's self-important concern with education and propriety—to be observed and judged by a different but equally bourgeois audience: his readers.

In the months that followed, Powell apparently noticed and responded to his mention in *The Tatler*, for on July 21 Steele writes that Powell "makes a prophane lewd Jester, whom he calls *Punch*, speak to the Dishonour of *Isaac Bickerstaff* with great familiarity" (no. 44). For the next six months or so Steele would refer several times to this "feud" between Powell and Bickerstaff, using it as the occasion for an elaborate political satire in which the histrionic process of literal inspiration becomes a metaphor for political manipulation and power. Steele initially declares to "Powell":

> I would have him know, that I can look beyond his Wires, and know very well the whole Trick of his Art, and that it is only by these Wires that the Eye of The Spectator is cheated, and hinder'd from seeing that there is a Thread on one of *Punch's* Chops, which draws it up, and lets it fall at the Discretion of the said *Powell*, who stands behind and plays him, and makes him speak sawcily of his Betters. . . . Therefore I shall command my self, and never trouble me further with this little Fellow, who is himself but a tall Puppet, and has not brains enough to make even Wood speak as it ought to do.[44]

The rhetorical categories of relative size evoke the assumptions of class: Powell is at once the authorial master of powerfully saucy puppets and merely a

---

[44] Steele is here referring to the custom of stretching a grid of thin wires across the opening of the puppet stage to conceal the threads attached to the puppets' limbs.

"little Fellow"; and his ventriloquistic craft potentially subverts a hierarchical class structure which its own conditions resemble. The rest of this essay, however, is a satirical defense of Steele's friend, the young Benjamin Hoadly (later to become the bishop of Bangor and a well-known Latitudinarian), who was then engaged in a pamphlet controversy with the bishop of Exeter over the Tory doctrine of passive obedience. By careful parodies of Exeter's language here and in a follow-up essay, Steele transforms Powell into a satiric analogue of the high churchman, who is then wittily accused of a design "to have all Men *Automata*, like your puppets."

In an essay on August 4 (no. 50), Steele printed the text of a fictitious letter from the puppet master which accuses Bickerstaff of "sowing the Seeds of Sedition and Disobedience among my Puppets":

> Your Zeal for the (good old) Cause would make you perswade *Punch* to pull the String from his Chops, and not move his Jaw when I have a mind he should harangue. Now I appeal to all Men, if this is not contrary to that uncontroulable, unaccountable Dominion, which by the Laws of nature I exercise over 'em; for all Sorts of Wood and Wire were made for the Use and Benefit of Man: I have therefore an unquestionable Right to frame, fashion, and put them together as I please; and having made them what they are, my Puppets are my Property, and therefore my Slaves.

Here, obviously enough, Steele belittles the Tory doctrines by comparing the subject's passive obedience to a sovereign authority to the puppet's literal passivity in the hands of its "author" and master. Eventually, however, the rhetorical momentum of this extraordinary passage itself starts to seem an instance of the "uncontroulable" and "unaccountable" domination against which Steele ostensibly writes. The carnivalesque power with which Punch speaks "sawcily of his Betters" is unmasked, revealed as no more than servitude and contrivance. The inexorable rhythm of framing and fashioning, pleasure and property, with which Steele's rhetoric transforms iconic objects into veritable slaves takes on its own implacable, demonic energy. A few lines later Powell proposes to reduce his dispute with Bickerstaff into two propositions: "The First, Whether I have not an Absolute Power, whenever I please, to light a Pipe with one of *Punch's* Legs, or warm my Fingers with his Whole Carcass? The second, Whether the Devil would not be in *Punch* should he by Word or Deed oppose my sovereign Will and Pleasure?" The rhetorical violence of this passage, even though submerged beneath an urbane wit, evokes the violence of cultural appropriation itself, whose logic constrains Steele to confirm the otherness of popular culture even as he uses it as a discursive tool in a project of liberal politics and bourgeois education.

Just as inevitably the passage not only evokes but exaggerates for parodic effect the theological model of theatrical authorship, and even the quasi-Platonic opposition of the flesh and the spirit that underlies such a model. Steele's version of Powell grounds his authorial "dominion" in the pure materiality of the performing object, and describes both in terms at once political and ontological:

> Nor is there in Nature any Thing more just, than the Homage which is paid by a less to a more excellent Being: so that by the Right therefore of a superior Genius, I am their supreme Moderator, altho' you would insinuate (agreeable to your levelling Principles) that I am my self but a great Puppet, and can therefore have but a co-ordinate Jurisdiction with them. I suppose I have now sufficiently made it appear, that I have a paternal Right to keep a Puppet-Show.

Thus, as one might put it, Steele is a Whig in real politics but an absolutist in the theater of culture, locked into the same basic assumptions about cultural distinction and social class that he instantiates in his ventriloquizing discourse. The ironically described "levelling Principles" of Bickerstaff, his "Zeal for the (good old) Cause," can manifest itself here only in the implicit class sneer directed toward Powell, who is repeatedly declared to be himself a "little Fellow" and a "great Puppet."

In January 1710 (following Powell's opening of a "Punch's Theatre" in London), Bickerstaff once again mentions his "feud" with Powell, in an essay that also construes the sheer materiality of the performing object as a figure of social class:

> As for *Punch*, who takes all Opportunities of bespattering me, I know very well his Original, and have been assured by the Joyner who put him together, that he was in long Dispute with himself, whether he should turn him into several Pegs and Utensils, or make him the Man he is. . . . As for his Scolding Wife, (however she may value her self at present) it is very well known, that she is but a Piece of Crabtree. This Artificer further whispered in my Ear, that all his Courtiers and Nobles were taken out of a Quickset Hedge not far from *Islington*; and that

Dr. *Faustus* himself, who is now so great a Conjurer, is supposd to have learned his whole Art from an old Woman in that Neighbourhood, whom he long served in the Figure of a Broomstaff. (no. 115, January 3, 1710)

Here again, the urbane wit draws an impermeable veil of irony over a passage that nevertheless exploits the system of social distinction which it satirizes, and ultimately shares the metaphysical assumptions at which it otherwise pokes fun. A cultural anxiety about scolding wives and witches' "poppets" seems to percolate just beneath the surface of a discourse whose freedom from such benighted ideas is otherwise so adamantly declared.

In the next few years both Steele and Addison would continue occasionally to mention Martin Powell and confirm his popularity with London theatergoers, while Powell himself avidly courted the attentions of society, eventually moving Punch's Theatre to the Little Piazza at Covent Garden, a site he claimed in an advertisement, "fitter to receive persons of quality."[45] The female spectators of London, Steele complains on January 3, 1710, "run gadding after a puppet show," (*Tatler*, no. 115). A little over a year later he confirms, with a similar double irony, that "the Opera at the *Hay-Market*, and that under the little *Piazza* in *Covent-Garden* [are] the Two leading Diversions of the Town" (*Spectator*, no. 14, March 16, 1711).[46] At about the same time, Addison similarly satirized the debased taste of the London audience by appending to one of his *Spectator* essays what purports to be a letter from a "projector" describing his plans to exhibit trained monkeys. "I will not say," writes the projector, "that a Monkey is a better Man than some of the Opera Heroes; but certainly he is a better Representative of a Man, than the most artificial Composition of Wood and Wire" (*Spectator*, no. 28, April 2, 1711). As so often, a satiric mockery of one kind of discourse (a pseudohierarchical argument privileging the monkey over what Addison had once called the "little man") participates in an implicit and equally hierarchical project of aesthetic distinction and bourgeois education.

Within a few years, however, after several successful seasons in the heart of fashionable London, Powell's popularity apparently waned. He is mentioned (in the previously cited ballad) at Bartholomew Fair in 1717 and occasionally elsewhere, but eventually he drops from sight. Thus Powell's career, no less than his performances, illustrates the violence with which popular and elite

[45] Quoted in Speaight, *History of the English Puppet Theatre*, 94.
[46] All citations from *The Spectator* are from the edition edited by Donald F. Bond, 3 vols. (Oxford: Clarendon Press, 1965), and are given parenthetically by date and number in the text.

modes of culture interact in a dynamic pattern of mutual appropriation. Punch invades and degrades the legitimate theater, only to become a discursive mouthpiece declaring his own subordination within a developing system of literary and theatrical taste. Meanwhile, the puppeteer moves from the carnival to Covent Garden and back again, at one and the same time a "great puppet" manipulated by discursive and cultural forces far beyond his own and the master of a theater whose conditions figurally embody not only the theological model of authorship but the very process of cultural appropriation itself.

"Borrowed Dress": Henry Fielding and Charlotte Charke

> I who in this puppet show
> Have played Punchinello
> Will now let all the audience know
> I am no common fellow.
>
> —Henry Fielding, *The Author's Farce*

At this point I turn back to the theater itself and pursue the figural and theatrical appropriation of the puppet in this period by considering two unusual figures of the eighteenth-century stage. Both Henry Fielding and Charlotte Charke, in different moments of their multifaceted careers, resorted to puppetry in ways that illuminate the precarious social position of eighteenth-century authors and actors and the shifting dynamics of bourgeois theatrical taste. Fielding, like Jonson before him, appropriated puppet theater both in his discourse and in his theatrical practice, even while apparently viewing it with a contempt that corresponds to his cultural and political allegiances and aspirations. Charke, the daughter of Colley Cibber and an actress recently much discussed for her cross-dressing and possible bisexuality, turned to puppet theater when other avenues of theatrical work were closed to her; she seems to have discovered in the performing object a symbolic equivalent to her own social and sexual marginality. Both figures resorted to puppetry out of sheer financial necessity and yet with a keen awareness of the puppet's participation in a multiply hierarchical system of literary, class, and gender distinction.

As Martin Battestin documents in his comprehensive biography, Henry Fielding's earliest literary efforts coincided with the coronation of King George II on October 11, 1727. This event inspired not only Fielding's first published work ("The Coronation: A Poem") but also a descending spiral of cultural appropriation that reflects some of the dynamics I will observe in Fielding's subsequent career. To exploit the public interest in the coronation, the managers of the Drury Lane Theatre produced Shakespeare's *Henry VIII*, including an elaborately staged version of the coronation of Anne Boleyn. John Rich retaliated at Lincoln's Inn Fields with his pantomime *Harlequin Anne Bullen*. Meanwhile, in the words of a contemporary newspaper, "in a certain Alley in Wapping during these Holidays the Coronation of Anne Bullen [was] represented by Punch's Company of Actors."[47] From Westminister Abbey to the legitimate theater, from the pantomime to the puppet, this repeatedly represented ritual of power evokes, as it were, the theological theater writ large: a collective image of culture as hierarchy. Fielding, too, over the course of the next two and a half years, followed two "regular" comedies with an unusual entertainment that used puppets to represent his own situation in miniature. His first play, *Love at Several Masques*, had been accepted for production by Cibber and the triumvirate at Drury Lane, a stunning success for a new playwright just twenty years old at the time. Unfortunately for Fielding, however, two other enormously successful plays from that season— Cibber's *Provoked Husband* at Drury Lane, and John Gay's *Beggar's Opera* at Lincoln's Inn Fields—completely overshadowed his theatrical premiere. Cibber and Wilks's rejection of Fielding's second comedy, *The Temple Beau*, forced him to offer it to the new theater in Goodman's Fields, where it had a reasonably good but unspectacular run. After this passage from the mainstream to the periphery of the legitimate theater, Fielding "threw in his lot with an even less reputable band of rogue comedians at the New Theatre in the Haymarket," where his play *The Author's Farce* opened on March 30, 1730.[48]

As its self-reflexive title suggests, Fielding's new play is a complexly metadramatic work which examines how theoretical ideas of authorship collide with the commodification of literature and the actual conditions of performance. *The Author's Farce* also exploits a broad spectrum of paratheatrical entertainment, especially puppet theater, and negotiates a delicate compromise between the literal author's aspirations to commercial success and the

---

[47] *Mist's Weekly Journal* for January 6, 1728, cited in Woods's edition of *The Author's Farce*, 41. On the regular theater productions inspired by the coronation, see also Battestin, *Henry Fielding*, 57; and Paul Sawyer, "John Rich's Contribution to the Eighteenth-Century London Stage," in *The Eighteenth-Century Stage*, ed. Kenneth Richards and Peter Thomson (London: Methuen, 1972), 92.

[48] Battestin, *Henry Fielding*, 82.

supposedly degenerate taste of his audience.[49] In this, as in his incorporation of a puppet show within his play, *The Author's Farce* begs comparison with Jonson's *Bartholomew Faire*. Fielding himself at one point alludes to his famous predecessor's work by allowing his play to be interrupted by the "Presbyterian" Murdertext, who contends—as the Puritan Zeal-of-the-Land Busy does in Jonson's play—that "a puppet show is the devil's house" (3.700). When he published the play almost immediately after its production, Fielding used the pseudonym "Scriblerus Secundus," thus alluding to Martinus Scriblerus, the fictitious author originally created by Swift, Pope, and other members of the Scriblerus Club.[50] Both allusions have the effect of positioning Fielding's play on the cultural high ground and announcing the young author's allegiance to the historical canon and the contemporary literary establishment.

Fielding's approach to his audience, as both enacted in and embodied by this play, seems similarly divided between imperious claims of literary privilege and an inescapable awareness of his own precarious authorial position. The first two acts paint a dismal picture of a situation that, as Battestin documents, was much like Fielding's own at the time: the young playwright Luckless is dunned by his landlady, Moneywould; swears romantic love to her daughter Harriot; and struggles fruitlessly to place a tragedy with either the theatrical managers or the booksellers. This framing story, despite its obvious autobiographical quality, is also, as contemporary critics complained, a thinly disguised adaptation of George Farquhar's popular play *Love and a Bottle* (1698)—or at least a deliberate invocation of the topos of the penniless poet.[51] Verisimilitude here merges with pure convention in a manner that Fielding later echoes in his deliberate confusion of puppets and players. The curious intimacy with which Fielding parades his own financial and authorial woes before the eyes of the public must have evoked in his audience a certain voyeuristic pleasure which contributed to the play's eventual success,

---

[49] On *The Author's Farce* as a play that critiques popular performance by embracing it, see Robert D. Hume, *Henry Fielding and the London Theatre, 1729–1737* (Oxford: Clarendon Press, 1988), 63; Peter Lewis, *Fielding's Burlesque Drama* (Edinburgh: Edinburgh University Press, 1987), 93; and Albert J. Rivero, *The Plays of Henry Fielding: A Critical Study of his Dramatic Career* (Charlottesville: University of Virginia Press, 1989), 34–35.

[50] This was an audacious gesture for a twenty-two-year-old playwright, as Fielding's subsequent difficult relations with Pope and the Scriblerian *Grub-Street Journal* confirm. See Lewis, *Fielding's Burlesque Drama*, 86–87; and James T. Hillhouse, *The Grub-Street Journal* (Durham: Duke University Press, 1928), 173–85.

[51] Hume, *Henry Fielding and the London Theatre*, 63; Battestin, *Henry Fielding*, 73, 77.

even as it collided with his public gestures of literary satire and authorial self-construction.

The early scenes of the play, it has often been observed, are an extended satire of the commodification of the literary text and the dominance of actor-managers in the contemporary theater. Bookweight, who suggests the notorious bookseller Edmund Curl, refuses to consider Luckless's tragedy before its acceptance by the players because, he says, "a play, like a bill, is of no value before it is accepted, nor indeed when it is, very often" (1.6.8). At the same time, Bookweight also stipulates that "a play which will do for them will not always do for us." As he explains:

There are your acting plays and your reading plays. . . . Your acting play is entirely supported by the merit of the actor, without any regard to the author at all. In this case, it signifies very little whether there be any sense in it or not. Now your reading play is of a different stamp and must have wit and meaning in it. These latter I call your substantive, as being able to support themselves. The former are your adjective, as what require the buffoonery and gestures of an actor to be joined to them to show their signification. (1.6.24–32)

As Fielding suggests in a passage that also parodies Bookweight's ponderous pretensions to learning, performance and publication now oppose each other in a relationship of inescapable cultural paradox. In Jonson's day the defense of the histrionic authority of the theatrical text went hand in hand with a defense of the book; but in Fielding's day, at least as envisioned here, the cooperative relationship between publication and production serves to confirm the apparent ascendancy of the histrionic over the literary. As Bookweight remarks, the "acting play" subverts the hierarchies of theatrical representation by subsisting on the "buffoonery and gestures" of the actor "without any regard to the author at all"; while the "reading play," precisely in its authorial "wit and meaning," tends to be debarred from further embodiment in the theater. Later, however, Bookweight contradicts even his modest claims here by confessing he would "rather venture" on an opera or puppet show "than a regular play" (2.7.33). The ascendancy of the marketplace both parallels and joins that of paratheatrical modes of performance to subvert both the textual and the histrionic transmission of the authorial voice.

A few scenes later Fielding depicts Luckless reading his tragedy to Marplay and Sparkish, who represent Colley Cibber and Robert Wilks. The actor-managers demonstrate their arbitrary power over the author by suggesting a variety of preposterous changes to Luckless's text and then rejecting his play out of hand when he refuses:

> *Luckless.* Could you convince me of any fault, I would amend it. But you argue in plays as the Pope does in religion or the Aristotelists in philosophy: you maintain your hypothesis with an *ipse dicit.*
> *Marplay.* I don't understand you [*sic*] hard words, sir. But I think it is very hard if a man who has been so long in a trade as I have should not understand the value of his merchandise, should not know what goods will best please the town.
>
> (2.1.41–49)

Here again, Fielding's satiric dialogue seems to rehearse the dynamics of the literary marketplace by depicting how the purely economic considerations of the actor-managers displace both classical learning and contemporary literary production.

In the next scene, similarly, Fielding depicts Bookweight's shop, where a team of starving hack writers is relentlessly turning out pamphlets and poems, each complete with its conventional Latin epigraph. When one Scarecrow offers Bookweight a translation of the *Aeneid,* Bookweight refuses, saying: "That, sir, is what I do not care to venture on. You may try by subscription if you please, but I would not advise you, for that bubble is almost down. People begin to be afraid of authors since they have writ and acted like stockjobbers" (2.6.7–10). Scarecrow himself is an exaggerated comic parody of cultural appropriation: a hack with no real knowledge of Latin who has translated Virgil, as he later confesses, out of Dryden's previous translation. But the joke about "stockjobbers"—that is, brokers who trade in stocks on their own behalf—is double-edged. Authors who claim not only a literary propriety but a commercial ownership of their own productions reveal the instability of the hypothetical vision of authorship precisely by subjecting it to the valuation of the marketplace. Fielding satirizes a situation in which the *agents* of textual or histrionic mediation—actors, booksellers, translators, and prompters—subvert the authority of the author even as both he and his theatrical surrogate wholeheartedly immerse themselves in the same marketplace they repeatedly allege has deformed the hierarchy of literary value.

Fielding's ensuing substitution of puppets for actors thus repeats such an inversion on the axes of both aesthetic taste and representation. In act 3 Luckless (and thus Fielding) capitulates to a cultural milieu in which "learn-

ing is decried, wit not understood [and] the theaters are puppet shows"
(1.5.27–30) by putting on his own puppet show with another self-reflexive
title, *The Pleasures of the Town*. Fielding had announced the obvious implications of this gesture in the prologue to the framing play:

> Beneath the tragic or the comic name,
> Farces and puppet shows ne'er miss of fame.
> Since then in borrowed dress they've pleased the town,
> Condemn them not, appearing in their own.
>
> (ll. 31–34)

Puppet shows pleased the town in "borrowed dress," that is, by usurping the
social and theatrical status of tragedy and comedy. Not just within their own
field of representation but *as* institution or cultural category, the puppets are
interlopers within a hypothetical comedy of manners set in the real conditions of contemporary theater. Puppets have thus moved up one level of cultural distinction and down one level of representation: they are "beneath the
tragic or the comic name," so to speak, both in the conventional cultural
sense and because they have dressed themselves in the "borrowed" status of
generic and aesthetic privilege. But what does it mean, as Fielding claims,
that puppets will now appear in their "own" dress, as "themselves"? Just as,
in the framing play, the obvious autobiographical references merge with
a virtually plagiaristic use of literary allusion, so Fielding's appropriative
project illustrates the essential impurity of the cultural categories by which
such a project defines itself. To strip puppets of their "borrowed dress"—as Jonson's Zeal-of-the-Land Busy discovered over a century earlier—is merely to reveal one more level of artifice. Similarly, this announced return to some hypothetical originary mode of puppetry by a poet or puppet master who "laughs at"
his audience is a theatrical gesture that moves in at least two cultural directions
at once: it appropriates and sophisticates the puppet performance it claims to
purify and shatters the limits of popular taste to which it pretends to surrender.

Moreover, Fielding's paradoxical claim to be returning puppets to their
"own" status is untrue, as the play's original audience soon learned. His puppet show was performed not by literal performing objects but by human actors playing puppets. Just before it begins a showman announces the forthcoming puppet show in a manner that parodies similar announcements of
real puppet theater—which conventionally boasted of the size and verisimilitude of the mechanical actors.[52] Luckless's showman announces, similarly,

[52] Richard Yeates in 1735 announced a performance of "large Wax-Work Figures, being five Foot

"the whole puppet show called *The Pleasures of the Town* . . . also the comical and diverting humors of . . . Punch and his wife Joan; to be performed by living figures, some of them six foot high" (2.8.1–8). As commentators have often suggested, Fielding's human puppets literalize the familiar critique of theatrical taste which suggests, as Luckless does to the player, that "all the playhouses" have been "for a long time but puppet shows" (2.7.30). Even this obvious joke, however, seems to overflow its own intentions. The theaters are puppet shows in the pernicious cultural sense but also in terms of a model of authorship and the concrete power relations of theatrical management with which Fielding himself is inevitably implicated. Fielding's "puppets" in this play are human bodies in their full natural amplitude, so that mere iconic resemblance or verisimilitude becomes absolute identity. But such bodies are degraded or deformed by their assumption of the squeaky voices and awkward movements of puppets. The entwined and transparent hierarchies of corporeal grace and representational fidelity here collide in a manner that parallels the author's own unwilling embrace of a performative mode that he considers "beneath the dignity of the stage" (3.5). Even later, when Murdertext attempts to disrupt the puppet show, the incident stands at the apex of another spiral of literary allusion and representational paradox. In an obvious echo of *Bartholomew Faire*, Murdertext seals off Fielding's play within a self-constructed historical canon of literature; and in his deliberate interruption of an already shapeless entertainment, he ironically subsumes the role of the carnivalesque puppet to which he objects. Nevertheless, Murdertext is also *himself* a (figural) performing object, whose theological objections to the puppet play are not only diverted by his sexual attraction to Mrs. Novel but also mocked by reference to the familiar eighteenth-century trope of Puritan-as-puppet: "The flesh hath subdued the spirit. I feel a motion in me, and whether it be of grace or not I am not certain. . . . I will abide the performing a dance, and will myself, being thereto moved by an inward working, accompany you therein" (3.759–64). Divine inspiration becomes at once mere sexuality (the body) and the figural equivalent of histrionic manipulation (the spirit).

Throughout the puppet show which continues for the rest of his play, Fielding keeps up a constant rhythm of appropriation and parody, involving at once the conventions of performance, specific literary models, and the categories of taste and aesthetic distinction. Luckless begins his show by pre-

high"; quoted by Woods in his introduction to *The Author's Farce*, xix. The performance advertised was, ironically, a puppet version of Fielding's play.

senting the audience with "Punchinello," who sings a song that repeats the
adversarial gesture of Fielding's prologue:

> Whilst the town's brimful of farces,
> Flocking whilst we see her asses
> Thick as grapes upon a bunch,
> Critics, whilst you smile on madness,
> And more stupid, solemn sadness,
> Sure you will not frown on Punch.
>
> (3.45–50)

Here Fielding's own cultural critique merges with the carnivalesque voice
of this most familiar of puppet characters, who at once invites and returns
a gaze of critical judgment thus rendered utterly problematic. Punch
and his wife, Joan, proceed to fight and dance, just as they had in the
shows of Martin Powell and other puppeteers of the period. But they
resolve:

> Since we hate, like people in vogue,
> Let us call not bitch and rogue,
> Gentler titles let us use,
> Hate each other, but not abuse.
> Pretty dear!
> Ah! my chère!
>
> (3.82–87)

So not only has Punch been marooned within a multiply parodic entertainment lacking even a "design or plot" (3.25) for him to disrupt, but he is also
forced, as it were, to repeat his own cultural appropriation on the level of the
bourgeois class dynamic.

   Little more needs to be said here about the obvious satire of literary and
theatrical taste that continues throughout the puppet show, with its parodic
representations of Cibber (Sir Farcical Comick), Theobald (Don Tragedio),
John Rich (Monsieur Pantomime), and others. At the end, in another frequently discussed metadramatic gesture, the "real" characters Luckless and
Harriot eventually prove, in a parody of the "recognition" scenes of contemporary drama, to be the King and Queen of Bantam, related by an ironic and
impossible consanguinity to the puppets Punch and Joan, who similarly

prove to be noble born.[53] As the revelation of the puppets' "origins" fulfills their previous aspiration to become people of fashion, so Luckless's familial relation to the puppets becomes a figure for Fielding's own inescapable connection to the popular culture he appropriates with such apparent ease. In the design of the whole multifaceted show, the Scriblerian author masters representation by representing himself, and reinscribes the puppets within a legitimate literary context. But both the play within and the play without are designed to produce the same effect (the town's pleasure) that they also satirize, and both character and playwright achieve success by using the very modes of popular performance that their respective entertainments relentlessly mock. Notice here again how the very idea of the performing object, whether construed either on the axis of cultural distinction or as a kind of paradigm of representation itself, seems to evoke a constant spiral of involution and self-reflection. Some twenty years ago Anthony J. Hassal went so far as to suggest that Luckless's role as the puppet "interpreter," who presents and comments on the action he also sets in motion, determined the narrative strategy later adapted by Fielding in the novels on which his reputation largely depends. "The structure of the puppet show," writes Hassal, "with its master animating and manipulating his perennial figures, reconstructing his traditional story, and appearing before the curtain to mediate between stage and audience, is, in all essentials, the structure of Fielding's novels."[54] Yet such resemblance is itself also a gesture of cultural appropriation. Fielding transmutes the conventions of low performance into a device of elite narrative, and the hypothetical puppeteer, plucked out of his real social conditions, is at once silenced and reborn as the magisterial author of the canonical text. This process, transacted within the larger dimensions of Fielding's whole career, is already adumbrated in the more specifically appropriative strategy of *The Author's Farce.*

If Fielding's general project in this play is, as I have observed more than once, generally comparable to Jonson's in *Bartholomew Faire,* the result also illuminates how a broadly similar cultural dynamic produces different results in a different cultural context. *Bartholomew Faire* has been, since its original production, one of Jonson's acknowledged masterpieces. By the Restoration period retrospective critics could consider this play's self-conscious appropriation of popular culture the ground of its literary achievement. Dryden in

---

[53] See Valerie C. Rudolph, "People and Puppets: Fielding's Burlesque of the Recognition Scene," *Papers on Language and Literature* 11 (1975): 31–38; cf. Rivero, *The Plays of Henry Fielding,* 51–52.

[54] Anthony J. Hassal, "Fielding's Puppet Image," *Philological Quarterly* 53.1. (1974):83.

1666 praised Jonson for a work in which "he does so raise his matter in that Prose, as to render it delightful; which he could never have performed, had he only said or done those very things that are daily spoken or practised in the Fair: for then the Fair it self would be as full of pleasure to an ingenious person as the Play; which we manifestly see it is not. But he hath made an excellent Lazar of it; the Copy is of price, though the Original be vile."[55] *The Author's Farce*, by contrast—although it did achieve a certain succès d'estime in the theatrical season of 1730—would subsequently be considered, even by its own author, little more than an idiosyncratic bit of apprentice work. (Indeed, in a striking instance of cultural reappropriation, the puppet show from *The Author's Farce* would eventually be performed by actual puppeteers at Bartholomew Fair and elsewhere.) In the next few years Fielding would write again for Cibber and the triumvirate at Drury Lane, and publicly lament his "Frolick Flights of Youth."[56] Nevertheless, by the season of 1733–34 he was induced to revise *The Author's Farce* for a new production. In the words of an anonymous poem attached to the published version of Fielding's ballad opera *The Intriguing Chambermaid*, Fielding's career seems a living acknowledgment that "the compliant bard" must conform to the "public taste," and "fill the scene, / With puppets" (3:282). Even later, as I will show, Fielding would return to literal puppetry at the very moment when he was writing the novels that would win for him the legitimate literary status to which he had previously aspired.

Whether as playwright, theatrical manager, essayist, or canonical novelist, Fielding may well seem from a twentieth-century perspective a central figure of his period's intellectual and cultural history. Charlotte Charke, by contrast, appears to be a thoroughly marginal figure, a minor player specializing in sensational cross-dressing roles, and an occasional writer whose most famous work, an autobiographical memoir, resembles a rogue narrative. Yet in fact both Fielding and Charke inhabited much the same cultural space, and similarly turned to puppetry in their respective struggles to make a precarious living in eighteenth-century show business. Charke's memoir, *A Narrative of the Life of Mrs. Charlotte Charke*, has been discussed in recent years by critics considering more generally how women's autobiographical writings of the eighteenth century participate in the construction of a "gendered female

[55] Dryden, "A Defence of an Essay of Dramatique Poesy," *Works*, 8:1.
[56] Henry Fielding, *The Modern Husband* (1732), prologue, in *The Complete Works of Henry Fielding*, ed. William Ernest Henley, 5 vols. (1902; rpt. New York: Barnes & Noble, 1967), 4:262. All further citations from Fielding are from this edition and are given parenthetically by volume and page in the text.

subject."[57] The various forms of trangressive behavior narrated in the book—Charke's quarrel with her famous father, Colley Cibber, her theatrical impersonations of Cibber in Fielding's *Pasquin* and elsewhere, her cross-dressing, her experiments with "an exhausting number of professions"—have also attracted the attention of scholars newly sensitive to the marginal and subversive in eighteenth-century culture.[58] Charke's recurrent activities as a puppeteer have, however, been virtually ignored, a fact that itself illustrates the continuing subordination of puppetry in the cultural equation. By contrast, I suggest here that Charke's efforts at puppet performance, as reconstructed from contemporary advertisements and her own brief account in *The Narrative*, embody in miniature the complex dynamics of class, gender, and culture which her whole difficult career can otherwise be seen to illuminate.

Charke acted a wide variety of roles at both Drury Lane and Lincoln's Inn Fields in the early 1730s, periodically quarreling with her father, her brother (the actor and manager Theophilus Cibber), and Charles Fleetwood, the manager of Covent Garden. She began to act in Fielding's Great Moguls's Company of Comedians at the Haymarket Theatre after the abortive production of her own play *The Art of Management* (1735), another parody of contemporary theatrical conditions and the taste of the town. The Licensing Act of 1737, which strictly limited performance to the two patent companies where neither Fielding nor Charke was welcome, ended both their careers in the mainstream London theater. At this point Charke undertook what would eventually prove to be a long series of commercial schemes to support herself and her daughter.

First, as she describes it in her own narrative, "I took it into my Head to dive into TRADE." Accordingly, she "took a shop in *Long-Acre*, and turn'd Oil-woman and Grocer."[59] Charke portrays her commercial life, however, as no

[57] The quoted phrase is from Felicity A. Nussbaum, "Eighteenth-Century Women's Autobiographical Commonplaces," in *The Private Self: Theory and Practice of Women's Autobiographical Writings*, ed. Shari Benstock (Chapel Hill: University of North Carolina Press, 1988), 167.

[58] See Lynne Friedli, " 'Passing Women': A Study of Gender Boundaries in the Eighteenth Century," in *Sexual Underworlds of the Enlightenment*, ed. G. S. Rousseau and Roy Porter (Chapel Hill: University of North Carolina Press, 1988), 234–60; Erin Mackie, "Desperate Measures: The Narrative of the Life of Mrs. Charlotte Charke," *ELH* 58 (1991): 841–65; Fidelis Morgan, *The Well-Known Trouble Maker: A Life of Charlotte Charke* (London: Faber & Faber, 1988); Sidonie Smith, *A Poetics of Women's Autobiography: Marginality and the Fictions of Self-Representation* (Bloomington: Indiana University Press, 1987), 102–22; and Kristina Straub, *Sexual Suspects: Eighteenth-Century Players and Sexual Ideology* (Princeton: Princeton University Press, 1992), 135, from which I take the phrase quoted in the text.

[59] *A Narrative of the Life of Mrs. Charlotte Charke*, 2d ed. (London, 1755), 70. All further citations are from this edition and are given parenthetically in the text.

better than a "ridiculous Scene" (70), a "Farce" (71), playacted in a kind of miniature theater. Her stock, she confesses, "did not exceed ten or a dozen Pounds at a Time of each Sort." Nevertheless, wearing a "mercantile face" and a "conceited . . . air of trade," she would talk "of 'myself and other DEAL-ERS,' as I was pleased to term it . . . with as much Discourse, as if I had the whole Lading of a Ship in my Shop" (70–71). When her self-confessed poor management compounded by a ruinous theft plunged her into "misfortunes and disgrace" (75), she "positively threw it up, possessed of a Hundred Pounds Stock, all paid for, to keep a grand Puppet-Show over the *Tennis-Court* in *James-Street*"(75). In this emphatic juxtaposition of the roles of fashionable urban grocer and "grand" puppeteer, Charke's text not only suggests the intricate process by which, in this period, a whole constellation of class-based meaning attaches itself to consumer goods, but also implicitly evokes that more general aura of commodification that seems inevitably to surround a theater of *objects*.[60] By literally exchanging her stock of sugar, tea, and oil for a company of marionettes, Charke highlights the tangible exchange value of the latter within the economic field of urban entertainment.

Charke's puppets were apparently built for her by a Mr. Yeates, a puppeteer and carnival showman who had previously been associated with Martin Powell's son, and whom Charke praises as a "skillful person . . . who has made [puppetry] his business from his youth upwards" (86).[61] Charke's performances, like Yeates's and her own careers, demonstrate the inseparability

[60] See J. H. Plumb, "Commercialization and Society," in *The Birth of a Consumer Society: The Commercialization of Eighteenth-Century England*, ed. Neil McKendrick, John Brewer, and J. H. Plumb (Bloomington: Indiana University Press, 1982), 265–334.

[61] There is some question about the "Mr Yeates" referred to by Charke (*Narrative*, 47). Fidelis Morgan identifies him as "Richard Yeates, actor, puppeteer and manager" (*The Well-Known Trouble Maker*, 47n.). But even the standard authorities on theater and puppetry in the period indicate a confusion between Richard Yates or Yeates—an actor who trained under Henry Giffard and acted both in the patent houses and at fairground booths from the 1730s to the 1780s—and a figure whom both Rosenfeld and Battestin identify as Thomas Yeates (fl. 1725–55), a puppeteer and booth holder at Bartholomew Fair and elsewhere, who worked with Charke's puppets and possibly with Fielding's. See Scouten, *The London Stage, 1729–1747;* the considerable listings in *The London Stage* index under "Richard Yates"; Rosenfeld, *The Theatre of the London Fairs*, 36–37, 45, 47, 48, 50, 51, 58, 100, 153, and passim; and Battestin, *Henry Fielding*, 435. Rosenfeld clearly distinguishes between Richard Yates and Thomas Yeates. Scouten, in his introduction to *The London Stage*, seems to conflate these two figures even while he distinguishes between a Richard Yates and a Richard Yeates, ascribing to the latter some of the activities otherwise attributed to Thomas Yeates (see his index). Speaight simply refers to "Yeates" with no first name (*History of the English Puppet Theatre*, 102–3) and identifies him as the puppeteer who worked with Charke and others. To make matters even more confusing, as early as 1728 there are references to a "Yeates Junior," who also worked as puppeteer and actor. As Speaight admits, "It is often extremely difficult to determine which is which" (156). I am inclined to think that Charke's Mr. Yeates was the puppeteer, not the actor, but this confusion itself further instantiates the interconnection of popular and elite practices for which I am arguing here.

of the cultural categories otherwise divided by the discourse of the period. In her satiric play *The Art of Management*, written just two years earlier, Charke had lamented—in roughly the same terms as Steele, Pope, Fielding, and many others—that "apes," "rough-hewn bears," and "mimic Andrews, from the Smithfield fairs" had driven from the stage the "proper rights" of the "tragic muse."[62] In fact, Charke herself not only acted in both the patent theaters and the booths of Bartholomew Fair (like most actors of the period), but also moved freely between the human and the puppet stages. Her career bridges the cultural divisions maintained in her discourse, and her puppets similarly mediated between popular and elite performance in both their content and their conditions.

Just as her puppets were quite literally objects of and for bourgeois acquisition, so were they also iconic representations of class aspiration. In Charke's words: "For some Time I resided at the *Tennis-Court* with my Puppet-Show, which was allowed to be the most elegant that was ever exhibited. I was so very curious, that I bought Mezzotinto's of several eminent Persons, and had the Faces carved from them. Then, in regard to my Cloaths, I spared for no Cost to make them splendidly magnificent, and the Scenes were agreeable to the rest" (82). Even these few sentences convey another multilevel process of cultural transmission and reception in which a variety of competing media and voices participate. The faces of "eminent Persons" descend from actuality to commercial mezzotint engravings to a puppet show, which is then "allowed," as though by some impersonal process of collective judgment, to be "the most elegant that was ever exhibited." The overall theatrical project is an obvious appropriation not only of puppets in general but of the techniques of previous "fashionable" puppeteers such as Martin Powell. At the same time, however, the "eminent" figures represented by the carved puppet heads were constrained, within the puppet show, to assume other roles and to act side by side with Punch and Joan in a kind of reverse cultural appropriation of the elite by the quasi-popular.

Charke's puppets acted fully realized plays from the "classical" repertory, including works by Shakespeare (among them *Henry IV*, with Punch as Falstaff), her father (*Damon and Phyllida*), and Fielding (*The Covent Garden Tragedy*, among others). While reproducing in miniature a conventional theatrical season of the period, Charke seems also to have reminded her audience deliberately of her stormy relations with her famous father and her earlier participation in Fielding's controversial seasons at the Little Theatre in

---

[62] Charlotte Charke, *The Art of Management; or Tragedy Expell'd* (London, 1735), 13.

the Haymarket (which was virtually next door to what Charke calls "Punch's Theatre" on James Street). Thus, she also indirectly represents herself within a performance that otherwise effaces her own identity behind the histrionic object. Charke's puppet shows, in their deliberate invocation of her own theatrical notoriety, their incongruous mix of carnivalesque comedy and the fashionable, must have offered a particular theatrical charge to an audience otherwise now limited to the two patent houses.

Her performance of Fielding's *Covent Garden Tragedy*, for example, no doubt evoked for its first audience an absolutely dizzying spiral of cultural appropriation. Originally performed as an afterpiece at Drury Lane in the season of 1732, and set among the bawds, pimps and whores of contemporary London, Fielding's play was already a metadramatic burlesque of pseudo-classical domestic tragedies such as *The Distrest Mother* by Ambrose Phillips (1712). The play also repeatedly uses metaphors drawn from puppet theater. Parodying the discourse of classical tragedy, one character laments that "man is a puppet which a woman moves / And dances as she will" (3:118). Later, enjoining one of her girls against sending away Captain Bilkum, Mother Punchbowl says, "A house like this without a bully left / Is like a puppet show without a Punch" (*Complete Works*, 3:124). Such lines would obviously reverberate with an additional comic effect when "spoken" by literal puppets. Moreover, Mother Punchbowl's name, as this passage seems intended further to underline, suggests a punning relationship with the most famous of puppet characters, just as her role in the play—which carnivalizes the topos of the suffering mother—broadly resembles the parodic function of Punch in conventional puppet shows.

The Covent Garden Tragedy also lampoons specific contemporary individuals: Captain Bilkum, for example, was intended to suggest Edward Braddock, a notorious bully; and Mother Punchbowl was intended to suggest Elizabeth Needham, a famous bawd also mentioned in *The Dunciad* and depicted in the first plate of Hogarth's *Harlot's Progress*. Shortly before both the print and the play appeared, Needham had been "set in the pillory," where she was "so ill used by the populace, that it put an end to her days."[63] In reality a lurid spectacle for a sadistic mob, Needham becomes, in Hogarth's print, an emblem within a cautionary tale of bourgeois morality, then in Fielding's play a satiric tool with which to *deflate* the moral pretensions of

---

[63] The description is from Pope's note to *The Dunciad* (1742 version), 1.324. For more on the connection between Needham and Mother Punchbowl, see Battestin, *Henry Fielding*, 135; and Paulson, *Hogarth's Graphic Works*, 1:144.

bourgeois theater. In Charke's puppet show, however, as she described it in a newspaper advertisement, "the part of Mother Punchbowl" was played "by Punch, being the first time of his appearing in petticoats."[64] The layers of cultural cross-referencing manifest in this gesture are almost impossible to separate. Most obviously, the bizarre cross-dressing of a puppet whose protruding hump and nose otherwise suggest a grotesque, exaggerated masculinity must inevitably have suggested Charke's own celebrated cross-dressed roles on the stage. Punch in petticoats must further have burlesqued and disrupted a role and a play that already carnivalized a particular mode of high theatrical seriousness. Moreover, in the phrasing of the advertisement itself, Charke burlesques the discourse of a commercial stage and pretends to treat puppetry with equal dignity by "constantly reminding her audience that the plays were to be performed by puppets while announcing them exactly as if they were to be acted by actors."[65] Such burlesque, however, in fact merely confirms the toylike preciosity of puppet theater and its consequent cultural subordination to the legitimate stage—a subordination already instantiated in Charke's own downward progress from the latter to the former.

In even larger political and social terms, the horrific punishment of the real Elizabeth Needham, in which the authorities employed the populace as the tool of its own punitive power, was itself but the dark side of the popular festivity to which Punch so commonly gives voice.[66] In *The Covent Garden Tragedy* Mother Punchbowl asks Captain Bilkum, and in effect the audience,

> Would it delight your eyes to see me dragged
> By base plebian hands to Westminister,
> The scoff of serjeants and attorneys' clerks,
> And then, exalted on the pillory,
> To stand the sneer of every virtuous whore?
> Oh, couldst thou bear to see the rotten egg
> Mix with my tears, that trickle down my cheeks,
> Like dew distilling from the full-blown rose:

[64] Cited in Speaight, *The History of the English Puppet Theatre*, 104; and in Morgan, *The Well-Known Trouble Maker*, 64.

[65] Morgan, *The Well-Known Trouble Maker*, 64.

[66] As E. P. Thompson suggests, in the eighteenth century "the rulers of England showed in practice a surprising degree of license towards the turbulence of the crowd"; and indeed, "there is a sense in which rulers and crowd needed each other, watched each other, performed theatre and countertheatre in each other's auditorium." E. P. Thompson, "The Patricians and the Plebs," in *Customs in Common* (New York: New Press, 1993), 57.

Or see me follow the attractive cart,
To see the hangman lift the virgal rod.

(*Complete Works*, 3:115)

The audience of the original play as performed at the Haymarket may have at least partially overlapped with the audience of Needham's brutal execution, just as they did for the public hangings at Tyburn. Yet this passage, with its witty deflation of tragic rhetoric and its comic skepticism about "virtuous whores," participates in the implicit construction of a hypothetical bourgeois audience that would separate itself from the "base plebian" actions of the London mob. Charke's version, however, goes perhaps one step further. In the transformation of a carnivalesque figure into the suffering victim of popular rage—the spectacle of Punch as at once cross-dressed actor, parodic mother, and pilloried bawd—multiple forms of trangression seem, as it were, to cancel one another out.

Charke's own position, as she confronts her audience through the faces and voices of her performing objects, seems similarly suspended within a kind of multiply self-contradictory cultural space. As I have observed, her own marginality (to which her status as puppeteer further contributed) was reproduced in the doubly-transgressive figure of Punch in petticoats. Yet Punch himself seems both empowered and exploited, constrained to embody at once the mob's violence and its victim. Just so, the puppet master who represents herself (in reverse) as a cross-dressed puppet both overcomes and yet merely repeats the forms of her own subordination (as daughter or as player). Even in a larger sense, as recent critics have argued, Charke's "impersonation of the masculine" in her dress and career finally "seeks to reinforce, reinstate and maintain the value of masculine, patriarchal conventions"; and "in her flight from conventional 'female' selfhood to 'male' selfhood, she reaffirms the lineaments of the ideology of gender and thus serves the very fictions that confine her."[67]

Charke discovered in puppetry an apparently free space within which, however, she merely re-created the theatrical and cultural hierarchies that otherwise excluded or subordinated her. In the end, her puppets were little more than a desperate and ultimately unsuccessful effort to exploit her own notoriety for financial gain. As she remarks in her memoir: "This Affair stood me in some Hundreds, and would have paid all Costs and Charges, if I had not, through excessive Fatigue in accomplishing it, acquired a violent

---

[67] Mackie, "Desperate Measures," 843; Smith, *Poetics of Women's Autobiography*, 121.

Fever, which had like to have carried me off, and consequently gave a Damp to the Run I should otherwise have had, as I one was one of the principal Exhibitors for those Gentry" (82). The syntactic ambiguity of the final reference to the "Gentry"—which seems to refer to either her intended audience or her puppets, those icons of "eminent persons"—embodies the ambiguity of Charke's position: at once the master of puppets who mirrored her audience and the servant of an audience whose social aspirations mirrored her own. Even after the collapse of her season at the Tennis Court, her name evidently continued to be associated with puppetry and to convey a certain commercial appeal. When Charke was forced to sell her original set of puppets at a considerable loss to Isaac Fawkes, another carnival showman and puppeteer, Fawkes advertised them at Bartholomew Fair in 1740 as "formerly Mrs. Charke's from the Theatre in the Haymarket."[68] Returned to their ostensibly "original" cultural frame, Charke's puppets reunited with her name to reproduce an aura of reflected fashion for a less privileged audience.[69]

Only three years later Henry Fielding also returned to puppetry in a manner that recalls, for contemporary audiences as for modern readers in retrospect, the actress and puppeteer with whom he had worked in his glory days at the Haymarket. Plagued by chronic financial problems, and "now more than ever in need of money" following the birth of a son,[70] Fielding adopted a public persona at once "fashionable" and female, Madame de la Nash, who on March 15, 1748, announced in the *Daily Advertiser* that

> at her large Breakfasting-Room, for the Nobility and Gentry, in
> Panton-Street, near the Haymarket, will sell the very best Tea,
> Coffee, Chocolate, and Jellies. At the same time she will entertain the
> company gratis with that Excellent old English Entertainment, call'd
>
> A PUPPET SHEW . . .

[68] Speaight, *History of the English Puppet Theatre*, 106.

[69] In 1739 Charke attempted to take her show to the resort town of Tunbridge Wells, but she found another puppeteer already well established there. Later she leased the puppets to Yeates, who performed for about a year at "Punch's Theatre" at the Tennis Court with some success. In 1745 another puppeteer, John Russell, attempted to mount a season of fashionable puppet performance at Mr. Hickford's Great Room in Brewer Street. Charke "was hired, after the first Night's Performance, at a Guinea [*sic*] per Diem, to move his *Punch* in particular." Charke, *Narrative*, 84–85, 177; Morgan, *The Well-Known Trouble Maker*, 129; and Speaight, *History of the English Puppet Theatre*, 105–7.

[70] Martin C. Battestin, introduction to Henry Fielding, *The History of Tom Jones, A Foundling*, ed. Fredson Bowers (Middletown, Conn.: Wesleyan University Press, 1975), xxxi.

With the Comical Humours of Punch, and his wife Joan, with all the
Original Jokes, F-rts, Songs, Battles, Kicking, &c.[71]

The unusual arrangement here described was a method of evading the Licensing Act. Whereas Charke had actually acquired a license for her puppet
shows, "Madame de la Nash" would pretend to be merely serving breakfast
while providing free entertainment for "her" customers. Fielding situates his
puppet show in between cultural extremes. The show was, as Battestin puts
it (repeating the cultural assumptions of the period),"no ordinary fairground
drollery but an entertainment aimed at fashionable audiences." Yet Fielding
also promises his audience that he will preserve intact all the scatological violence of the "Original" entertainment. At least in retrospect Fielding's puppet show seems, so to speak, the very primal scene of cultural appropriation.
An audience explicitly defined as genteel consumes its tea and jellies (an attenuated version of carnivalesque consumption) and reproduces the popular
festivity from which it is at the same time insulated within a carefully defined
literal and cultural space. And on the first day, according to a newspaper re-
port, "a great many Persons of the politest taste . . . express'd the highest
Satisfaction at the Performance."[72]

"Visions of Graver Puppetry":
Punch and Judy and Cultural Appropriation

It is a drama in two acts, is Punch. . . . Ah, it's a beautiful history;
there's a deal of morals with it, and there's a large volume wrote
about it.
     —Henry Mayhew, *London Labour and the London Poor*

In a cultural progress repeatedly described by theater historians, sometime
around the end of the eighteenth century Punch, the "fashionable" marionette reemerged as a glove puppet in a street puppet show called "Punch
and Judy." In 1828, only a little more than fifty years after the earliest references to this new, simpler version of Punch, John Payne Collier (later a famous and controversial Shakespearean) published a text of the show as performed by "a very old Italian way-faring puppet-showman of the name of

[71] Cited in Speaight, *History of the English Puppet Theatre*, 108; and Battestin, *Henry Fielding*, 435.
[72] Battestin, *Henry Fielding*, 435.

Piccini," with illustrations by George Cruikshank and a slightly tongue-in-cheek scholarly preface.[73] This well-known volume initiated what would prove to be a continuing process of transcription, investigation, and celebration of this oral and ephemeral form of street theater. Various other memoirs and versions of Punch and Judy appear throughout the nineteenth and early twentieth centuries, and in recent decades several full-length studies have documented its history and evolution in detail. Here I want to discuss not so much the show itself, which has already been exhaustively described and analyzed, but instead the process by which Punch was appropriated as a cultural icon of the popular. For Punch and Judy had just barely emerged in its current form before it began to be observed and positioned by commentators who confirm its otherness in the very process of analysis.

In broad terms, what happened to Punch at the end of the eighteenth century is a double process that has proved almost impossible to describe without recourse to the hierarchical terms that so commonly accompany the analysis of popular culture. At the beginning of the nineteenth century, for example, the antiquarian Joseph Strutt mentions Punch's various appearances in fashionable London venues, but then concludes:

In the present day (1801) the puppet-show man travels about the streets when the weather will permit, and carries his motions, with the theatre itself, upon his back! The exhibition takes place in the open air; and the precarious income of the miserable itinerant depends entirely on the voluntary contributions of the spectators, which, as far as one may judge from the square appearance he usually makes, is very trifling.[74]

In fact, of course, the conditions Strutt describes had characterized most forms of puppetry since at least the Middle Ages; but the exclamation point at the end of his first sentence is an index of the cultural weight he attaches to the change for the worse he mistakenly observes. Both practically and economically, Punch is seen to "descend" from the theater and breakfast rooms of fashionable London to the streets and "open air," even as he also changes from an elaborate and sometimes nearly life-size marionette (like those of Martin Powell and his followers) to a crude and diminutive glove puppet on a movable booth stage.

[73] *Punch and Judy with illustrations, designed and engraved by George Cruikshank* (London, 1828), 74. Subsequent citations are given parenthetically in the text.

[74] Joseph Strutt, *The Sports and Pastimes of the People of England* (1810), 2d ed. (London: Methuen, 1903), 146.

Figure 6. A "representative sample" of London society watches a Punch-and-Judy show. Benjamin Robert Haydon, *Punch, or May Day* (1846). Reproduced by permission of the Tate Gallery, London.

Strutt also highlights the puppeteer's new dependence "on the voluntary contributions of the spectators." Although all performers are in some sense dependent in this way, Strutt intends to contrast the uncertain rewards of "passing the hat" to the rights and privileges of an organized system of remuneration, suggesting with some justification that the first method is "popular" in a particularly literal way. As far as can be determined from the famous engravings of Cruikshank and Thomas Rowlandson, from Benjamin Robert Haydon's 1846 painting *Punch, or May Day* (Figure 6), and from a variety of other visual representations of the street show, Punch's audience tended to come from the lower classes, but also encompassed the full spectrum of society. Haydon's painting (whose academic polish deliberately contrasts with the popular practice it documents) shows a shoeless orange-girl and a street sweeper listening intently to the show while several well-dressed gentlemen, ladies, and their children also crowd around the puppet booth. In 1826 one writer observed that Punch's "squeaking of those little snatches of tunes" had a "talismanic power upon the locomotive faculties of all the peripatetics within hearing, attracting everybody to the traveling stage, young and old, gentle and simple."[75] About a century later another writer remembered among the spectators at the puppet show "an errand-boy, . . . several school children, several grown-up people, a policeman, a clerk, a postman, a bookmaker—in fact, a representative audience."[76] Only gradually did Punch and Judy come to be seen, as it is today, as an entertainment primarily for children.

Punch's ethnic and geographic origins, as I have mentioned briefly, have been incessantly debated, a process beginning at least as early as the glove puppet show itself. An Italian puppeteer was believed to have first brought the marionette Punchinello to London in Pepys's day, and the Italian puppeteer interviewed by Collier in the early nineteenth century claims to have been the first performer of the glove puppet show. Yet Collier also suggests that the apparent foreignness of Punch had become, in effect, a theatrical convention. He observes that "the performers of 'Punch and Judy,' who are natives of Great Britain, generally endeavour to imitate an 'outlandish dialect.' " Henry Mayhew's Punchman claims to speak with his fellow puppeteers in an Italianate patois.[77] Today scholars continue to question whether or not (to cite Michael Byrom's positive assertion) "the English Punch is essentially the same person as the Italian Pulcinella," or whether (to cite George Speaight's contrary point) Punch and Judy "is essentially an English show."[78] Either way, however, Punch is considered to be descended from an ancient carnivalesque tradition traceable back "to the religious plays of medieval England, and to the improvised farces of the Italian comedians, and to

[75] Quoted in Leach, *The Punch and Judy Show*, 50.

[76] Maurice Baring, *Punch and Judy and Other Essays* (London: William Heinemann, 1924), 4.

[77] " 'Bona parlare' means language; name of patter," says the Punchman, and " 'Tambora'—drum; that's Italian. 'Pipares'—pipes,' " and so forth. Henry Mayhew, *London Labour and the London Poor*, vol. 3 of 3 (1861–62; rpt. New York: Augustus Kelly, 1967), 47. Subsequent citations are given parenthetically in the text.

[78] Michael Byrom, *Punch and Judy: Its Origin and Evolution* (Norwich, England: DaSilva Puppet Books, 1988), 12–14; Speaight, *History of the English Puppet Theatre*, 229. Punch's Italianate origins are also assumed by Collier, *Punch and Judy*, 11–18; and by Philip John Stead, *Mr. Punch* (London: Evans Brothers, 1950).

the folk festivals of pagan Greece."[79] And yet the emergence of the street show is seen by the same commentators as the glorious birth (or rebirth) of a vital, subversive, and truly popular form of performance. Having "broken free from his strings and like some butterfly emerging from its chrysalis," writes Byrom, Punch "appeared, transformed, as a glove puppet." Although "Punch was, literally, thrown on to the streets" in the early nineteenth century, writes Speaight, it was there that he "found his soul once again." Robert Leach suggests more specifically that, at the end of the eighteenth century, "there sprouted, awkwardly and haphazardly, what may legitimately be called a working class culture" out of which Punch and Judy was born.[80] These and other scholars seem to construe the puppet as the authentically illegitimate voice of the people, even as they abstract from an unruly cultural history an organic, teleological narrative of evolution and transmission—one of those stories that, in the words of Donna Haraway, "begins with original innocence and privileges the return to wholeness," and that is thus "ruled by a reproductive politics—rebirth without flaw, perfection, abstraction."[81] Punch is positioned as at once profoundly historical (the heir to an ancient and primeval European tradition) and vitally contemporary (the pure expression of working-class culture) in a process that begins with the writers I have been discussing throughout this chapter and far transcends the puppet's actual existence as a street performer.

In fact, however, Punch and Judy manifests, in its content and its conditions, a complex dialogue between relatively more popular and more elite forms of culture. If, on a practical level, Punch "descended" from the theater back to the street, he simultaneously "ascended" from a mere interpolator within preexisting stories to the hero of his own apparently unique and inimitable drama. As recorded by Collier and many subsequent writers, the "Punch-and-Judy" show has a formulaic structure (determined, at least in

---

[79] Speaight, *History of the English Puppet Theatre*, 230. Byrom similarly claims that Punch's origins are to be found "in the pagan dawn of European civilization, that is, in ancient Greece," and that "Punch could have been a puppet all the way from his prehistoric origins in the pagan folk plays" (*Punch and Judy*, xi).

[80] Byrom, *Punch and Judy*, 12; Speaight, *History of the English Puppet Theatre*, 180–81; Leach, *The Punch and Judy Show*, 30.

[81] Donna J. Haraway, *Simians, Cyborgs and Women: The Reinvention of Nature* (New York: Routledge, 1991), 177. These common descriptions of Punch and Judy are also instances of what Stuart Hall has described as "self-enclosed approaches to popular culture which . . . analyze popular cultural forms as if they contained within themselves, from their moment of origin, some fixed and unchanging meaning of value." Stuart Hall, "Notes on Deconstructing 'the Popular,' " in *People's History and Socialist Theory*, ed. Raphael Samuel (London: Routledge & Kegan Paul, 1981), 237.

part, by the two hands of the puppeteer) in which the central figure presents himself directly to the audience and then fights with or kills a series of antagonists. In the beginning he kills his wife, Judy, and their baby, and then faces a series of other figures who attempt to call him to account—a constable, a beadle, a hangman, and so on—prior to a concluding confrontation with the devil. As early and recent commentators alike observe, the show is a condensed, vestigial version of a variety of conventional dramatic stories. Its basic structure of confrontation between a central figure and a succession of opponents, leading to a final judgment, resembles a morality play or *Doctor Faustus*.[82]

In the earliest transcribed version of the show, Punch dances with and romances a puppet named Pretty Polly, who then sings one of the well-known airs from John Gay's immensely successful play *The Beggar's Opera*.[83] The Punchman interviewed at length by Henry Mayhew in the mid-nineteenth century asserts that he "frequently went to theatres to learn knowledge," claims that he "took my ghost from Romeau and Juliet," and observes that "Otheller murders his wife, ye know, like Punch does" (48). As contemporary illustrations also make clear, those "perambulatory" booths in which Punch performed were sometimes carved to suggest diminutive versions of the grand proscenium arches and ornate pediments in contemporary theaters; and the show was sometimes billed under elaborate titles such as "The Dominion of Fancy: or, Punch's Opera."[84] Mayhew's Punchman describes his theater in a passage that also attempts to record and explain his Cockney pronunciation, and in so doing further evokes the cultural distance between oral performance and text: "This here is the stage front, or *proceedings* (proscenium), and is painted over with flags and banners, or any different things. Sometimes there's George and the Dragging, and the Rile Queen's Arms, (we can have them up when we like, cos we are sanctioned, and I've played afore the rile princes)" (53). Situated at the fluid boundary of culture and class, Punch embodies at once the aspirations of the low toward the forms of a legitimate drama against which it still defines itself, and

---

[82] Cf. Leach, *The Punch and Judy Show*, 163. *Doctor Faustus* itself was a common subject for puppet plays in England and in Germany, where it was still performed in the nineteenth century. On Dr. Faustus as puppet play, see T. C. H. Hedderwick, *The Old German Puppet Play of Doctor Faust* (London, 1887); and Philip Mason Palmer and Robert Pattison More, *The Sources of the Faust Tradition: From Simon Magus to Lessing* (1936; rpt. New York: Octagon, 1966), 241–65.

[83] The Polly of Punch and Judy is, of course, presumably derived from Polly Peachum in John Gay's *Beggar's Opera*.

[84] This is the title given by Mayhew's Punchman to his show (*London Labour*, 53).

the "downward" inertia with which conventions and stories of the legitimate stage reemerge and persist in the oral traditions of popular performance.

Even more broadly, however, I want to suggest that the Punch-and-Judy
show is neither as simply nor as "purely" trangressive and carnivalesque
as both early and recent commentators almost uniformly claim. To be
sure, the show's rapid emergence in the last quarter of the eighteenth century through the first quarter of the nineteenth is undoubtedly conditioned in part by the radical social restructuring that accompanied the industrial revolution. In the Punch who discomfits and beats a constable, a
doctor, and a beadle, and who—in his most famous single bit of comic
business—tricks the hangman "Jack Ketch" into putting his own head in
the noose to escape the gallows, it is not hard to perceive a festive working-
class inversion of authority. In the Punch who kills his wife and baby
with comic nonchalance, it is not hard to see an element of wish fulfillment that might appeal to men of a class in which divorce was virtually impossible. Punch's story seems inevitably to manifest what E. P. Thompson
suggests were the "Brechtian values—the fatalism, the irony in the face of
Establishment homilies, the tenacity of self-preservation"—that characterized English working-class culture.[85] Thus, modern critics conclude that
Punch simply "strikes out against family (wife, child), state (the constable
and hangman), and church (the devil)," and is thus "dangerously subversive,
. . . concerned with freedom from oppression [and] a fierce assertion of disobedience."[86]

But just as Mayhew's Punchman shows a keen awareness of his subordinate position within a much larger cultural landscape, so the Punch-and-
Judy show seems to embody something more (or less) than its own manifestly trangressive content. Among the considerable variations within
surviving transcripts of the show, two incidents seem nearly universal:
Punch's beating and killing of his wife and baby, and his subsequent escape
from the gallows. To place these two parts of the show in historical context is
to see once again the inadequacy of a cultural viewpoint that, in the Bakhtinian manner, simply naturalizes "festivity" as a purely benevolent voice of
"the people." For one thing, it is clear that the show in no sense represents
liberation for its second titular character (see Figure 7), an utterly obvious

---

[85] E. P. Thompson, *The Making of the English Working Class* (1963; rpt. New York: Vintage, 1966), 59.
[86] James B. Twitchell, *Preposterous Violence: Fables of Aggression in Modern Culture* (New York: Oxford
University Press, 1989), 83; Leach, *The Punch and Judy Show*, 125, 165.

Figure 7. Punch kills his wife. An engraving from George Cruikshank's *Punch and Judy with twenty-four illustrations* (1828). Reproduced by permission of the Houghton Library, Harvard University.

point to which commentators, with their celebratory rhetoric, often seem strangely blind. More specifically, Punch's violent relations with his wife manifest not just masculine wish fulfillment but also what numerous recent scholars suggest is a bourgeois displacement of wife beating onto the lower classes. As far back as the seventeenth century, as Joy Wiltenburg documents, a certain mode of popular literature began to depict wife beating as "a plebeian activity," thus offering "respectable audiences a means of distancing themselves from the violence while still enjoying it." By the eighteenth century, as Margaret Hunt suggests, "wife beating became, for literate people, a particular mark of the inferiority and animality of the poor."[87] Even the name of Punch's wife inexplicably changes in the early nineteenth century from Joan to Judy, the latter recorded in a dictionary of 1812 as meaning "blowen," that is, a woman who cohabits with a man outside of marriage.[88] So when Punch knocks his wife's block off, he is not only revolting against the constraints of authority but also confirming a bourgeois vision of working-class brutality and immorality.

Similarly, the miniature drama of Punch's arrest, imprisonment, and impending execution which appears in most versions of the show is usually assumed to derive from the tradition of the so-called Tyburn Fair—the popular festivity that surrounded public hangings in the eighteenth century.[89] As contemporary writers such as Mandeville, Defoe, and Fielding observe, and as modern historians suggest, such executions themselves presented a quasi-theatrical spectacle: "the condemned in their carts—the men in gaudy attire, the women in white, with baskets of flowers and oranges which they threw to the crowds."[90] Here too, however, a focus on the Punch show as simply a wish-fulfilling vision of escape from punishment ignores the obvious. As Peter Linebaugh puts it, Punch and Judy "expressed class rage against family, police, courtiers, physicians and householders"; but at the same time,

[87] Joy Wiltenburg, *Disorderly Women and Female Power in the Street Literature of Early Modern England and Germany* (Charlottesville: University Press of Virginia, 1992), 128; Margaret Hunt, "Wife Beating, Domesticity, and Women's Independence in Eighteenth-Century London," *Gender and History* 4.1 (1992): 27. See also Anna Clark, "Humanity or Justice: Wifebeating and the Law in the Eighteenth and Nineteenth Centuries," in *Regulating Womanhood: Historical Essays on Marriage, Motherhood, and Sexuality*, ed. Carol Smart (London: Routledge, 1992), 187–206.

[88] *OED*, s.v. "Judy" and "blowen"; cf. Speaight, *History of the English Puppet Theatre*, 192.

[89] See Thompson, *Making of the English Working Class*, 61, who calls Tyburn Fair "the ritual at the heart of London's popular culture"; Thomas W. Laqueur, "Crowds, Carnival, and the State in English Executions, 1604–1868," in *The First Modern Society: Essays in English History in Honour of Lawrence Stone*, ed. A. L. Beier, David Cannadine, and James M. Rosenheim (Cambridge: Cambridge University Press, 1989), 305–55; and Peter Linebaugh, *The London Hanged: Crime and Civil Society in the Eighteenth Century* (New York: Cambridge University Press, 1992). Linebaugh suggests that Laqueur overstates the festive nature of the Tyburn Fair, and argues, conversely, that the lower classes attended public hangings to evince their "scorn . . . against law and authority" (xvii-iii). As some of my readings in this chapter suggest, I am inclined to think that both responses—a festive callousness toward the suffering victim and a class solidarity against the punitive power of authority—were possible and extant among the popular spectators at executions.

[90] Thompson, *Making of the English Working Class*, 61. Certain well-known executed criminals, as Laqueur observes, were "represented as harlequin" in contemporary pantomime ("Crowds, Carnival, and the State," 341). In Hogarth's engraving "A Just View of the British Stage" (Figure 3), which I discussed earlier, Colley Cibber holds a puppet of Jack Sheppard—whose life had been dramatized in John Thurmond's *Harlequin Sheppard* at Drury Lane in 1724—while Robert Wilks holds Punch. See Paulson, *Hogarth's Graphic Works*, 1:110; and Linebaugh, *The London Hanged*, 39.

The Violence of Appropriation 169

"Punch, in murdering friend and foe alike, suggests to us that the London working class was doing Jack Ketch's job for him."[91] The show is a miniature representation of violent crime and violent punishment which acknowledges their interconnection; it embodies at once a working-class cynicism about law and an authoritarian insistence on social control.

To be sure, I would not wish to deny the energy with which Punch, for at least some of his performers and audiences, must have given voice to "the people's unofficial truth." In its full social context, however, the Punch-and-Judy show must be seen to express an impulse of undifferentiated aggression and thus to reproduce the impulse of domination against which it otherwise seems to rebel. Punch lords it over both Judy *and* the hangman; that both figures become his precisely analogous antagonists and victims suggests the cultural and ideological forces that were inevitably also brought to bear on a show that instantiates as well as overcomes (its own) otherness. If the show undoubtedly does emerge in part from the social ferment of the industrial revolution, it nevertheless embodies a variety of competing class interests just as it bridges popular and elite forms of culture. As Leach persuasively argues (at the outset of a book that goes on repeatedly to contradict such an insight), the "absolute egotism" so clearly manifest in the show expresses not merely a "refusal to accept the dictates of alien authority" but also "the thrusting individualism of industrial capitalism."[92] Popular festivity, just slightly reconstrued, becomes the restless energy of class aspiration. To interpret Punch and Judy as simply "festive," subversive, or liberational is to assume not only a masculine viewer but also a working-class and literally paternal one, whereas in fact the very breadth of the show's evident appeal must suggest precisely how hierarchies of class, age, and gender intertwine.

Collier's version, for example, featured a run-in between Punch and a blind beggar:

Punch. Hollo! You old blind blackguard, can't you see?
Blind Man. No Mr. Punch. Pray, sir, bestow your charity upon a poor blind man, with a bad cough (Coughs.)
Punch. Hollo! Was my face the dirtiest place you could find to spit in? Get away! you nasty old blackguard! Get away! (seizes the Blind Man's staff, and knocks him off the stage.—Punch hums a tune, and dances to it).

(100–101)

[91] Linebaugh, *The London Hanged*, 404.
[92] Leach, *The Punch and Judy Show*, 16.

Another common figure of the show throughout its history was a black servant whom Mayhew's Punchman describes as "a nigger [who] says, 'me like
ebery body'; not 'every,' but 'ebery,' cos that's nigger" (51). The black man
was sometimes also presented as a vaguely Eastern or African foreigner who
could utter only the single word "Shallaballa."[93] The obvious alterity of such
figures once again betrays the show's participation within the same process of
cultural subordination which it has so often been seen to overturn. This conventional black character was eventually renamed Jim Crow after a popular
song sung by Thomas Rice, the minstrel singer, who had been the rage in
London in the summer of 1836. In another dizzying spiral of multiple reappropriation, this one moving freely between the boundaries of nation and
race, a counterfeit version of African American culture, transmuted by way of
the blackface singer, reemerges as a performing object embodying a popular
English fantasy of cultural otherness. Much as Collier stipulates that he has
"in a degree preserved [the] foreign dialect" of the Punchman he records
(94), so Mayhew's text carefully reproduces the cockney's own reproduction
of an imagined black dialect, and as such crystallizes a multilevel dynamic of
linguistic distinction.

Moreover, if Punch's apparent festive rebellion slips on the one side toward
mere brutality and xenophobia, it also slips on the other side toward a contrasting impulse of bourgeois self-containment. Across its various versions
the show incorporates within itself an ambivalent moral judgment on
Punch's festive license. The two most famous literary versions of the play,
Collier's and Mayhew's, end with Punch destroying his last opponent, the
devil; and in Mayhew's, the show closes with Punch crying out, "Satan is
dead! . . . We can now all do as we like!" (59). But various other versions
retain what may be an older conclusion in which the devil carries Punch
away as punishment for his crimes. In the early twentieth century, for example, two different writers remembered Punch and Judy filtered through a
similar veil of sentimental literary associations but, nevertheless, with opposite endings. "Punch is the Beowulf, the St. George [who slays] that old ser-
pent" the devil, writes Samuel McKechnie, with characteristic rhetorical
overstatement. "He is the most powerful of all legendary heroes, the most
human, the most amusing, the most imperfect, and the most lovable."[94] The
novelist Maurice Baring, by contrast, remembers Punch finally meeting

[93] According to Speaight, from 1825 to 1939 a black man "appears in eleven out of fourteen versions"
(*History of the English Puppet Theatre*, 193).
[94] Samuel McKechnie, *Popular Entertainments through the Ages* (1931; rpt. New York: Benjamin Blom,
1969), 82–83.

"with the doom of Doctor Faustus [and] crying out the Cockney equivalent for 'O lente, lente currite, nocti equi.' "[95] Even in relatively more popular forms of discourse from the show's heyday, Punch's story was frequently construed in crude, moralistic terms. A surviving text of the late eighteenth century (1792), which Henry Morley describes as "a sixpenny mechanical sheet of pictures opening and shutting" so as to illustrate and summarize the puppet show, concludes of its final scene:

Here's a sad sight poor Punch is going
To pay for all his former doing.
Consider this and mend your lives
Each action bad but badly thrives
Contrive to keep your minds from evil
And then you need not fear the devil.[96]

The Punchmen themselves were also sometimes concerned about the anarchic quality of their shows. Collier mentions one "showman" who got "lamentably pelted with mud, because, from some scruple or other, he refused to allow the victory over the Devil to Punch" (56). Mayhew's Punchman, as he describes various details of his version to the gentleman journalist, repeatedly insists "that's moral" (49), "that's the moral you see" (59), or "that's well worded, sir . . . so that the young children may not be taught anything wrong" (57).

Even Punch's apparent practical freedom from an organized market economy—the essential characteristic of its popular status—was only partial. To be sure, the typical Punchman often did perform in the street and earned much of his living through the "voluntary contributions" earnestly solicited by his partner. But listen to Mayhew's Punchman describe some of the other financial details of his profession:

We make much more by horders for performance houtside the gennelmen's houses, than we do by performing in public in the hopen streets. Monday is the best day for street business; Friday is no day at all, because then the poor people has spent all their money. If we was to pitch on a Friday, we shouldn't take a halfpenny in the streets, so we in general on that day goes round for horders. . . . We do most at

[95] Baring, *Punch and Judy*, 4.
[96] As with several previous texts, I cite this one from the original copy included in an 1890 extra-illustrated copy of Morley's *Memoirs of Bartholomew Fair*.

hevening parties in the holiday time, and if there's a pin to choose between them, I should say Christmas holidays was the best. For attending hevening parties now we generally get one pound and our refreshments—as much more as they like to give us. . . . It looks like rain this evening, and I'm uncommon glad on it, to be sure. You see, the vet keeps the children in-doors all day, and then they wants something to quiet 'em a bit; and the mothers and fathers, to pacify the dears, gives us a horder to perform. (46)

Such a description suggests how easily Punch and Judy moved from the streets to the drawing room, where its apparent working-class rebellion became an amusement to "pacify" children. Punch thus participates both literally and figuratively in the cultural construction of bourgeois childhood, which took place, as several scholars suggest, during the extended period surveyed in this chapter. In the eighteenth century, J. H. Plumb argues, children became "luxury objects upon which their mothers and fathers were willing to spend larger and larger sums of money, not only for their education, but also for their entertainment and amusement." As such, children also became, for the first time, "a field of commercial enterprise for the sharp-eyed entrepreneur."[97] Thus, the gradual redefinition of Punch and Judy into an entertainment for children, the status it enjoys today, was shaped by a particular economy of exchange which had the further effect of expropriating the show into a new, carefully insulated social space.

Correspondingly, Punch was also subject throughout the same period to an impulse of social and moral reform in the name of bourgeois propriety. "As for *Punch*," wrote the authors of *A Second Tale of a Tub* as far back as 1712, "who used heretofore to be nothing but a roaring, lewd, rakish, empty Fellow, a perfect *Mohock*, he now speaks choice Apothegms and sterling Wit" (xxvi-vii). One George Yates, at Bartholomew Fair in 1779, stipulated of his performance that "though it goes under the mean appellation of a Puppet Show," yet it will be "diverting and rational . . . the chaste ear will not be offended, as is usual with people in the profession, to amuse by low and obscene language."[98] Later, the obvious violence of Punch and Judy provoked a Victorian concern about its moral effect on the body politic not unlike contemporary fears about children's television. George Meredith in the 1870s, for example, worried "whether the puppet–show of Punch and Judy inspires our

---

[97] Plumb, "Commercialization and Society," 310.
[98] Speaight, *History of the English Puppet Theatre*, 174.

street-urchins to have instant recourse to their fists in a dispute, after the fashion of every one of the actors in that public entertainment."[99] A few years later Frances Power Cobbe decried the prevalence of wife beating in England and suggested that "in view of . . . our criminal statistics there is something ominous to the circumstance that 'Punch' should have been our national English street-drama for more than two centuries," especially since "so much of the enjoyment should concentrate about the thwacking of poor Judy."[100] Accordingly, Punch was sometimes stripped of his traditional violence and dislocated into Victorian drawing rooms and nurseries, where he also reappeared in the form of "paper cutouts" or "dolls and models" and as a common subject for children's books.[101] I have already cited Mayhew's Punchman's inconsistent but unmistakable concern for the morality of his performance, as well as his eagerness to perform in genteel households. J. M. Barrie in the 1890s imagined a Punch and Judy performance in which "Punch did chuck his baby out at the window . . . in his jovial, time-honoured way, but immediately thereafter up popped the showman to say, 'Ah, my dear boys and girls, let this be a lesson to you never to destroy your offsprings. Oh, shame on Punch, for to do the wicked deed; he will be catched in the end, and serve him right.' "[102] Today, as the puppeteer and scholar Michael Byrom remarks ruefully, "the hanging scene has almost disappeared from the repertory, [and] Punch's destruction of the Baby . . . is already halfway gone."[103]

The intimate relationship between the Punchman and his paying customers, seen as the defining characteristic of the show's truly popular status, was therefore also the conduit by which bourgeois values could interpenetrate and transform its most basic conventions. Such a process is even adumbrated in the conventions and physical appearance of the puppet itself. A kind of overdetermined, parodic image of phallic masculinity—his humped back, protruding nose, and omnipresent cudgel or stick—clashes with what eighteenth-century writers conventionally called his "eunuch voice";[104] and this

[99] George Meredith, *An Essay on Comedy and the Uses of the Comic Spirit*, ed. Lane Cooper (New York: Charles Scribner's Sons, 1918), 84.

[100] Frances Power Cobbe, "Wife Torture in England" (1878), in *Femicide: The Politics of Woman Killing*, ed. Jill Radford and Diana E. H. Russell (New York: Twayne, 1978), 46.

[101] Leach, *The Punch and Judy Show*, 87.

[102] J. M. Barrie, *Sentimental Tommie* (New York: Charles Scribner's Sons, 1915), 442.

[103] Byrom, *Punch and Judy*, 80. Contemporary puppeteers with whom I have spoken similarly describe how parents and teachers often insist on changes and omissions in the Punch-and-Judy script.

[104] This characteristic "squeak" was deliberately created by the prized "swazzle" which Punchmen placed in their mouths. On the swazzle, see Mayhew, *London Labour and the London Poor*, 3:45, 53; and

odd combination inevitably recalls Jonson's "motion" ("neyther Male nor Female"), and Shakespeare's Eros (who "has broke his arrows"). Together such examples suggest once more the peculiar doubleness with which bourgeois audiences imagine the puppet as both fiercely potent and always already emasculated, a violent performer "exhibited" only "after castration."[105]

I have been suggesting that the history of Punch is specifically a history of appropriation, in which the actual puppet show seems to recede against a vast backdrop of description and analysis. The canonization and celebration of Punch as the authentic voice of the popular finally offers, in Bourdieu's words, little more than "a sham inversion of dominant values," which produces "the fiction of a unity of the social world, thereby confirming the dominated in their subordination and the dominant in their superordination."[106] The cultural history I have been surveying in this chapter takes the form of a delicate balancing act: by turns writers domesticate the puppet (making it an "instructive" and "respectable" amusement) or celebrate its lowness as a kind of homegrown treasure, a uniquely English entertainment. As far back as the 1670s, Samuel Butler critiqued the neoclassical dramatic theory of Thomas Rymer and others by mocking those who would

> Reforme & Regulate a Puppet-Play,
> According to the tru & ancient way,
> That not an Actor shal Presume to Squeek
> Unless he hav a License for 't in Greek,
> Nor Whittington Henceforward sel his Cat in
> Plaine vulgar English, without Mewing Latin . . .
> Nor Devil in the Puppet Play b'allowd
> To Rore & Spit fire but to fright the Crowd,

Speaight, *History of the English Puppet Theatre*, 212–13. In the Latin poem discussed earlier in this chapter, Addison refers to Punch's "voces . . . tenues," which the contemporary translator gives as "treble voice and eunuch tone" (quoted in Speaight, *History of the English Puppet Theatre*, 90); and Steele, in an essay I discuss later in the chapter, refers to Punch as a "eunuch" (*Spectator*, no. 14, March 16, 1711). See also Kristina Straub's observation of the "pervasive characterization of actors" in the eighteenth century "as not quite 'manly,' even 'feminine' by progression." Straub, *Sexual Suspects*, 33.

[105] The quoted phrase is from Henry Fielding, "Some Thoughts on the Present State of the Theatres, and the Consequences of an Act to Destroy the Liberty of the Stage," *Occasional Prompter*, March 25, 1736, cited in Battestin, *Henry Fielding*, 218.

[106] Pierre Bourdieu and Loïc J. D. Wacquant, *An Invitation to Reflexive Sociology* (Chicago: University of Chicago Press, 1992), 82–83.

Unless some God or Dev'l chance t'have Piques
Against an Antient Family of Greeks.[107]

Butler's ostensible "defense" of the puppet play is really, of course, a defense
of the "tragedies of the last age," which, in a book of that title, had been
attacked by Thomas Rymer in the name of neoclassical regulation. Striking a
comic analogy between puppetry and this legitimate drama, Butler ascribes
to the latter the former's assumed Englishness (exemplified by its common
depictions of Dick Whittington) and its disingenuous theatrical simplicity
(exemplified by its histrionic "Dev'l" designed only to "fright the Crowd").
   This vision of the puppet as a homespun entertainment whose cultural
subordination becomes, paradoxically, the ground of its appeal would become a familiar topos in eighteenth-century discourse, though one often invoked with tongue in cheek. Richard Steele, in one more of his intricately
nuanced satires of public taste from *The Spectator*, contrasted the Italian
"Opera at the Haymarket" with Martin Powell's puppet performances "under the little Piazza in Covent-Garden." These, Steele observes,

> being at present the Two leading Diversions of the Town; and Mr.
> Powell professing in his Advertisements to set up Whittington and his
> Cat against Rinaldo and Armida, my Curiosity led me the Beginning of
> last Week to view both these Performances, and make my Observations
> upon them. . . . I shall only observe one thing further, in which both
> Dramas agree; which is, that by the Squeak of their Voices the Heroes
> of each are Eunuchs; and as the Wit in both Pieces is equal, I must
> prefer the Performance of Mr. Powell, because it is in our own
> Language. (*Spectator*, no. 14, March 16, 1711)

The comparison between opera and puppetry had actually been introduced
by Powell himself, who had advertised the show here referred to as "The History of Whittington, thrice Lord Mayor of London: with a variety of new
scenes in imitation of the Italian Opera's."[108] If Steele's preference for the
puppet show on the grounds of its language and subject is a joke that further
deflates the elite pretensions of the opera, the whole descending series of
frames and contexts (from opera to puppets to witty essay) nonetheless em-

---

[107] Samuel Butler, "Upon Critics who Judge of Modern Plays Precisely by the Rules of the Antients,"
in *Critical Essays of the Seventeenth Century*, ed. J. E. Spingarn, 3 vols. (Oxford: Oxford University Press,
1908), 2:278–79.
[108] Note to *Spectator*, no. 14, 1:61.

bodies a process of cultural domestication. The oppositions of high and low, English and Other, here contradict each other, and the low is reconstrued as acceptable to a bourgeois audience on the grounds of a sort of quasi-nationalist appeal. Several decades later, when Henry Fielding (as "Madame de la Nash") turned puppeteer in what I have described as a gesture of personal and cultural reappropriation, he advertised what he called an "Excellent old *English* Entertainment, call'd A PUPPET SHEW" (emphasis added). Samuel Foote, announcing his "Primitive Puppet Show" in 1773, similarly boasted that "all our actors are the produce of England."[109] These allusions to the domesticity of the puppet must be placed against the frequent early modern allusions, many cited in the preceding chapter, to "French puppets," "Dutch drolleries," and the like. Throughout this period and beyond, the puppet in general, and Punch in particular, was being reclaimed as preeminently English with a half seriousness that corresponds to puppetry's own place in the cultural hierarchy.

This ironic pride in English popular culture participates in the construction of British nationalism, which, as recent historians such as Benedict Anderson and Linda Colley have argued, dates from this period.[110] It is also one aspect of that more general bourgeois rethinking of popular culture that Peter Stallybrass and Allon White have described so eloquently, and that, with puppet theater, manifests itself sometimes as deliberate reformation and control and sometimes, conversely, as a "defense" of a cultural purity supposedly threatened by the former. James Ralph, a boyhood friend of Benjamin Franklin and later an associate of Henry Fielding, produced in 1728 a series of essays called *The Touchstone*, which surveys "the reigning Diversions of the Town." Ralph's work is a largely serious disquisition on the moral and social effect of entertainment. He discusses puppetry in some detail near the end of the book, beginning with a proud assertion of its essential if not quite historical Englishness: "The Mechanical Genius of the *English* is obvious to every body in many Cases, but in none more properly, than in the Contrivance and Conduct of our PUPPET-SHEWS: The Improvement of which is certainly owing to us, if not the Invention; and indeed, it has often prov'd our Province to refine upon the first Thoughts of others, in Works of Art and Ingenuity." Ralph goes on to defend the native tradition of puppetry, much as he also defends a variety of English festive customs such as sports and mar-

[109] Foote, "Primitive Puppet-Shew," 19.
[110] Benedict Anderson, *Imagined Communities: Reflections on the Origin and Spread of Nationalism* (London: Verso, 1983), 16; Linda Colley, *Britons: Forging the Nation, 1707–1837* (New Haven: Yale University Press, 1992).

ket fairs. Puppetry is, for Ralph, a kind of reasonable facsimile of the legitimate drama which can thus bring the advantages of the latter to the rural bourgeoisie:

> These portable Stages are of infinite Advantage to most Country Towns, where *Play-houses* cannot be maintain'd; and in my mind, superior to any company of Strollers; the Amusement is innocent and instructive, the Expence is moderate, and the whole Equipage easily carry'd about; as I have seen some Couples of King and Queens, with a suitable Retinue of Courtiers and Guards, very well accommodated in a single Band-box, with Room for *Punch* and his Family, in the same Machine.[111]

Notice how what later writers would refer to condescendingly as the "perambulatory" qualities of the puppet show—its microcosmic accommodation of plebeian and patrician within the same miniature "Band-box"—seems to become a figure for a bourgeois fantasy of thrift, comfort, and social harmony.

About twenty years later, similarly, Fielding in *Tom Jones* both records and satirizes the moral self-consciousness of provincial puppet theater. Jones and his companion Partridge encounter a puppet master on their travels and accompany him to an inn to view the performance:

> The Puppet-show was performed with great Regularity and Decency. It was called the fine and serious Part of the *Provok'd Husband*; and it was indeed a very grave and solemn Entertainment, without any low Wit or Humour, or Jests; or, to do it no more than Justice, without any thing which could provoke a Laugh. The Audience were all highly pleased. A grave Matron told the Master she would bring her two Daughters the next Night, as he did not shew any Stuff. . . . The Master was so highly elated with these Encomiums, that he could not refrain from adding some more of his own. He said, "The present Age was not improved in any Thing so much as their Puppet-shows; which, by throwing out *Punch* and his Wife *Joan*, and such idle Trumpery, were at last brought to be a rational Entertainment." . . . "I would by no Means degrade the Ingenuity of your Profession," answered *Jones*; but I should have been glad to have seen my old Acquaintance Master *Punch* for all that; and

[111] James Ralph, *The Touch-Stone, or . . . Essays on the Reigning Diversions of the Town* (London, 1728), 228.

so far from improving, I think, by leaving out him and his merry Wife *Joan*, you have spoiled your Puppet-show.[112]

A project of bourgeois cultural discernment takes place both within and without this fascinating passage. Both Jones and "Master Punch" must, as it were, singlehandedly face down a broad spectrum of bourgeois values—education, moral improvement, aesthetic reform, disdain for the low—and both Jones and Punch are similarly construed as healthy voices of common sense silenced by the obsessive demands of middle-class distinction. Fielding also clearly invites his own reader to sympathize with Jones's preference for his "old Acquaintance Master *Punch* . . . and his merry Wife *Joan*," who, in Fielding's discourse, are empowered precisely through their reappropriation as figures of an implicitly redefined category of the popular.

Thus, the actual reform to which puppetry was periodically subjected throughout this extended period was as nothing compared to the show's more sweeping appropriation within a discourse *about* culture that, as I have been suggesting all along, insulates itself from the same "lowness" it also celebrates. Throughout the period I have surveyed in this chapter, the explicitly assumed cultural subordination of puppet theater also seems to alternate with a particular sentimentality that attributes to puppets an imaginary transcendence of their real conditions, an enduring, carnivalesque social power. In 1648, as I have previously noted, the Lord Mayor of London attempted to suppress the puppet performers at Bartholomew Fair. A few months later a broadside presented "An Elegy, on the Timely Death of John Warner, late Lord Mayor." It concludes:

> Here lies my Lord Mayor under this Stone,
> That last Bartholomew-fair, no Puppets would owne,
> But next Bartholomew-faire, who liveth to see,
> Shall view my Lord Mayor a Puppet to bee.[113]

In historical retrospect, the descending cycle of representation that transmutes the real suppression of carnival performance into scurrilous broadside and puppet play almost obscures the power relations that underlie the events themselves. Ten years later, after the death of Olivier Cromwell and on the

---

[112] Fielding, *Tom Jones*, bk. 12, chap. 5, 637–39. Note the similarity between this account and Steele's description of Martin Powell in *Tatler*, no. 16, previously cited.

[113] Quoted in Rollins, "A Contribution to the History of the English Commonwealth Drama," 283.

eve of the restoration of the monarchy, Cromwell's son Henry eulogized his father in a speech to Parliament and imagined him recast as the subject of a puppet show:

> Me thinks I hear 'em already crying thirty year hence at Bartholomew Fair, "Step in and see the Life and Death of brave Cromwell." Me thinks I see him with a velvet cragg about his shoulders, and a little pasteboard hat on his head riding a tittup a tittup to his parliament house, and a man with a bay leaf in his mouth crying in his behalf, "By the living God I will dissolve 'em," which makes the porters cry, "O brave Englishman." Then the Devil carries him away in a tempest, which makes the nurses squeak and the children cry.[114]

This extraordinary nostalgia before the fact evokes, even if unintentionally, a savagely ironic equivalence between Cromwell's dictatorial dissolution of representative government and the literal conditions of puppet performance, in which a man "with a bay leaf in his mouth" (to produce the characteristic squeak) now speaks the famous words on Cromwell's behalf. Recast at once as both Punch and Faustus, Cromwell is also simultaneously diminished and exalted by this cultural gesture in which an elite voice presumes to speak for the popular, much as the imagined puppeteer would speak for a Lord Protector now consigned to history.

The full cultural existence of Punch is thus marked by a recurrent sentimentality about the popular which discovers a discursive transcendence in the socially marginal even while utterly subsuming the latter within the absorbent material of bourgeois culture itself. Perhaps the clearest of all examples of this process, as well as the single most famous cultural production to appropriate the voice and iconography of Punch, is the magazine of that name founded by Mark Lemon, Henry Mayhew, Douglas Jerrold, and others in 1841.[115] According to one of the many versions of the magazine's founding, the idea for the name came from Mayhew, who in the first decade of the magazine's life was also conducting the interviews that would constitute his *London Labour and the London Poor.* A relative of one of the founders remembers "hearing Henry Mayhew suddenly exclaim, 'Let the name be

---

[114] Quoted in Speaight, *History of the English Puppet Theatre,* 71.

[115] The history of *Punch* magazine is chronicled and discussed in Arthur A. Adrian, *Mark Lemon: First Editor of "Punch"* (London: Oxford University Press, 1966); Walter Jerrold, *Douglas Jerrold and "Punch"* (London: Macmillan, 1910); Arthur Prager, *The Mahogany Tree: An Informal History of Punch* (New York: Hawthorn Books, 1979); and M. H. Spielman, *The History of "Punch"* (London: Cassell & Co., 1895).

'Punch'!'—a fact engraven on her memory through her childish passion for the reprobate old puppet."[116] In the founding manifesto of the magazine, published in its first issue, Lemon wrote:

> Few of the admirers of our prototype, merry Master PUNCH, have looked upon his vagaries but as the practical outpouring of a rude and boisterous mirth. We have considered him as a teacher of no mean pretensions, and have, therefore, adapted him as the sponsor for our weekly sheet of pleasant instruction. When we have seen him parading in the glories of his motley, flourishing his baton . . . in time with his own unrivalled discord, by which he seeks to win the attention and admiration of the crowd, what visions of graver puppetry have passed before our eyes![117]

Here again, Punch is silenced by celebration: the figural music to which he flourishes his "baton" is drowned out by the same rhetoric with which the writer reenvisions and transforms him.[118] Even this word itself declares—in its own pointed paradigmatic substitution for the expected "cudgel" or "stick"—the cultural space between the observer and the social fact.

In the long ensuing history of *Punch* magazine, itself frequently chronicled and celebrated, the "rude and boisterous mirth," the "unrivaled discord" of the ephemeral performing object would be not merely described and appropriated in print (as it had been so many times throughout the period covered in this chapter) but literally flattened—into a logo, a cartoon, the very personification of the printed page. M. H. Spielman, writing just after the magazine's jubilee (1895), concluded rhapsodically that its founders had converted Punch "from a mere strolling puppet, an irresponsible jester, into the laughing philosopher and man of letters, the essence of all wit, the concentration of all wisdom, the soul of honour, the foundation of goodness, and the paragon of every virtue."[119] This particular kind of appropriation seems to depend not just on Punch's status as popular, carnivalesque, and authentically English, but also on childhood memories that engrave on the

---

[116] Spielman, *History of "Punch,"* 24.

[117] *Punch*, July 17, 1841, 1.

[118] Interestingly, when Spielman transcribes this well-known passage, he gives the word as "bâton"—the diacritical mark emphasizing the word's Gallic origin and hence its semantic distance from the object it describes (*History of "Punch,"* 2).

[119] Spielman, *History of "Punch,"* 28.

mind a sentimental fantasy of reprobation. Having been diminished into a denizen of the Victorian nursery, the puppet reemerges as the very icon of a bourgeois intelligentsia who appear, as they might have put it, as pleased as Punch. If it is difficult not to regret the complacency with which the historian records and reproduces the transformation of carnivalesque performance into the "graver puppetry" of (his own) discourse, to do so is simply to reverse the process; attributing to Punch some imagined power or purity which his history disarms or contaminates. But cultural production and cultural appropriation, as the evidence presented in this chapter suggests, are not only inseparable but virtually coterminous. The sense of loss that pervades the discursive history of Punch and Judy, like the retrospective celebration of an authentic and distinctly popular culture, is a nostalgia for something that was never there in the first place, and that is, in any case, still alive and well.

Four

Modern and Postmodern Puppets in Theory and in Practice

My focus necessarily becomes more diffuse in this final chapter, as I pursue the continuing appropriation of the puppet by a cosmopolitan twentieth-century culture in which the distinction between the popular and the elite beomes ever more problematic. I consider here how the puppet figures in three distinctly different fields of cultural theory and practice: the early modernist theater; the contemporaneous theories of theater developed by philosophers, critics, and semioticians; and the mass culture of film and television. In our century the actual performing object of ancient folk practice would be not merely appropriated as metaphor, and occasionally interpolated into the literary drama, but, as it were, swallowed whole—construed as the primal reality (or theoretical paradigm) of theater itself, and reappropriated within new forms of quasipopular performance. As in the preceding chapters, I attempt no comprehensive account of modernist theory and practice or, still less, of the emergence of a truly cosmopolitan mass culture. Rather, I suggest here, as I have throughout, that apparently unrelated instances of dramatic theory and practice represent broadly similar instances of cultural appropriation, and finally join in a much larger process of cultural distinction in general.

"The Omnipotence of a Methodical Will":
Performing Objects and the Theatrical Avant-Garde

The Germans even forbade us to use the words "corpse" or "victim"
[and] made us refer to the bodies as *Figuren*, that is, as puppets.
—from *Shoah*, a film by Claude Lanzmann

Heinrich von Kleist's celebrated dialogue "On the Puppet Theater" (1810) is
but the earliest example of what would become a virtual obsession with the
puppet in the theory and practice of European drama. In this brief and enig-
matic text, the author and a well-known dancer identified only as "Mr. C."
meet by chance at "a puppet theater which had been hammered together in
the marketplace, to entertain the crowds with little mock-heroic dramas, in-
terspersed with songs and dances."[1] Mr. C. expresses his fascination with
these mechanical actors, and goes on to argue that the puppet might actually
be more graceful than a living dancer, might indeed "present a dance such as
no other accomplished dancer of the time . . . was ever likely to achieve"
(212). Mr. C. thus presents his aesthetic judgment in the form of a paradox
which evokes, even as it apparently contradicts, the structure of the theological theater and its underlying ontological hierarchy, within which matter is
subordinate to spirit, the icon to its object, and the puppet to the human
actor or dancer. The carefully described setting further suggests, as I have
done throughout this book, that these representational hierarchies reflect
and embody a more specific system of social and cultural distinction. Mr. C.
and the narrator converse in the "marketplace," among "crowds" enter-
tained by an outdoor puppet theater pointedly contrasted to the opera,
where Mr. C. "had lately been appointed chief dancer." In the course of the
dialogue the two men thus appropriate the puppet in precisely the sense I
have been using the term: they discover in a "toy version of high art, contrived for the populace" (212) the vehicle for a hypothetical perfection of
high culture. Thus, their discourse simply moves the puppet from the bottom to the top of transparent hierarchies of representation and social distinction.
    But if the dialogue as a whole thus acknowledges the interdependence of
the aesthetic and the social, Mr. C's ensuing remarks emphasize, by contrast,

[1] Heinrich von Kleist, *An Abyss Deep Enough: Letters of Heinrich von Kleist with a Selection of Essays and Anecdotes*, ed. Phillip B. Miller (New York: E. P. Dutton, 1982), 211. Subsequent citations are given parenthetically in the text.

a quasi-theological opposition of corporeality and consciousness. "More charm might inhere in a mechanical doll than in . . . the human body" (214), Mr. C. concludes, because puppets are "incapable of affectation" as well as of those aesthetic "blunders" which are "unavoidable, since we have eaten of the tree of knowledge" (213). At this level of argument, the relationship of puppeteer to puppet no longer corresponds to the relationship of the mind to the body—as it might, for example, within the broadly Platonic and Christian tradition against which Kleist's argument otherwise defines itself. For Kleist, the inanimate puppet is *more* capable of being filled with the *vis motrix*, the "dancer's soul," than the animate body. The actor's or dancer's art depends on the fallible and imperfect union of conscious intention and bodily motion. Kleist's argument by contrast privileges an *authorial* relationship by which intention expresses itself by inspiring some passive, external vehicle. It is the disjunction of mind and body, rather than puppet theater as such, that is Kleist's basic point in the dialogue; and he proceeds to illustrate this disjunction further by telling a story about a young boy of "marvelous grace" with whom he had seen "the famous statue called the Spinario, the youth removing a thorn from his foot." Once, when this youth "happened to raise his foot to a stool" while glancing in the mirror, he noticed his own resemblance to the statue and called it to the attention of his observer:

> I indeed had noticed it too in the very same instant, but either to test the self-assurance of the grace with which he was endowed, or to challenge his vanity in a salutary way, I laughed and said he was seeing phantoms. He blushed and raised his foot a second time to prove it to me, but the attempt, as might easily have been foreseen, did not succeed. . . . He was unable to produce the same movement again. And the movements that he did make had so comical an effect that I could hardly suppress my laughter. (215)

Within a year, Kleist concludes, "not a trace could be detected of that sweetness which had once so delighted the sight of all who surrounded him (215)."

Beyond the obvious point about self-consciousness and affectation, one also notices that even as the statue was already an emblem of the thorn in the flesh, the painful intersection of matter and spirit, so does the ruinous power of apparent "*self*-consciousness" actually originate in the eye of the beholder. In a setting that irresistibly suggests the classical gymnasium, a young man of veritable beauty looks to a figure who is at once observer, narrator, and literal author of this text for confirmation of his own representational and corporeal meaning—and encounters the laughter of parodic (mis)recognition. Thus the power of the authorial gaze masters and transforms its object. Through the anecdote Kleist in effect transforms the graceful, classical body into the "mock-heroic" or grotesque body which the dialogue otherwise associates with the puppet, thus reasserting the same hierarchy of representation that Mr. C.'s opening paradox had apparently overturned. In the celebrated concluding lines of the dialogue, Mr. C. proclaims that "grace" will appear "most purely in that bodily form that has either no consciousness at all or an infinite one, which is to say, either in the puppet or a god" (216). This "teleological and apocalyptic history of consciousness" is, as Paul de Man remarks, "one of the most seductive, powerful, and deluded topoi of the idealist and romantic period."[2] Here, however, the theoretical gesture is also inseparable from an implicit affirmation of authorship and from an act of cultural appropriation which Kleist otherwise effaces under an elegant veil of paradox and quasi-mystical rhetoric.

I have lingered on the figural and narrative strategies of Kleist's essay to suggest some of the theoretical themes that began to reemerge in European dramatic theory and practice about a century later. As Kleist's text seems to foreshadow, from the late nineteenth century up to more or less the present day, the European theater has revealed a pervasive fascination with puppets and performing objects. Starting with what sometimes appear to be radically different aesthetic goals, and producing (when they did produce) radically different kinds of performance, the theorists and playwrights of the modernist tradition in some way share Kleist's distrust of the animate body and his paradoxical privileging of the object as a vehicle for histrionic transmission. The symbolist theater of the fin de siècle, which also represents the first stage in the development of a modernist theatrical aesthetic, found in the puppet "a model of concise, symbolic expression" and a serviceable avant-garde technique that might "unseat the gestural authority of naturalistic performance."[3] Later, the idea of the performing object conveniently merged with the more general modernist aestheticization of the machine and a corresponding effort to rethink the practical technology of the stage.

[2] Paul de Man, *The Rhetoric of Romanticism* (New York: Columbia University Press, 1984), 267.

[3] Irène Eynat-Confino, *Beyond the Mask: Gordon Craig, Movement, and the Actor* (Carbondale: Southern Illinois University Press, 1987), 32–33; William B. Worthen, "The Discipline of the Theatrical Sense: *At the Hawk's Well* and the Rhetoric of the Stage," *Modern Drama* 30 (1987): 94. Worthen has also generously shared with me his manuscript essay "Of Actors and Automata: Hieroglyphics of Modernism," forthcoming in the *Journal of Dramatic Theory and Criticism*, which discusses many of the same examples I do in this chapter, in the course of exploring "how stage automata participate in the modern theater's imaging of its audience."

The modernist puppet is obviously also a deliberate appropriation of popular (or, sometimes, non-Western) cultural practices, a fact that scholars and theater historians sometimes dismiss as an incidental or methodological consequence of much "larger" aesthetic strategies.[4] The cultural history previously sketched in this book suggests, conversely, that appropriation is central to the modernist theatrical project. In the discussion that follows I track the evolution of a particular strain in modernist dramatic theory across five examples: from the avant-garde theaters of Alfred Jarry and Maurice Maeterlinck in the 1890s, through the idiosyncratic but influential work of Edward Gordon Craig just after the turn of the century, to the futurist and Bauhaus theorists and designers in the ensuing decades. By tracing a particular thread of connection among these apparently quite dissimilar figures and schools, I suggest how, in each case, a primary appropriation of a theatrical practice associated with the popular masks a broader theoretical form of cultural appropriation, a bold reclamation of the whole histrionic process in the name of an imperious author-creator. The historical self-consciousness of modernist drama—its radical attempt to rethink and renew a supposedly exhausted tradition—similarly masks a different theoretical project: the reestablishment of a hypothetical theater whose theological hierarchy has been contaminated by its own vehicle, the human actor. As I also suggest, the aestheticism with which the modernist theater privileges, even mystifies, the notion of performance is inseparable from its continuing attempt to recast the power relations of the histrionic process itself, both in theory and in practice.

The premiere of Alfred Jarry's *Ubu Roi* on December 11, 1896, is still commonly viewed as the inaugural event of the modern avant-garde theater, and the epitome of its relentless, continuing effort to affront the middle class. In the simplest terms, however, Jarry's intention was also, in his own words, "to write a puppet play."[5] Jarry had performed earlier versions of *Ubu* with actual puppets both as a schoolboy at the lycée in Rennes and again, later, in a

---

[4] For example, while conceding that the modernist rediscovery of performing objects sometimes involved a "misuse" of "traditional" cultures, John Bell goes on to conclude that "questions about the politics of cultural appropration do not affect the central importance of the western re-evaluation of theater-techniques." John Bell, "Theater of the Twentieth Century as Theater of the Performing Object," in *The Theatrical Inanimate: A Conference on Changing Perceptions* (New York: The Jim Henson Foundation, 1992), 42–43.

[5] Alfred Jarry to Aurélian Lugné-Poe, director of the Théâtre de l'Oeuvre, in *Selected Works of Alfred Jarry*, ed. Roger Shattuck and Simon Watson Taylor (New York: Grove Press, 1965), 67.

small puppet theater in his Paris apartment.[6] At the celebrated production at the Théâtre de l'Oeuvre the play was performed by actors, but Jarry instructed them to imitate the mechanical movements of marionettes; he attempted, in the entire production, to "poussez au *guignol* le plus possible"—to suggest, as far as possible, a Punch-and-Judy show.[7] William Butler Yeats attended the premiere and, in an account now almost as well known as the event itself, remembered the actors "hopping like wooden frogs" and looking like "dolls, toys, marionettes."[8] As Jarry himself enjoined the audience in an address before the play began, "Vous serez libres de voir en M. Ubu les multiples allusions que vous voudrez, ou un simple fantoche" (you are free to see in Mr. Ubu as many allusions you like, or, if you prefer, just a plain puppet).[9] In all this Jarry is obviously one more example of a playwright whose aspiration to cultural authority manifests itself in an attraction to a popular mode of theatrical performance.

Many other writers of the period were similarly attracted to puppet theater or the conceptual idea of the performing object. In 1889 the Belgian playwright Maurice Maeterlinck published his first play, *La Princess Maleine*, intending it "pour un théâtre de fantoches," a puppet theater. Three years later Maeterlinck formally titled a volume of three other plays "drames pour marionettes."[10] These unusual symbolist plays had a profound influence on avant-garde theater over the next few decades: Jarry in France, Gordon Craig in England, Vsevolod Meyerhold in Russia, and other theatrical reformers throughout Europe would later claim Maeterlinck as an inspiration or artistic ally.[11] In the 1880s many of the writers of the symbolist community in

[6] Roger Shattuck, *The Banquet Years*, rev. ed. (New York: Harcourt, Brace, 1968), 191, 195; Keith Beaumont, *Alfred Jarry: A Critical and Biographical Study* (New York: St. Martin's, 1984), 26–27, 33.

[7] These instructions appear in a letter to Aurélian Lugné-Poe from Jarry's friend Rachilde (the pen name of Marguerite Eymery); cited in Beaumont, *Alfred Jarry*, 97. The French word *guignol* refers to a crude and farcical glove puppet show, much like the English Punch and Judy, which is why the term is often idiomatically translated as it is here. *Guignol* may be contrasted to the more generic *pantin* or *fantoche*, and to *marionette*, which usually refers to relatively larger and more elaborate performing objects such as the stringed puppets known by the same name in English.

[8] *The Autobiography of William Butler Yeats* (New York: Collier, 1965), 233.

[9] Alfred Jarry, *Oeuvres complètes*, ed. Michael Arrivé (Paris: Gallimard, 1972), 1:399; Jarry, *Selected Works*, 76.

[10] Marvin Carlson, *The French Stage in the Nineteenth Century* (Metuchen, N.J.: Scarecrow, 1972), 211; Jacques Robichez, *Le symbolisme au théâtre: Lugné-Poe et les débuts de l'Oeuvre* (Paris: L'Arche, 1957), 76 n.173. On Maeterlinck's interest in puppets, see also Bettina Knapp, *Maurice Maeterlinck* (Boston: Twayne, 1975), 77.

[11] See Alfred Jarry, "Réponses à un questionnaire sur l'art dramatique," in *Oeuvres complètes*, 410; translated as "Twelve Theatrical Topics," in *Selected Works*, 86. Maeterlinck is also one of the authors listed among the library of the titular character of *Gestes et opinions du docteur Faustroll, pataphysician*

Paris were also attending Henri Signoret's Petit Théâtre des Marionettes, where large and elaborate puppets operated from below by a unique system of rods and levers performed examples of high literary drama, including Greek tragedy and Shakespeare.[12] In the 1890s, similarly, the Nabi painter Paul Ranson had a puppet theater in his studio on Montparnasse, and Jarry and several other writers and painters organized a Théâtre des Pantins, where they put on a new production of *Ubu Roi* in 1897.[13]

As a schematic or merely iconic representation of character and the human form, the performing object was obviously well suited to the symbolist attempt to transcend the particulars of individual personality and achieve what Maeterlinck calls "la révélation de l'infini et de la grandeur ainsi que la beauté secrète, de l'homme" (the revelation of the infinitude and grandeur and secret beauty of man).[14] As a literally inanimate object, passive matter available for authorial form, the puppet was also well suited, as I will suggest, to the intense reaffirmation of a sovereign author which was another key aspect of the symbolist project. In any case, an impulse of depersonalization and abstraction, a kind of simplified and sentimental Platonism, is the common thread that unites Jarry's grotesque and scatological *Ubu* (which strips down to its bare bones a *Macbeth*-like story of political usurpation and tyranny) and Maeterlinck's apparently quite dissimilar plays, with their exaggerated tragic fatalism, pseudo-medieval settings, and oppressively monosyllabic dialogue.

Jarry and Maeterlinck construed their revolt against naturalism as taking place on a practical and also a theoretical level, with corresponding social and metaphysical implications. That is, both playwrights attempted to reform the actual conditions of late nineteenth-century bourgeois theater (whose formalistic "well-made" plays they considered mere empty amusement), and also to rethink the very process of histrionic representation. As the two playwrights suggest in various prefatorial and theoretical statements, they were revolting not so much against naturalism in the strict sense of the term (the school of Zola and his followers) as against the very possibility of theatrical realism in the broadest sense. Such realism they envisioned in the terms of the theological model of authorship. The theatrical performance, a literal *embodiment* of the playwright's singular "truth," would conventionally be con-

---

(1898), in *Oeuvres complètes*, 660.

[12] Max von Boehn, *Dolls and Puppets*, trans. Josephine Nicoll (New York: Cooper Square, 1966), 346.

[13] Eynat-Confino, *Beyond the Mask*, 32–33; Beaumont, *Alfred Jarry*, 143.

[14] Maurice Maeterlinck, preface to "Pelléas and Mélisande" and Other Plays, trans. Richard Hovey (New York: Dodd, Mead, 1911), 8. The preface is in French in this edition.

sidered as either more or less *verisimilar* insofar as it succeeds or fails in such embodiment. To Jarry and Maeterlinck this process was desirable in principle but inadequate in practice. They accordingly reconstrued the prevailing conditions of theatrical performance as a *subversion* of authorship, precisely because a human actor must interpose his body and personality between the author's vision and its practical realization. In a retrospective preface to one of his best-known plays, *Pelléas and Mélisande*, Maeterlinck reiterates his preference for a "theater of marionettes" because, as he puts it, the human actor inevitably "usurps" the power of the poem. Indeed, Maeterlinck insists that "masterpieces" such as Shakespeare's plays are "incapable of being represented" on the stage. He once saw *Hamlet* performed by an illustrious actor, but, he writes,

> a single one of his looks showed me that he was not Hamlet. . . . I saw clearly that he had his own destinies, and those that he wanted to represent were decidedly different from his. I saw his health and his habits, his passions and his sorrows, his thoughts and his works, and he tried vainly to interest me in a life which was not his and which his mere presence had rendered factitious. . . . The whole masterpiece is a symbol, and the symbol will not support the active presence of man. The crow of the cock is sufficient, says Hamlet, to make the specters of night vanish. In the same way, the poem loses its life "of the second sphere" as soon as a being of the inferior sphere is introduced in it.[15]

This passage repeats but surpasses a certain familiar romantic idealism which exalts the idea of drama while mistrusting practical performance: Hazlitt, Lamb, and other romantic writers, for example, similarly expressed their skepticism that a literal actor could ever adequately represent Shakespeare's heroes. Beneath Maeterlinck's mystical rhetoric, however, lurks a more visceral distaste for the corporeal body, with its "santé" and its "passions." Even the example of *Hamlet*, chosen as if by chance, reinforces the figural momentum with which Maeterlinck construes the process of histrionic embodiment as a subversion of authority. Maeterlinck writes that *Hamlet* has been "dethroned" by "the actor," so that "we are no longer able to separate the usurper from our dreams." The actor is a "force enemie," a "specter" who has overthrown the authority of the character and the play, at once the usurping Claudius and the ghostly father with all the sins of nature on his head.

---

[15] Ibid., 8–10.

In Jarry's scattered writings on the theater, a similar attempt to rethink the histrionic process merges with a social discourse about theater and its audiences. In one text, for example, Jarry contrasts the taste of "the crowd," for whom drama was merely "a pastime," with what he calls the "minority theater," in which "the elite join in the creation of one of themselves who, among this elite, sees a being come to life in himself that was created by himself, an active pleasure which is God's sole pleasure and which the holiday mob achieves in caricature in the carnal act."[16] Here the involuted syntax embodies the supposed interrelationship of a discursive hierarchy that descends from God to the author to an elite group of spectators whose cultural perception is itself an analogous form of "creation." By contrast, the merely carnal procreation of the "holiday mob" is itself seen as a reproduction or parody of this higher aesthetic process. The acute sense of social distinction manifest in these lines merges with an implicit misogyny, even as the latter similarly merges, elsewhere in Jarry's writings, with a symbolist distrust of histrionic impersonation. "On the Paris stage," Jarry writes, " a boy of fourteen is traditionally played . . . by a twenty-year-old woman who, being six years older, has much more experience. This is small compensation for her ridiculous profile and unaesthetic walk, or for the way the outline of all her muscles is vitiated by adipose tissue, which is odious because it has a function—it produces *milk*."[17] Here again, a quasi-Platonic critique of theatrical representation tries to mask or justify a distaste for the female body, now construed as the paradigm of corporeality itself.[18]

And yet *Ubu Roi* may well seem to contradict this apparent symbolist distrust of the body. The avant-garde scandal of the play lies precisely in its appropriation of the grotesque and scatological qualities of folk puppetry—Père Ubu's toilet-brush scepter and protruding belly, his infamous opening cry of "Merdre!," and so forth. But Jarry's adolescent indulgence in the carnivalesque is a displacement by inversion of a different theatrical project. For Jarry also conceptualizes the performing object quite precisely as a vehicle for performance unmediated by corporeality or personality, a performance of absolute self-presence and authorial mastery: "We have always been bored at what is called 'the Theater.' Could it be because the actor, however brilliant he may be, betrays—and all the more so the more brilliant or personal he is—the thought of the poet? Only puppets, of which one is master, sover-

---

[16] Jarry, *Selected Works*, 87; Jarry, *Oeuvres complètes*, 411–12.
[17] Jarry, *Selected Works*, 74; Jarry, *Oeuvres complètes*, 409.
[18] For more on Jarry's misogyny, see Shattuck, *The Banquet Years*, 231–34.

eign, and Creator, translate, passively and in the most rudimentary and precise manner, our thoughts."[19] Here again, Jarry's rhetoric moves freely between a quasi-theological vision of representation and a more specific disdain for the social institution "ce qu'on appelle le Théâtre," just as the abstract and hypothetical vision of a sovereign author-creator reifies the social attitudes otherwise manifest in Jarry's writings. In a famous anecdote Aurélian Lugné-Poe, director of the Théâtre de l'Oeuvre, is said to have suggested to the actor who played Ubu in the celebrated production that he "imitate the author's own voice and jerky stylized gestures"—gestures a schoolmate remembered as appearing "puppet-like."[20] Thus, the play and event that was *Ubu Roi* inscribes at once an implicit representational hierarchy and its inversion: from the author to the titular character to the literal puppet and back again. As with Maeterlinck, Jarry's palpable rejection of theatrical realism is but the practical consequence of his desire to reaffirm the uncompromising sovereignty of the authorial voice. It is as such that one must understand what Keith Beaumont calls the "paradox" of a playwright who "takes up a defiantly elitist and anti-democratic standpoint" yet also "champions such distinctly popular forms of expression as the *guignol*."[21] Jarry's appropriation of popular performance corresponds precisely to his avant-garde assault on naturalism and the bourgeois stage, and both gestures clearly instantiate the same system of cultural distinction that they seem to overturn.

In short, when Jarry, Maeterlinck, and many succeeding writers declare the superiority of the puppet to the actor (as Kleist's Mr. C. had also done nearly a century earlier), the apparent paradox nevertheless evokes (and reconfirms) the hierarchical structure of a theological theater. These writers seem to overturn that hierarchy, but only by replacing the mediated and dialogical structure of conventional performance (in which the artist speaks through other artists) with a monological relationship between the author and his art. Theatrical critics of the fin de siècle and later continued to affirm the supreme value of what they vaguely called the author's "thought" or "dreams" through this same strategy of indirection: by celebrating the puppet's supposed superiority over the actor as a histrionic vehicle. In the late 1880s, for example, Anatole France reviewed several different puppet performances at Henri Signoret's Petit Théâtre in texts that would later be repeatedly cited by Gordon Craig. France's argument about the aesthetic effect of

<hr />

[19] Alfred Jarry, "Conference sur les pantins," in *Oeuvres Complètes*, 421–22.
[20] Shattuck, *The Banquet Years*, 207, 192.
[21] Beaumont, *Alfred Jarry*, 322 n.45.

puppets closely parallels Maeterlinck's and also evokes a broad spectrum of the puppet's inherited figural associations. "If I must speak my whole mind, actors spoil comedy for me," France writes, because "their personality effaces the work they represent." By contrast, "those dolls of M. Signoret" are "worthy of giving form to the dreams of the poet."[22] In a later piece France argues, similarly, that marionettes " have a simple grace, the divine clumsiness of statues who condescend to behave as dolls, and it is delightful to watch these little figures enact a play. . . . These marionettes are like the Egyptian hieroglyphs, that is, they have a certain pure and mysterious quality, and when they represent a drama of Shakespeare or Aristophanes, I seem to watch the poet's thought unfolded in sacred characters along the temple's wall."[23]

As he attempts to reproduce the intoxicating magic of the puppets in the rhythms of his own prose, France's rhetoric systematically invokes dualistic oppositions of history (past and present), culture (Eastern and Western), and class (high and low). His marionettes are at once ancient idols slumming in the contemporary world (having consented "à faire les poupées") and the "naive" figures of folk art whose grace lies precisely in their dislocation from any meaningful sense of time or place: thus the indecipherable mystery of the hieroglyph. Oscar Wilde saw *The Tempest* at the same theater, one of the productions that France had reviewed, and he discussed it in a letter to the *London Daily Telegraph* (February 19, 1892). Observing that "the personality of the actor is often a source of danger in the perfect presentation of a work of art," Wilde argues that puppets, conversely, "are admirably docile," and "recognize the presiding intellect of the dramatist."[24] In 1902 the critic Arthur Symons similarly contrasted the human actor, with his "intrusive little personality," to the puppet, which "may be relied on."[25] The rhetoric in either case attributes to the puppet a kind of pseudo-agency, an ability to "recognize" or respond to the authorial vision, while also conversely grounding the puppet's histrionic power in its passivity or docility. The puppet can thus become the paradoxical site for a kind of philosophic realism which caricatures Plato even while evoking and, as it were, short-circuiting the Platonic hierarchy of representation: Symons muses that one might see among

[22] Anatole France, "M. Signoret's Marionettes," in *On Life and Letters, Second Series*, trans. A. W. Evans, vol. 27 of *The Works of Anatole France*, 30 vols. (New York: Gabriel Wells, 1924), 137–39.

[23] Anatole France, "Hrotswitha and the Marionettes," in *On Life and Letters, Third Series*, trans. D. B. Stewart, vol. 28 of *Works of Anatole France*, 9–10.

[24] *The Letters of Oscar Wilde*, ed. Rupert Hart-Davis (New York: Harcourt, Brace & World, 1962), 311.

[25] Arthur Symons, *Plays, Acting, and Music* (New York: E. P. Dutton, 1909), 3–4.

the puppets a face that makes "all other faces in the world [seem] but spoilt copies of this inspired piece of painted wood."[26] Here again, the urbane paradox with which Symons transforms the crude icon into the quasi-Platonic form merely reaffirms the representational hierarchy by foreshortening it, opening up an unmediated passage from inspired author to inspiring performance.

In the same years, too, the young Edward Gordon Craig, another performer and aspiring theorist who had grown up in the milieu of fin de siècle symbolism, was beginning to develop what would be the most elaborate version of this theatrical fascination with the puppet.[27] Craig's ideas seem to have emerged as the theoretical aftermath of his early experience and recurrent frustration with the practical exigencies of the theater. After directing several interesting and influential amateur productions in London, and working fitfully on abortive projects in Germany and elsewhere, Craig settled in Florence in 1907 and began to publish his journal *The Mask*. Throughout its life Craig wrote nearly all of *The Mask* under both his own name and a variety of pseudonyms, attempting by this curious literary ventriloquism to convey the illusion of a thriving theatrical community where there was, in fact, but a single idiosyncratic voice. Right from the beginning Craig employed an explicit strategy of cultural appropriation in his polemical efforts to reform the modern stage. For example, in "A Note on Masks," published in his journal's first issue (March 1908) under the pseudonym John Balance, Craig argues that paratheatrical modes of performance—"dancing, pantomime, marionettes, masks"—would be central to the revival of modern theater. No mere primitivist, however, Craig insists on the use of such forms not because they are "popular" but because, as he claims, their popular manifestations are themselves appropriations of some more primal mode of cultural expression.[28] Thus, the "Clown and Pantaloon" of popular pantomime are merely attenuated versions of "Buddha teaching symbolic gesture," and literal marionettes are (as Craig suggests, citing Anatole France's reviews) only the vestige of ancient ritual images, what France had called "caractères sacrés sur les

[26] Ibid., 6.

[27] When Gordon Craig was growing up with his mother, the celebrated actress Ellen Terry, and his father, the architect Edward William Godwin, the family friends, "among them William Burges, Whistler, Burne-Jones, and Oscar Wilde, belonged to the Pre-Raphaelite and Aesthete circles" (Eynat-Confino, *Beyond the Mask*, 4). On Craig's life and career, see also Christopher Innes, *Edward Gordon Craig* (Cambridge: Cambridge University Press, 1983); and Charles R. Lyons, "Gordon Craig's Concept of the Actor," in *Total Theatre: A Critical Anthology*, ed. E. T. Kirby (New York: E. P. Dutton, 1969), 58–77.

[28] Edward Gordon Craig, *Craig on Theatre* (London: Methuen, 1983), 18.

murailles d'un temple" (sacred characters on the walls of a temple). Craig's point thus inverts the more common strategy of Western dramatic theory, which, as I have suggested, has often attempted to subordinate the paratheatrical in the name of a legitimate, literary, and theological theater. Craig, however, remains clearly within this same cultural logic. For Craig, as he suggests with these explicitly theological images, the paratheatrical is paradoxically more legitimate because more originary; his discourse simply makes an end run around more conventional formulations while retaining an essentially similar hierarchical habit of thought.

In "The Actor and the Über-Marionette" (*The Mask*, April 1908) Craig goes much farther, envisioning a kind of "super puppet" that could literally replace the human actor—and thus undo not only the imagined descent of theater from ritual to representation but even the belittling materiality of corporeal existence. Restating but intensifying a conventional symbolist point, Craig asserts, with deliberate rhetorical bravura, that the human actor's inevitable personality makes him a figural puppet, for "emotion *possesses* him, it seizes upon his limbs; moving them whither it will."[29] Craig goes on to present a kind of myth or parable about the origins of performance, which began, he speculates, with staged animal fights, "an elephant and a tiger in an arena" (58). Eventually a man with "greater learning" met a man with "greater temperament" and persuaded him to "speak my lines" in an address to the people (58–59). Afterwards, Craig suggests,

> other authors found it an excellent thing to use handsome and buoyant
> men *as instruments.* It mattered nothing to them that the instrument
> was a human creature. Although they knew not the stops of the
> instrument, they could play rudely upon him and they found him
> useful. And so to-day we have the strange picture of a man content to
> give forth the thoughts of another, which that other has given form to
> while at the same time he exhibits his person to the public view. . . .
> But all the time, and however long the world may last, the nature in
> man will fight for freedom, and will revolt against being made a slave
> or medium for the expression of another's thoughts. (60)

[29] Edward Gordon Craig, *On the Art of the Theatre* (New York: Theater Arts, 1956), 56. All further citations from Craig's work are from this edition and are given parenthetically in the text. Craig's texts as printed in *The Mask* are frequently inconsistent in spelling and punctuation; and although *Craig on Theatre* is generally the most useful and reliable selection of his work, the volume includes only a portion of "The Actor and the Über-Marionette."

In this conception the theater is theological in precisely the sense in which I have used the term: describing a hierarchy that reflects or resembles at once the ontological hierarchy of a quasi-Platonic idealism and the social and political hierarchies of domination and subordination. Thus, Craig's critique of the actor masquerades as a defense of the actor's freedom. I also observe how, in Craig's rhetoric, the actor as "medium" (one who "give[s] forth the thoughts of another") corresponds precisely to the actor as self-exhibitor, both roles foregrounding the actor's general status as body, object, vessel, or container.

Within a few lines, however, what has been sounding like a critique of the actual social conditions of theater slips back into that Kleistian critique of the disjunction of corporeality and consciousness. "Even if the actor was to present none but the ideas which he himself should compose," Craig suggests, "his nature would still be in servitude, his body would have to become the slave of his mind, and that as I have shown is what the healthy body refuses to do" (60–61). With this extraordinary vision of the body enslaved to an authorial intention that which is somehow always external even when self-embodied, Craig projects a hypothetical theater in which, as he insists, "the body of man . . . is *by nature* utterly useless as material" (61). But then Craig pulls back from the implications of such an argument and describes, by contrast, a hypothetical new form of human acting that would no longer attempt "to reproduce Nature" (62). Citing Plato's attack on mimesis from *The Republic*, Craig dismisses the traditional actor as "an imitator, not an artist," someone who "looks upon life as a photo-machine looks upon life" and who might "claim kinship with the ventriloquist" (62–63). True acting, by contrast, would transform the body into a "machine" that obeys the mind "in every movement," allowing the actor to rid himself of the authorial text, to "put aside Shakespeare's poem" (70–71).

The fundamental instability of Craig's position manifests itself in this self-contradictory digression and even in the infelicity of its metaphors. For, one might ask, is the traditional actor the photographer or the photograph, the ventriloquist or the dummy? Craig calls for actors to become themselves true "artists" after just having "proved" the intrinsic unreliability of their instrument (the body); and at the same time he calls for a master artist (author or director) who *requires* a docile and reliable vehicle of histrionic expression. Thus, a few pages later Craig finally reasserts the much more radical conclusion that emerges inevitably from his earlier argument. "The actor must go," he states flatly, "and in his place comes the inanimate figure—the Über-marionette" (81). The allusion to Nietzsche's *Übermensch* has little specific meaning, and seems intended merely to lend an aura of philosophic legitimacy to this vague concept of a performing object somehow "beyond" the mere puppet both practically and conceptually. With its imagined fluidity of motion like "the body in trance," clothed with "death-like beauty" (85), the über-marionette will replace the "living figure in which the weakness and tremors of the flesh were perceptible" and in so doing lift theater out of mere "debased stage-realism" (81). This fantastic metapuppet will manifest the intentions of its author-creator in a double movement of absolute paradox: first, because the puppet is a slave, passive matter untroubled by emotion or personality, and second, because the puppet was once a mystic image of the divine, himself a worshiped and adored master.

Similarly, Craig locates the über-marionette either in the primeval past or in a hypothetical future. Here again, he assumes the existence of a reverse cultural teleology in which high practices incessantly descend into the grasp of the low:

> Today, in his least happy period many people come to regard [the marionette] as rather a superior doll—and to think he has developed from the doll. This is incorrect. He is a descendant of the stone images of the old temples—he is today a rather degenerate form of a god. . . . The marionette appears to me to be the last echo of some noble and beautiful art of a past civilization. But as with all art which has passed into fat or vulgar hands, the puppet has become a reproach. All puppets are now but low comedians. (81–82)

Thus, Craig envisions himself as a crucial figure in a historical narrative of loss and restoration. In his own description he is not appropriating a mode of primitive or folk culture but simply restoring a misappropriated practice to its "original" status and meaning. Craig's nostalgia for a primeval past recalls a familiar theme in Western discourse about the puppet, and elevates to the level of serious dramatic theory a claim that had been repeatedly made in jest throughout the previous two centuries. In 1773, for example, the comedian Samuel Foote had introduced his "Primitive Puppet Shew" (a parody of sentimental drama acted by large, cutout puppets) by praising "the antiquity and utility of this truly elegant art" which "came to Rome from Egypt, through Grecian strainers" and yet now, "from the corruption of its original principles, and the inability of its latter professors, has sunk into . . . disrepute" (17). In 1828, as I have previously observed, John Payne Collier's speculations on the ancient roots of the Punch-and-Judy show seemed like an elaborate parody of scholarship. By the end of the nineteenth century, however, Anatole France could write in complete seriousness of an "august" marionette who "emerges from the sanctuary" and "great religious festivals," citing a "learned historian" as evidence.[30] Around the time of his first notes on the über-marionette, Craig too had evidently been reading a scholarly treatise on puppetry, Richard Pischel's *Home of the Puppet-Play* (1900).[31] In this book Pischel marshals an impressive-sounding array of etymological and ethnographic evidence in order to claim that puppets are "the most ancient form of dramatic representation" and to trace back both puppetry in general and celebrated European puppet characters such as Pulcinella and Punch to the ancient culture of India.[32] This pedantic argument, a minor instance of a much larger effort to prove the "Aryan" roots of European culture, incites Craig to a bizarre orientalizing fantasy, with which his essay closes in a crescendo of increasingly rhapsodic rhetoric:

> Let me again repeat that [puppets] are the descendants of a great and noble family of Images, images which were indeed made "in the likeness of God." . . . In Asia lay his first Kingdom. On the banks of the Ganges they built him his home . . . a vast palace springing from column to column into the air. . . . And then, one day, the ceremony . . . a celebration once more in praise of the Creation. . . . And during this ceremony there appeared before the eyes of the brown worshippers the symbols of all things on earth and in Nirvana. . . . I pray earnestly for the return of the image—the Über-marionette—to the Theatre; and when he comes again and is but seen, he will be loved so well that once more will it be possible for the people to return to their ancient joy in ceremonies—once more will Creation be celebrated—homage rendered to existence—and divine and happy intercession made to Death. (90–94)

Betraying once again an unresolved dialectic of the singular and the communal, Craig seems to envision himself as joined in worship of the über-marionette and yet also as the master of ceremonies, at once the spectacle and the spectator. Craig places his über-marionette quite literally on a pedestal, sepa-

---

[30] Charles Magnin, *Histoire des marionettes en Europe: depuis l'antiquité jusqu'à nos jours* (1861; rpt. Paris: Slatkin, 1981), does in fact argue that "les marionettes et les automates ont été partout les hôtes révérés des temples" (puppets and automata have been the honored guests in temples everywhere [8]).

[31] Eynat-Confino, *Beyond the Mask*, 86.

[32] Richard Pischel, *The Home of the Puppet-Play*, trans. Mildred C. Tawney (London: Luzac, 1902), 5, 22.

rated from an expected reader, whom he repeatedly implores to "let me tell you" (91, 93), by an impermeable veil of historicity and cultural otherness.

I have observed how Craig's basic argument begins with an analogy between the corporeal microcosm and the theatrical macrocosm: the opposition of mind and body corresponds to that of author and actor. At the end of the essay, this analogy implicitly returns in the form of another myth or parable about the origins of theater.

> Now let me tell you who it was that came to disturb the calm air which surrounded this curiously perfect thing. It is on record that somewhat later he took up his abode on the Far Eastern coast, and there came two women to look upon him. . . . He charged them full of a desire too great to be quenched; the desire to stand as the direct symbol of the divinity in man. No sooner thought than done; and arraying themselves as best they could in garments ("like his" they thought), moving with gestures ("like his" they said) and being able to cause wonderment in the minds of the beholders ("even as he does" they cried), they built themselves a temple ("like his," "like his"), and supplied the demand of the vulgar, the whole thing a poor parody. . . . In fifty or a hundred years, places for such parodies were to be found in all parts of the land. . . . Weeds, they say, grow quickly, and that wilderness of weeds, the modern theatre, soon sprang up. The figure of the divine puppet attracted fewer and fewer lovers, and the women were quite the latest thing. With the fading of the puppet and the advance of these women who exhibited themselves on the stage in his place, came that darker spirit which is called Chaos, and in its wake the triumph of the riotous personality. (93–94)

Having previously associated the actor with an empty corporeality, Craig here construes this status as *female*; and he suggests that histrionic illusion, mimesis itself, is causally linked to a physical attraction of the female for the male, construed as a female desire to represent "the divinity in man." This outlandish argument seems to telescope the cultural history outlined in this book, in which the puppet constantly figures within intricately interlocking hierarchies of social, sexual, and ontological distinction. One notices, too, the conceptual slippage with which the corporeal (and female) arts of imitation and exhibition lead to a triumph of "the riotous personality"—that same intrusive "emotion" which otherwise "conspires against art" (57). In this passage the über-marionette appears to be male in opposition to the parodic and primeval actresses who parody his mystic grandeur. Earlier, however, Craig had similarly rhapsodized about the "symbolic movements" of a "fair brown Queen," whom he relates to the puppetlike figures seen by Herodotus at "the temple-theatre in Thebes" (83).[33] Similarly, his son and biographer would later note that Craig first conceived of the über-marionette just after meeting the celebrated dancer Isadora Duncan, with whom he would also have a passionate but troubled personal relationship. In a curiously literal way, then, Craig conceives his hypothetical superpuppet as a kind of female automaton which would have Duncan's exquisite physical grace but not her consciousness or agency; a being that, unlike her, "could be controlled" and "would not suffer from, or be affected by emotions."[34] Histrionic performance thus represents the unity of an active, masculine form and a passive, feminine matter.[35] Craig's vision of histrionic mastery is a confused but unmistakable evocation of conventional Western habits of thought. His über-marionette is male when he construes it as a mystic idol or transcendent image but female (and culturally Other) when he construes it as a literal performing object, the figural servant or slave of authorial intention. Much as Renaissance discourse, for example, associated woman with the pernicious aspects of both nature and of art, Craig associates woman with both the body (motion and exhibition) and the mind (the intrusive personality), insofar as he subordinates each term to a vague and indefinite "art of theater."

I am suggesting that Craig's mystical flights of fancy and his rhetoric of theatrical liberation mask a fantasy of overwhelming personal power, a theater whose methodology and theoretical structure are alike grounded in domination and subordination. In the pages of *The Mask* Craig repeatedly quotes Flaubert's claim that "the artist in his work must be like God in creation, invisible and all-powerful". He dedicates his essay "The Artists of the Theatre of the Future" first "to the young race of athletic workers in all the theatres," and then, in an explicit second thought, "to the single courageous

[33] Craig refers only to "the old Greek Traveller of 800 B.C." It is ironic, or perhaps curiously appropriate, that Craig should think of Herodotus in this context, since in fact (as I briefly noted in the first chapter) the "puppets" or ritual figures observed by Herodotus represented male gods with movable, oversized phalluses, who were carried by female worshipers.

[34] Edward Craig, *Gordon Craig: The Story of His Life* (New York: Knopf, 1968), 198.

[35] "It seems to me," Craig writes in discussing dance, "that before the female spirit gives herself up, and with the male goes in quest of this vast treasure, perfect movement will not be discovered" (*Art of the Theater*, 51–52). Eynat-Confino, who elucidates Craig's idiosyncratic mystical ideas at some length, concurs that his aesthetic system is contingent on a "union of the male and the female 'spirit'—possible only, according to him, by the submission of woman to man" (*Beyond the Mask*, 134).

individuality in the world of the theatre who will some day master and re-mould it" (1). Nearly thirty years later, still living in Italy, Craig presented Mussolini with two of his books and, according to his son, "was very disappointed" that he received no response, for "Mussolini had always appealed to him as a man of genius and a man of power combined, a man who controlled everything—rather as he himself imagined his 'stage director' would do in the theatre."[36]

To be sure, the specific figure who masters the histrionic process alternates, in Craig's discourse, between the literal author and the stage manager or director, an ambiguity that is a virtually inevitable consequence of his emphasis on paratheatrical modes of performance such as movement and dance.[37] Indeed, Craig's most lasting influence on the modernist stage lies in his contribution to the idea of the modernist auteur: the director as theatrical artist of a self-sufficient work distinct from the text. "The theatre must not forever rely upon having a play to perform," he insists in another of his essays, "but must in time perform pieces of its own art" (144). Nevertheless, Craig's vision of an über-marionette suspended between an (ir)recoverable past and an indescribable future begs comparision to his literal career, in which he continually projected grandiose theatrical productions which remained unrealized or unrealizable.[38] Similarly, Craig's unresolved dialectic between the singular artist and the multiplicity of performance corresponds to the other contradiction of his career: his obsessive lifelong fear of plagiarism versus his constant, unsuccessful efforts to found a school and the yearning for community in general so clearly manifest in his ventriloquistic

---

[36] Craig, *Gordon Craig,* 337.

[37] The idea of a pure art of histrionic movement seems inevitably to suggest dance; and it is indeed partially as a theorist and critic of dance that Craig enters the mainstream of modernist performance theory. See, for example, Arnold Rood's introduction to his anthology *Gordon Craig on Movement and Dance* (New York: Dance Horizons, 1977). An ambiguity between author and director reveals itself frequently in Craig's writings; for example, although he often writes about eliminating the authorial text altogether (as he does in various passages cited here), in one essay he argues against the director's cutting a single line from one of Shakespeare's plays. "This liberty with great plays is no sign of civilization," he writes, "it is barbarous in the extreme." Gordon Craig, "Shakespeare's Plays," *The Mask* 1.7 (September 1908): 142–43.

[38] In *The Stage Is Set* (New York: Harcourt, Brace, 1932), the scenic designer Lee Simonson strongly critiques Craig's work, suggesting that many of his published set designs would be literally impossible to build, and arguing that Craig's failure to realize his theoretical ideas was the result of "his own lack of authentic creative power" (317–31). Frederick Brown, in *Theater and Revolution: The Culture of the French Stage* (1980; rpt. New York: Vintage, 1989), similarly suggests that Craig's myths were "made to accommodate emotions he could neither control nor satisfy in his own name" (219).

journal and multiple pseudonyms.[39] Although he lived until 1966, after his youth he never again finished a single fully realized theatrical project. His continuing influence rests on a slender corpus of drawings and essays, and some celebrated but fragmentary work on the productions of other companies (such as Stanislavsky's Moscow production of *Hamlet* in 1908). That such influence remains considerable suggests how Craig (rather like Ben Jonson) found in discourse and theory, in the singular relation of author to an absent and invisible reader, the kind of theater he truly aimed to achieve: a theater uncontaminated by actors, by multiplicity, by otherness itself.

If Craig's total project remains idiosyncratic, his approach to the histrionic process, as I have suggested, both reflected and fostered a continuing modernist effort to rethink and reaffirm the power relations of the stage. At approximately the same time Craig was developing his grandiose fantasies of theatrical reform, a group of young artists in Italy, who called themselves futurists, were similarly trying to dislocate the authority of psychological realism and experimenting with a theater of objects. Scholars have increasingly come to recognize the wide-ranging influence of futurist performance, and acknowledged its role within an avant-garde theatrical tradition encompassing Dada, the Living Theater, the "happenings" of the 1960s, and even contemporary "performance art."[40] By contrast, I want to place the futurist theater within the rather different theoretical tradition I am tracing here, and to suggest that its attempt to radically reconstitute theatrical practice was actually grounded in a wholly conventional, even reactionary, reaffirmation of authorship. Various scholars have documented and discussed the complex relationship between and brief alliance of Filippo Marinetti, founder and central figure of the futurist movement, and Mussolini's fascism.[41] I suggest, using the terms of my argument here, that a protofascist vision of totalizing authority is already adumbrated in Marinetti's vision of a radically theologi-

[39] On these characteristics of Craig's personality and career, see Craig, *Edward Gordon Craig*.

[40] Michael Kirby and Victoria Nes Kirby, eds., *Futurist Performance* (New York: PAJ Publications, 1986), 6–8; Henry M. Sayre, *The Object of Performance: The American Avant-Garde since 1970* (Chicago: University of Chicago Press, 1989), 9.

[41] Perhaps the most celebrated statement of the relationship between Marinetti's futurist movement and Fascism is the epilogue of Walter Benjamin's essay "The Work of Art in an Age of Mechanical Reproduction," in *Illuminations*, ed. Hannah Arendt, trans. Harry Zohn (New York: Schocken, 1968), 241–42. See also Andrew Hewitt, *Fascist Modernism: Aesthetics, Politics, and the Avant-Garde* (Stanford: Stanford University Press, 1993); Marjorie Perloff, *The Futurist Moment: Avant-Garde, Avant-Guerre, and the Language of Rupture* (Chicago: University of Chicago Press, 1986), 29–36; and Caroline Tisdall and Angelo Bozzolla, *Futurism* (New York: Oxford University Press, 1978), 200–209.

cal theater in which the resources of technology become extensions of an all-powerful authorial "will."

Marinetti's first theatrical manifesto, "The Variety Theater" (1913), relies for its effect, like most of his texts, on an ecstatic cascade of imagery. Like Craig before him, Marinetti attempts in this polemical text to transcend a drama of mere "photographic reproduction" by embracing a carnivalesque mode of nonnarrative performance. Marinetti calls for a theater of "jugglers, ballerinas, gymnasts," and "new significations of light, sound, noise, and language," a sort of vaudeville circus devoted to "astonishment" and "the Futurist destruction of immortal masterworks."[42] Marinetti describes an "anti-academic, primitive and naïve" mode of performance that incorporates the "gymnastics and acrobatics of the Japanese" and the "muscular frenzy of the Negroes," unfolding before "honeyed dandies" with frock coats and cigars, and resembling "café-concert performances in the open air on the terraces of casinos" (118–20). This is precisely a vision of infinite and incessant cultural appropriation, in which not only the histrionic variety of the past but even "the joy that will shake men for another century" is spread out to be "sampled" by an imagined audience who combine the evident privileges of wealth and the self-congratulatory complacency of a bohemian avant-garde.

Marinetti's familiar attack on the cultural authority of representational theater is, however, but the ironic counterpart of an equally familiar vision of the histrionic process, one based on a singularity of power and control. Futurist performance, he asserts, has "no masters" (116), yet it will dramatize "the omnipotence of a methodical will" (119); futurist performance disparages "the robot-like monotony" of the "inner life" and yet is meant to "mechanize sentiment" (119–20). Moreover, futurist theater will celebrate what Marinetti calls "the rapacious spirits" of man while it "snatches every veil from woman" and "brings to light [her] marvelous animal qualities, her grasp, her powers of seduction" (118). One notices the subtle shift of figural meaning in which an almost explicit image of rape becomes an image of the voyeur or pimp exhibiting a female body, which in this exhibition reaches out to grasp or seduce the viewer. This image of the rapist-male and the seducer-female, an essentialism that remains familiar in certain modes of contemporary discourse, is the counterpart, on the level of gender, of a dramatic

[42] Filippo Marinetti, *Selected Writings*, ed. R. W. Flint, trans. R. W. Flint and Arthur A. Coppotelli (New York: Farrar, Straus & Giroux, 1972), 116–117, 119. Subsequent citations are given parenthetically in the text.

theory that attacks the mere "psychology" of "conventional theater" only to exalt what Marinetti calls "the authority of instinct" (120).

Marinetti's vision of an anarchic Variety Theater nonetheless controlled by some mysterious omnipotent "will" provides the theoretical background for the futurist experimentation with kinetic stages and performing objects.[43] In the early years of the futurist movement, Marinetti and his colleagues began staging outrageous quasi-theatrical events with readings, exhibits of futurist art, and short dramatic sketches or scenes. These scenes, called *sintesi* or "synthetic" plays, sometimes were radically condensed and schematic versions of conventional dramatic narratives (which thus reveal the indirect influence of Maeterlinck and symbolist drama); and sometimes employed light, color, and mechanical effects to reach toward a wholly nonrepresentational form of theater. In the years just following the First World War, futurists such as Fortunato Depero and Enrico Prampolini staged several performances at the Teatro dei Piccoli, a marionette theater in Rome. The *Plastic Dances*, designed and choreographed by Depero in 1918, featured exotic marionettes and a large wooden puppet referred to as "the great Savage," whose belly opened at one point to reveal other smaller puppets dancing within.[44] Such a spectacle would seem to realize Marinetti's vision, in the "Variety Theatre" manifesto, of "fantastic pregnancies that give birth to objects and weird mechanisms" (118), and, more generally, to recall the anxieties about corporeal reproduction that periodically emerge in the writings of both Marinetti and his symbolist "masters."[45] In one essay Marinetti "confesses," as he puts it, that "we strong futurists have felt ourselves suddenly detached from women [and] have even dreamed of one day being able to create a mechanical son, the fruit of pure will, a synthesis of all the laws that science is on the brink of discovering" (75). Here, betraying that ancient habit of thought which has so often linked the theater to specifically feminine modes of corporeality, Marinetti imagines the same "will" that represents itself in futurist theater as reproducing itself in some vague form of mechanical parthenogenesis.

At the same time, Depero and Prampolini also produced several theoreti-

---

[43] Even in plays written before the founding of the futurist movement, Marinetti had revealed a familiar symbolist fascination with the puppet. His play *Le Roi Bombance*, for example, was a near parody of *Ubu Roi*, and was staged in 1909 at the same theater where Jarry's famous work had been performed; and his *Poupées électriques* of the same year depicts the manufacture of mechanical people. See Kirby and Kirby, *Futurist Performance*, 13, 92; also R. W. Flint's introduction to Marinetti, *Selected Writings*, 10.

[44] Kirby and Kirby, *Futurist Performance*, 105–10.

[45] Marinetti refers to the symbolists as his "masters" and "glorious intellectual fathers" even while "abjuring" their influence (*Selected Works*, 66).

cal texts that similarly indulge in elaborate utopian fantasies about a fully mechanized theater. "*The stage must be completely redone and amplified in all electrical and mechanical senses*," wrote Depero in 1916, "in order that every intention of the artist can be rendered feasible."[46] The logic of this vision—suggesting a theater that might be "played" like an instrument by a single artist—would also quickly lead the futurists toward the ideas of Gordon Craig, with whom some of them had been corresponding, and who had re-printed Marinetti's manifesto "The Variety Theater" in *The Mask* in January 1914. Prampolini, in his own manifesto "Futurist Scenography" (1915), ac-knowledges the influence of Craig in the process of going even one step fur-ther in the same theoretical direction. He agrees with Craig that "human actors will no longer be tolerated," but neither will the "supermarionettes recommended by recent reformers." Prampolini calls instead for a theater of "vibrations, luminous forms," and "exhilarant, explosive gases." Perfor-mance must be reduced to these improbable and unimaginable "actor gases" (a term that painfully suggests the trenches of a world war just ended and the death camps of the war to come) because, he argues, only such inanimate vehicles of performance can "express the soul of the character conceived by the author" or "the multiple aspects conceived by the playwright."[47] Pram-polini reaches, as it were, the very bottom of the hierarchy of representation in a theater of formless materiality, only to reaffirm, finally, a hypothetical author whose histrionic power is but the aesthetic mirror of domination itself.

Both Craig and the futurists demanded a hierarchical theater absolutely con-trolled by an author-creator even as they paradoxically called for a theater freed from the dramatic text. Thus, both Craig's hypothetical über-mari-onettes and the futurist mechanical stages radicalized the very concept of a theological theater, whose earlier advocates (as I have suggested throughout) combined a logocentric privileging of the word with a corresponding subor-dination of paratheatrical (and popular) modes of performance. In the par-ticular modernist tradition I am sketching here, the extralinguistic aspects of performance—movement, light, sound, and so forth—became the domi-nant techniques of a hypothetical theater whose central figure would no

[46] Kirby and Kirby, *Futurist Performance*, 207. Compare Marinetti's manifesto "The Futurist Syn-thetic Theater," which concludes by anticipating performances in a "great metal building . . . enlivened by all the electromechanical inventions that alone will permit us to realize our most free conceptions on the stage" (*Selected Works*, 129).
[47] Kirby and Kirby, *Futurist Performance*, 203–6.

longer be the literal and literary author but instead the *manipulator* of a unified and technologized theatrical instrument.

The practical implications of this theoretical approach were further pursued in the stage workshops of the Bauhaus, the celebrated and influential art school founded by Walter Gropius in 1919 in Weimar, Germany. Gropius's initial vision for the Bauhaus was preeminently one of artistic unity and community, an ideal he hoped to manifest in the school's curriculum, in the relation between its "masters" and students, and in the character of its products. Such unity would therefore be both aesthetic and social. In various texts from the school's first few years, for example, Gropius called enthusiastically for the cooperation of "architects, painters and sculptors" in a "collective work of art," and also for "a new guild of craftsmen without the class distinctions that raise an arrogant barrier between craftsman and artist!"[48] Correspondingly, Gropius argued that "theatrical performance, which has a kind of orchestral unity, is closely related to architecture," for in both "a multitude of artistic problems form a higher unity with a life of its own."[49] The underlying assertion of authorial control, which can be seen in subsequent Bauhaus dramatic theory, is thus a deeply paradoxical by-product of an aesthetic theory otherwise dedicated to collectivity, both in theory and in practice, both among artists and in works of art.

The central figure of Bauhaus theater was Oskar Schlemmer, who joined the school's staff in 1921 as a sculpture master, but who soon organized a stage workshop with Gropius's encouragement.[50] Schlemmer's most celebrated productions were dancelike, nonnarrative performances that featured both human actors wearing what he described as "padded fabrics and rigid plastic configurations" (*Triadic Ballet*), and "metallic figures" that "float, soar, rotate, whir, rattle, speak or sing" (*Figural Cabinet*).[51] In his major theoretical statements from the same years, as Gropius puts it, Schlemmer "transformed into abstract terms of geometry or mechanics his observation of the human figure moving in space" (8). Schlemmer also positioned this quasi-scientific project in a diagrammatic hierarchy of cultural and historical distinction (see

---

[48] Walter Gropius, "Program of the Staatliche Bauhaus in Weimar" (1919), reprinted in Hans M. Wingler, *The Bauhaus* (Cambridge: MIT Press, 1978), 31; idem, "The Theory and Organization of the Bauhaus" (1923), in *Bauhaus: 1919–1928*, ed. Herbert Bayer, Walter Gropius, and Ise Gropius (Boston: Charles T. Branford, 1952), 23.

[49] Bayer, Gropius, and Gropius, *Bauhaus*, 29.

[50] Walter Gropius, ed., *Theater of the Bauhaus* (Middletown, Conn.: Wesleyan University Press, 1961), 8.

[51] Both productions were first performed in 1922; for these descriptions, see Wingler, *The Bauhaus*, 363; and Gropius, *Theater of the Bauhaus*, 42. Unless otherwise identified, all subsequent citations of Bauhaus writings are from the latter book and are given parenthetically in the text.

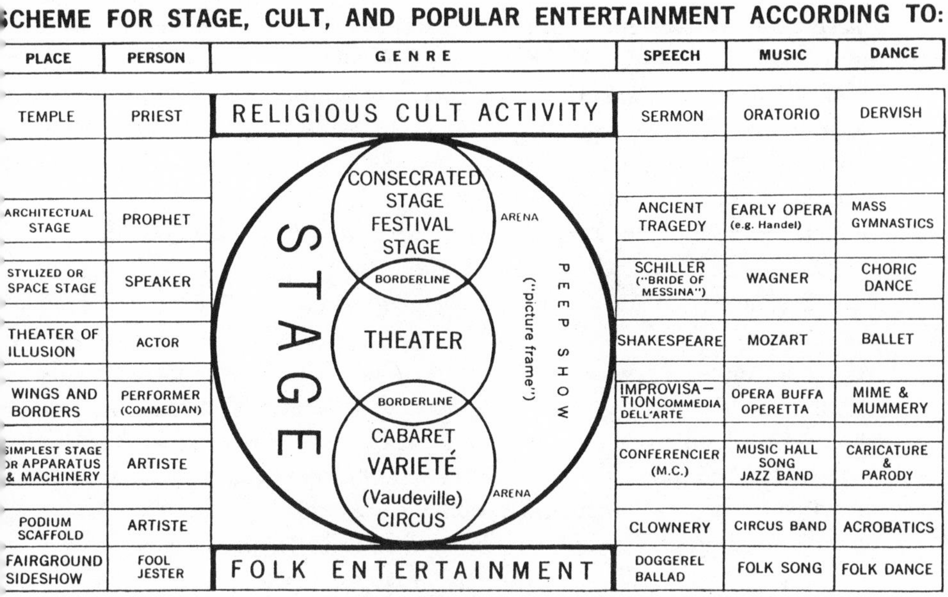
SCHEME FOR STAGE, CULT, AND POPULAR ENTERTAINMENT ACCORDING TO:
PLACE
PERSON
GENRE
SPEECH
MUSIC
DANCE
TEMPLE
PRIEST
RELIGIOUS CULT ACTIVITY
SERMON
ORATORIO
DERVISH
ARCHITECTURAL STAGE
PROPHET
CONSECRATED STAGE FESTIVAL STAGE
ARENA
ANCIENT TRAGEDY
EARLY OPERA (e.g. Handel)
MASS GYMNASTICS
STYLIZED OR SPACE STAGE
SPEAKER
BORDERLINE
SCHILLER ("BRIDE OF MESSINA")
WAGNER
CHORIC DANCE
THEATER OF ILLUSION
ACTOR
STAGE
THEATER
PEEP SHOW
("picture frame")
SHAKESPEARE
MOZART
BALLET
WINGS AND BORDERS
PERFORMER (COMMEDIAN)
BORDERLINE
IMPROVISA-TION COMMEDIA DELL'ARTE
OPERA BUFFA OPERETTA
MIME & MUMMERY
SIMPLEST STAGE OR APPARATUS & MACHINERY
ARTISTE
CABARET VARIETÉ (Vaudeville) CIRCUS
ARENA
CONFERENCIER (M.C.)
MUSIC HALL SONG JAZZ BAND
CARICATURE & PARODY
PODIUM SCAFFOLD
ARTISTE
CLOWNERY
CIRCUS BAND
ACROBATICS
FAIRGROUND SIDESHOW
FOOL JESTER
FOLK ENTERTAINMENT
DOGGEREL BALLAD
FOLK SONG
FOLK DANCE

Figure 8. Oskar Schlemmer's "Scheme for Stage, Cult, and Popular Entertainment," from "Man and Art Figure." Adapted from *Die Bühne im Bauhaus* (Munich: Albert Langen Verlag, 1925).

Figure 8). In this conception "theater" itself has a mediate position between what Schlemmer calls "religious cult activity" at the top and "folk entertainment" at the bottom, so that, as he puts it, "between cult and theater lies 'the stage seen as moral institution'; between theater and popular entertainment lie variety (vaudeville) and circus, the stage as an institution for the artiste" (18–19). As Schlemmer's detailed diagram makes clear, his vision of theatrical history is one of universal appropriation, a process at once diachronic and synchronic, in which a master genre of theater constantly absorbs the aura of the high and the vitality of the low. Schlemmer's "stage" partakes at once of (primitive) religious ritual (compare Craig's mystic "ceremonies") and the (primitive) histrionic forms of carnival and marketplace (compare the futurist "Variety Theatre"). Gropius similarly designed a "synthetic total theater" in 1926, which he claimed could unite in one building the "arena" (which Schlemmer associates with both high and low, the "consecrated stage" and the vaudeville or circus), the Greek proscenium theater, and the modern "deep" (or "picture frame") stage (12–14). Thus, the ideal of "aesthetic unity" to which both Gropius and Schlemmer remained committed appears to have required a revision of the conventional cultural hierarchy: a subordination not of the low to the high but of both extremes to a vital center. But if Bauhaus theater is thus conceptualized as mediate (as opposed to high), the theoretical system itself nevertheless privileges the supposed cultural efficacy of such mediation and unity, whose products presumably transcend the historical categories from which they emerge.[52]

In Schlemmer's major theoretical statement "Man and Art Figure," even the title announces the text's participation in the continuing modernist conversation about the actor and the object. Schlemmer's strategy in this text is reminiscent of Craig's in that he alternately pursues a speculative fantasy about a purely objective theater and pulls back into more practical efforts to systematize the human actor. His initial vision is of a theater of "linear, flat or plastic forms," of "fluctuating, mobile space" and "transformable architectonic structures." This purely abstract theater, he frankly admits, "would constitute—theoretically—the *absolute* visual stage. Man, the animated being, would be banned from view in this mechanistic organism. He would stand as 'the perfect engineer' at the central switchboard, from where he would direct this feast for the eyes" (22). Schlemmer's authorial figure is neither the producer of the text nor even a conventional director but a literal "engineer" who presides over a theater otherwise purged of "animated being."

In the pages that immediately follow this rigorous vision, Schlemmer retreats briefly into more practical remarks about movement and costume, revealing the influence of, for example, Meyerhold's "biomechanics" and other contemporary efforts to systemize the art of acting along scientific lines.[53] But soon he returns to the idea of the performing object, in remarks that

[52] Gropius's initial statements to the Bauhaus community were explicitly utopian. See, for example, his frequently cited address to students in July 1919, in which he imagined a "cathedral of the future" that would "shine with its abundance of light into the smallest objects of everyday life." Although "we will not live to see the day," he told his students, "we are. . . . the precursors and first instruments of such a new, universal idea" (Wingler, *The Bauhaus*, 36).

[53] On biomechanics, see Vsevolod Meyerhold, *Meyerhold on Theatre*, trans. Edward Braun (New York: Hill & Wang, 1969); Joseph R. Roach, *The Player's Passion: Studies in the Science of Acting* (Newark: University of Delaware Press, 1985), 202–4; and Marvin Carlson, *Theories of the Theatre: A Historical and Critical Survey from the Greeks to the Present* (Ithaca: Cornell University Press, 1984), 356–59. Meyerhold's well-known essay "The Fairground Booth" defends the histrionic efficacy of paratheatrical and popular modes of performance such as the puppet and the mask, and in so doing has obvious affinities with the theoretical work I am discussing here.

concede his debt to the theoretical tradition I have been sketching. He cites both Kleist and Craig as exemplars of a continuing "endeavor to free man from his physical bondage and to heighten his freedom of movement beyond his native potential," an endeavor that will eventually result "in substituting for the organism the mechanical human figure (*Kunstfigure*): *the automaton or marionette.*" Kleist's Mr. C., one recalls, had made his highest theoretical claims for a hypothetical marionette that "a mechanic" might construct "according to his specific requirements"—by using, for example, the "mechanical legs that English craftsmen manufacture for hapless accident victims" (212–13). A century later Schlemmer claims, in effect, to unite Mr. C. (the artist and theorist) with this hypothetical mechanic (the technological craftsman), asserting that, for the theater, "possibilities are extraordinary in light of today's technological advances: precision machinery, scientific apparatus of glass and metal, the artificial limbs developed by surgery, the fantastic costumes of the deep sea diver and the modern soldier, and so forth" (28). The performing object will thus be the terminal destination for all the resources of scientific, medical and military technology, and this technology in turn becomes both cause and counterpart of the performing object's newly refurbished cultural status: "The artificial human figure (*Kunstfigure*) permits any kind of movement and any kind of position for as long a time as desired. It also permits—an artistic device from the periods of greatest art—a variable relative scale for figures: important ones can be large, unimportant ones small" (29). Here again Schlemmer inscribes the sheer mechanical efficiency of the performing object as a particular value within an assumed multihierarchical system in which literal magnitude and aesthetic distinction similarly conjoin.

A few years later, in a public lecture to a group of "Friends of the Bauhaus" after the school moved to Dessau in 1925, Schlemmer speculated about "plays whose 'plots' consist of nothing more than the pure movement of forms, color and light," and a theater "without human involvement of any sort (except for the man at the control panel)." In an extraordinary passage Schlemmer first projects this wholly abstract, mechanized stage, and then seems, in a sort of momentary rhetorical suspension of disbelief, to go one step further, envisioning a theater purged not only of the literal author, but even of the engineer-director, and perhaps even of the audience:

Today's technology already has the necessary apparatus. It is a question of money—and, more importantly, a question as to how successfully such a technical expenditure can meet the desired effect. How long, that is, can any rotating, vibrating, whirring contrivance, together with an infinite variety of forms, colors, and lights, sustain the interest of the spectator? The question, in short, is whether the purely mechanical stage can be accepted as an independent genre, and whether, in the long run, it will be able to do without that being who would be acting here solely as the "perfect machinist" and inventor, namely, the *human* being. (88)

Two different visions, each an absolute terminus of a particular line of theoretical speculation, seem to face each other: on the one hand, a solipsistic, authorial theater in which an individual consciousness plays what Gropius would later call "a great keyboard for light and space" (12); on the other, a theater existing, as it were, in and for itself, a sort of perpetual motion machine against whose "infinite variety"[54] both creator and spectator would necessarily be found wanting.

The Object of Signification: Vitalism, Semiotics, and the Puppet

> The human intellect feels at home among inanimate objects.
> —Henri Bergson, *Creative Evolution*

In a series of lectures on Shakespearean tragedy delivered at Trinity College, Cambridge, in 1946–47, H. B. Charlton delivered a summary judgment on *Titus Andronicus*, Shakespeare's earliest and least-loved tragic play. "There is no inner world to it," Charlton complained. "Hence its plot is factitious; its people are mechanized puppets wearing masks of human faces, but seldom reacting even with a faint semblance of humanity."[55] The casual metaphor of character-as-puppet strikes me with a peculiar irony in the context of the modernist exaltation of the performing object. Despite a contemporaneous theatrical tradition that construed the puppet as somehow "truer" than the "debased stage realism" of human actors, most Anglo-American academic critics since the early decades of the century have retained more conventional assumptions about naturalism and verisimilitude, and have projected such assumptions onto the opposition of the player and the puppet, the actor and

---

[54] Gropius used this phrase when speaking at the Volta Congress in Rome on the "'Teatro Dramatico'" in 1935, during which he also outlined his plans for the "synthetic total theater," mentioned earlier. Gordon Craig also attended this event, along with Maeterlinck, Marinetti, and William Butler Yeats. See Craig, *Gordon Craig*, 337.

[55] H. B. Charlton, *Shakespearean Tragedy* (Cambridge: Cambridge University Press, 1948), 24.

the object. Thus L. C. Knights could observe in 1937 that the comedies of a relatively "minor" Renaissance dramatist, Thomas Middleton, offer "little more than the pleasure of a well-contrived marionette show"; and Leo Salingar could argue in 1955 that in Shakespeare's later history plays "the English people are represented concretely, no longer by means of puppets."[56] These examples of academic critical discourse, chosen almost at random, seem to suggest that the evolution of English Renaissance drama was a kind of Pinocchio story, in which the wooden, artificial puppets of the early or lesser playwrights somehow came to life in later masterpieces. The critical metaphor of the puppet is thus inevitably pejorative; it imposes on an individual career or an evolving national tradition the terms of an assumed system of aesthetic distinction. The same metaphor also conveys a certain feigned sense of liberation, suggesting that successful dramatic characters somehow break free from the conventions and techniques by which they were created to become (as Shakespeare had put it) a *living* drollery."

In this way, the puppet metaphor again reveals itself as inseparable from a representational hierarchy against which, in this case, it also stands in a relation of absolute paradox. For characters who thus "live," as one commonly puts it, also embody and manifest, precisely in this appearance of life, the guiding intentions of their authors. Consider, for further example, how in roughly the same period when Gordon Craig and others were calling for "super puppets" to reform the mere verisimilitude of the stage, George Bernard Shaw's characters were commonly attacked by reviewers (in an image eventually parodied by the author) as "mere puppets stuck up to spout Shaw."[57] Whereas dramatic characters are dismissed as puppetlike, in the former instances because they fail to convey the intentions of their respective authors, here Shaw's characters are said to convey his intentions, as it were, not wisely but too well. Thus, the figural meaning of the puppet as tool or instrument, servant or slave, collides with the rather different meaning that underlies this recurrent critical metaphor: the puppet as inanimate, mechanical, or merely artificial. These interrelated meanings circulate between academic critics and theatrical theorists with a paradoxical (il)logic: puppets convey the illusion of freedom precisely in their "docility," or achieve a kind of presence precisely in their inevitable condition as icon, figure, or representation.

[56] L. C. Knights, *Drama and Society in the Age of Jonson* (1937; rpt. New York: Norton, 1968), 261; Leo Salingar, "The Elizabethan Literary Renaissance," in *The Age of Shakespeare*, vol. 1 of *The Pelican Guide to English Literature*, ed. Boris Ford (London: Penguin, 1955), 64.
[57] George Bernard Shaw, *Fanny's First Play* (1911), in *Complete Plays with Prefaces*, 6 vols. (New York: Dodd, Mead, 1963), 6:168.

Although the critical metaphor of the puppet seems bluntly to contradict the modernist theatrical theory discussed in the previous section, in fact both converge on the shared theoretical ground of a Bergsonian vitalism. Around the turn of the century and in the ensuing decades, Henri Bergson's philosophic critique of mechanism became one of the underpinnings of European intellectual life, including some of the writers I have been discussing here. In the 1890s Jarry had heard Bergson lecture at the Lycée Henry IV, and Jarry's puppetlike King Ubu exemplifies certain aspects of Bergson's mechanistic vision of comedy.[58] In 1928 Maeterlinck declared in an interview that Bergson was "a great writer and a great artist" and "the greatest thinker in the world."[59] Bergsonian phenomenology, with its emphasis on perception, dynamism, and intuition, shaped not only the futurist obsession with movement and speed, but also Marinetti's concept of the "will to change."[60] Just as the pejorative opposition of puppet and player seems to require a kind of teleology—an assumption that representation proceeds toward ever finer approximations of life—so the modernist theater declared itself a precursor of some vaguely utopian "theater of the future." Both visions thus resemble Bergson's "creative evolution," which (although carefully distinguished from the teleology or "finalism" of Leibniz and the Enlightenment) nevertheless suggests that biological evolution proceeds from an "original impetus of life" and always involves "at least a rudiment of choice."[61]

In another convergence of cultural reference, the puppet or "marionette" serves as the guiding metaphor of Bergson's celebrated study of theatrical comedy, Le rire (1900), a text that also interconnects the two contrasting figural meanings of the puppet which I identified a moment ago. "We laugh," Bergson concludes in a celebrated formulation, "every time a person gives us the impression of being a thing."[62] Thus, more specifically, a drawing "is generally comic in proportion to the clearness, as well as the subtleness, with which it enables us to see a man as a jointed puppet" (80), and "on stage, actors who "come and go, dance and gesticulate together" make us "distinctly think of marionettes" (83). But Bergson also argues that the function of laughter "is to intimidate by humiliating," and that "the laugher" tends

---

[58] Shattuck, The Banquet Years, 238.

[59] R. C. Grogin, The Bergsonian Controversy in France, 1900–1914 (Calgary: University of Calgary Press, 1988), 43.

[60] Tisdall and Bozzolla, Futurism, 21–22.

[61] Henri Bergson, Creative Evolution, trans. Arthur Mitchell (1911; rpt. New York: Modern Library, 1944), 107.

[62] Henri Bergson, "Laughter" (1900), in Comedy, ed. Wylie Sypher (1956; rpt. Baltimore: Johns Hopkins University Press, 1980), 97. Subsequent citations are given parenthetically in the text.

"to look upon another's personality as a marionette of which he pulls the strings" (188–89). The comic effect is at once spectatorial and authorial, stemming either from a peception of the body as mechanized and puppetlike or from an impulse of specifically social power and domination directed at an Other. This ambiguity permits the Bergsonian position to influence or produce, as it does in the previous examples, what appear to be entirely different modes of discourse: either the organicism of academic critics or the triumphant mechanism of the early modernists.

I am suggesting with these disparate observations that certain habits of thought manifest in twentieth-century theatrical theory and practice also emerge from the critics and philosophers who influenced or commented on that tradition. The fact that puppet theater has, until recently, attracted relatively little serious theoretical interest while continuing to serve as a pejorative standard of reference obviously also reflects and confirms the puppet's continuing cultural subordination. Performing objects were, however, a central topic of interest in one particular theoretical tradition of the last half century: the structural semiotics pioneered by the so-called Prague Linguistic Circle, a group of linguists and literary critics who first formed a loose association in the 1920s to advance a functionalist model for linguistic phenomena and verbal art. In the 1930s and later, members of the Circle pioneered a specifically theatrical semiotics which continues to exert a narrow but distinct influence on contemporary dramatic theory, and found in the puppet a particularly useful subject for analysis.[63] For the Prague critics, in fact, the performing object would serve as an irreplaceable conceptual link within a systematic and totalizing vision of signification, extending from the essential duality of signifier and signified to the larger "codes" or "systems" that govern particular signifying practices. Inside the bounds of the theatrical experience, the puppet offered itself up for analysis as a "pure" signifier free from the excess signifying content of the human actor's biological and psychological life. As Jiri Veltrusky writes, in a retrospective essay written many decades after the Prague school's pioneering work, the actor "oscillates between being a sign, that is, a reality standing for another reality, and being a reality in its

---

[63] On the Prague school, see Victor Erlich, *Russian Formalism: History-Doctrine*, 3d ed. (The Hague: Mouton, 1969), 154–60; and Peter Steiner, "The Roots of Structuralist Esthetics," in *The Prague School: Selected Writings, 1929–1946*, ed. Peter Steiner (Austin: University of Texas Press, 1982), 174–219. On the theatrical semiotics of the Prague school, see Keir Elam, *The Semiotics of Theatre and Drama* (London: Methuen, 1980), 5–10. For a recent example of a formalist and semiotic approach to puppet theater, see Steve Tillis, *Toward an Aesthetics of the Puppet: Puppetry as a Theatrical Art* (Westport, Conn.: Greenwood Press, 1992).

own right"; but, conversely, "the puppet is a pure sign because all its components are intentional."[64] This theoretical privileging of the puppet as "pure sign" reveals an obvious affinity with the modernist distrust of the human actor's "intrusive" personality and also corresponds, on the hypothetical level of signification itself, to nineteenth-century scholarly arguments in which the puppet was viewed as the primal or originary form of theatrical performance.

In the discourse of the Prague school as a whole, the conceptual opposition of actor and puppet, animate and inanimate, expands into an intricate hierarchy encompassing the social conditions and psychological effects of performance. Otkar Zich addressed the puppet in a passage from his 1931 book *The Esthetics of Dramatic Art*, which was re-cited and discussed in a widening circle of subsequent theoretical work over the next half century. Zich postulates a basic duality in an audience's possible perception of puppet theater ("Puppets can be understood either as living people or as lifeless puppets") which will lead correspondingly to two diametrically opposed responses:

a) We may consider the puppets as puppets, i.e., we will emphasize their lifeless material. This material then is something real for us and we cannot take seriously their speech and movements, their "expressions of life"; they strike us as comic, *grotesque*. The fact that the puppets are small, that they are at least partially (in fact, in body) rigid, and that their movements are accordingly awkward, "wooden," contributes even more to their comical appearance. . . . We consider them puppets, but they want us to consider them people, and they certainly make us merry! Everyone knows that puppets really do have such an effect.

b) There is, however, another possibility. Puppets can be understood as living beings, if we emphasize their manifestations of life (movements and speech), and conceive of these expressions as real. Consciousness of the actual lifelessness of the puppets then recedes and surfaces only as a sense of something inexplicable, as a mystery evoking our wonder. In this case the puppets affect us *mysteriously*.[65]

[64] Jiri Veltrusky, "Puppetry and Acting," *Semiotica* 47.1–4 (1983): 79.
[65] Zich was not formally a member of the Prague Linguistic Circle, but he is generally conceded to be a major influence on it. I am citing his book, as yet untranslated into English, as quoted by Petr Bogatyrev in a 1937 essay reprinted as "A Contribution to the Study of Theatrical Signs," in Steiner, *The Prague School*, 58. A revised and expanded version of Bogatyrev's essay appears as "The Interconnection of Two Similar Semiotic Systems: The Puppet Theater and the Theater of Living Actors," *Semiotica* 47.1–4 (1983): 47–68.

Zich postulates a symmetry of audience response by assuming a consensus of viewers (and readers) that is manifest in the insistently repeated "we," "us," and "everyone"—a consensus otherwise contradicted, as subsequent commentators have suggested, by the basic duality itself. Zich argues that audiences respond to puppets with one of two reactions, each of which proceeds from cognition to emotion, the latter implying a certain kind of aesthetic effect:

unreal	real
inanimate (merely material)	animate (illusion of life)
grotesque and comic	mysterious and wondrous

These categories inevitably suggest a variety of the historical themes and actual instances of puppet theater considered in this book, for example, the implicit distinction between the wonder and the trick that emerges both in Plato's dialogues and in the Judaeo-Christian tradition of iconophobia; or the evident contrast between Punch and Judy and the *Kunstfigure*, between the *guignol* and the über-marionette. Zich's opposition also recalls Bergson's identification of the laughable with mechanism and materiality. But the instability of the opposition emerges even in such comparisions, for Zich's hypothetical reaction of "wonder" to a puppet performance would be merely the (temporary) product of histrionic illusion, whereas symbolist puppets were said to convey wonder precisely in their refusal to counterfeit life. Or to put it another way, the first term in the opposition as summarized in the list slips from one side to the other. We see puppets as mysterious when, in Zich's words, we "emphasize their manifestations of life . . . and conceive of these expressions as *real*"; yet we similarly conceive them as grotesque and comic when we perceive them accurately as wooden and inanimate, for then the "material . . . is something *real* for us." The terms on the left-hand side of the opposition name a viewer's "correct" apprehension of mundane reality: the puppets are actually made of inanimate matter. But the right-hand is constituted precisely by a kind of perceptual short-circuit in which (because the puppet's expressions and motions invest it with an appearance of animate life) a viewer attributes reality to the stage sign. Morever, Zich also suggests that puppets strike us as grotesque and comic because "we consider them puppets, but they *want* us to consider them people"; that is, the comic effect arises from an incongruous (and hence comic) attribution of agency to the mere stage sign. But then, here again, the reverse is also true: puppets strike one as mysterious when one attributes to them agency and life.

Now, when Petr Bogatyrev discussed Zich's opposition, both in 1937 and again nearly half a century later (in a special issue of the journal *Semiotica*, "The Semiotic Study of Puppets, Masks, and Performing Objects"), he asserted that Zich was incorrect from the point of view of a more rigidly semiotic concept of human perception. Zich's "mistake," Bogatyrev contends,

lies in failing to recognize the puppet theater as a unique system of signs: without such recognition no work of art can be perceived correctly. Everything that Zich says about puppetry can be applied to every other art: whenever we perceive artistic signs in comparison with a real thing, that is, proceeding from a real thing and not from the sign system that constitutes the work of art, we have the same impression that Zich describes. . . . Zich's basic error was that he did not recognize a separate sign system for puppets, but compared them to living actors. . . . If we consider puppet theater as equal to any other theater and, finally (like all art) as a system of signs, then the puppet will not seem funny to us.[66]

There are three "systems" implicit in Bogatyrev's argument: the basic semiotic (or, perhaps, phenomenological) system by which a human subject interprets the signs of reality itself, and the two specific systems of theater and puppetry, both of which relate to the former by a network of expectations and conventions. Thus, as Frank Proschan summarizes in introducing the special issue of *Semiotica*, we may misperceive signs "when we perceive them as objects rather than as signs, and when we perceive them as signs from one system when they are in fact signs from another system."[67] Bogatyrev suggests, in effect, that Zich fails to consider the real agency or aesthetic intention of the puppet show; that is, he treats puppets as if they simply existed, outside the institution of performance and its underlying semiotic "codes." According to Bogatyrev, a viewer "literate" only in the "sign system" of human theater will find puppet theater grotesque and comical in a manner in which it need not be to the viewer literate in the independent sign system of puppetry.

But Bogatyrev's own account seems inevitably to suggest, even as he pointedly refrains from mentioning it, a further dimension to this semiotic process of interaction between viewer and object. As Henryk Jurkowski suggests in

[66] Bogatyrev, "The Interconnection of Two Similar Semiotic Systems," 49.

[67] Frank Proschan, "The Semiotic Study of Puppets, Masks, and Performing Objects," *Semiotica* 47.1–4 (1983): 14.

yet another comment on this fundamental opposition, Bogatyrev's description really implies "the perceptions of two kinds of publics: the folk audience's perception (puppets are mysterious) and the erudite audience's perception (puppets are puppets)."[68] A semiotic system, at least with reference to drama, takes the shape of a collection of expectations shaped by custom, education, and experience, and so the response of different social classes to the same performance may (presumably) vary. Jurkowski thus claims that Zich's basic perceptual oppositions and Bogatyrev's systemization of them correspond to analogous oppositions of social subject and object: high and low forms of performance, and erudite and folk audiences. Therefore the set of oppositions might be extended as follows:

unreal   real
grotesque and comic   mysterious and wonderous
erudite audience   folk audience

But it should be obvious how this set of correspondences betrays a similar instability, and does justice to the response of neither hypothetical audience. For it is precisely the grotesque and carnivalesque mode of theater and puppetry that, both in historical practice and in the Bakhtinian tradition of cultural critique, is associated with folk or popular culture. Moreover, as the celebrated director Peter Brook suggests, forms of performance considered popular typically speak "a very sophisticated and stylish language: a popular audience usually has no difficulty in accepting inconsistencies of accent and dress, or in darting between mime and dialogue, realism and suggestion."[69] And as even Brook's remark (and his own theater) exemplifies, the supposed naïveté or purity of popular performance is often considered, as I have repeatedly observed, an aesthetic asset susceptible to appropriation by the literary drama.

I have lingered on this particular theoretical conversation to suggest how the semiotic concept of system, which Bogatyrev anchors on the opposition of puppetry and acting, inevitably devolves into a cultural hierarchy whose categories (aesthetic effect or audience response) thoroughly interpenetrate each other. The recognition that high and low audiences are no more distinct than the abstract cognitive responses of real and unreal evidently decon-

[68] Henryk Jurkowski, "Transcodifications of the Sign Systems of Puppetry," *Semiotica* 47.1–4 (1983): 124.
[69] Peter Brook, *The Empty Space* (New York: Atheneum, 1968), 67.

structs the notion of semiotic system (as Jacques Derrida has argued about the semiotic sign in general) "at the very moment when . . . its exigency is recognized."[70] Jurkowski, for example, insists that "puppets have belonged to many different sign systems, [which] are constituted by the relations between puppet and puppeteers or actors, thereby producing different functions of the puppet." This characteristic functionalism, revealing the continuing influence of the Prague school approach, seems headed toward a usefully relational vision of culture. In enumerating these different "systems" of puppetry, however, Jurkowski merely reinscribes a representational hierarchy even while, of course, refraining from overt aesthetic judgment: "In antiquity and the Middle Ages," he suggests, "in live theater, the puppet was a copy of an actor; in jugglers' presentation, a copy of a human being; in the storytellers' system, an illustration; and in the embryonic puppet theater, a real theatrical puppet."[71] But where could one possibly draw the line between puppet as "human being" and puppet as "actor"? When does a performing object become a *real* puppet?

Two contrasting theoretical impulses thus seem to structure the Prague school project and the work produced under its continuing influence. On the one hand, Bogatyrev's studies in Czech folklore, like Jurkowski's work on historical sign systems, begin with a salutary appreciation of culture as appropriation, a recognition that the function of cultural artifacts and practices can change when they pass "from one milieu to the other"—that is, to cite one of Bogatyrev's examples, when particular folk songs pass "from aristocratic classes and the milieu of towns to the peasantry and vice versa."[72] On the other hand, the concept of a semiotic system seems to embody a contradictory effort to reify (for analytic purposes) a distinct hierarchy of cultural production and consumption. A constant effort to understand how particular cultural practices function in specific contexts coexists with a radical leveling of cultural difference, the latter a more or less inevitable consequence of the totalizing aspirations of semiotics. "There are numerous elements that unite the diverse traditions [of puppetry]," argues Frank Proschan, and "consideration of the entire gamut can ensure the soundness of our analyses of particular traditions." But even while insisting that scholars must "avoid any definition that privileges our elite western notions of . . . puppetry,"

[70] Jacques Derrida, *Of Grammatology*, trans. Gayatri Chakravorty Spivak (Baltimore: Johns Hopkins University Press, 1976), 50.

[71] Jurkowski, "Transcodifications of the Sign Systems of Puppetry," 134.

[72] Petr Bogatyrev, "Folk Song from a Functional Point of View" (1936), in *Semiotics of Art: Prague School Contributions*, ed. Ladislav Matejka and Irwin R. Titunik (Cambridge: MIT Press, 1976), 31.

Proschan and his fellow essayists seem unavoidably to instantiate just such a perspective in the way traditions relentlessly categorized as "elite" or "exotic," "classical" or "contemporary," "folk" or "avant-garde" are yoked by violence together into a mastering, quasi-scientific discourse.[73]

The semiotic project as a whole, as Derrida suggests, and as the semiotic study of puppetry illustrates with a particular clarity, is inextricably bound up in a metaphysics of presence which reveals its interconnection with the theological model of theatrical authorship. Proschan explicitly refers to Plato's allegory of the Cave as "protosemiotic," and suggests that Plato's vision of reality as a kind of puppet show consisting of "shadows . . . twice removed from natural things" is a paradigm of the semiotic project.[74] Correspondingly, the most widely accepted of all Prague school concepts, particularly by students of drama, is the idea that all vehicles of performance are "signs of signs," secondary versions of the (already double) signs that constitute human experience in general. In one essay Bogatyrev yet again anchors this quintessential semiotic concept on the opposition between the puppet and the actor. "In the puppet theatre," he writes, "an actor does not exist as a live person," and therefore "the movements of the puppet actor are pure sign of sign."[75] One need only compare such an argument to Veltrusky's apparently similar but ultimately quite different assertion, cited earlier, that the puppet is "a pure sign because all its components are *intentional*" (emphasis added). The semiotic attempt to systematize representation finally reproduces the conceptual ambiguity whose consequences I have been tracing throughout: the puppet is the paradigm of both secondariness and authorial intention, offering at once a confirming example of the supposed representational descent from "truth" to embodiment and the possibility of a "pure" vehicle for the authorial voice. Semiotics seems inevitably to place not only the puppet but performance itself in an ontological and representational hierarchy descending from an imagined author-creator who serves, within the hypothetical space of this theological theater, as the equivalent of what Derrida has famously called a "'transcendental signified." In the terms of my argument here, the "fundamental quest" of semiotics for "a concept independent of language," a "truth" that might "exceed the chain of signs," corresponds to its (re)construction of a theater once again dominated by what Michael Is-

---

[73] Proschan, "The Semiotic Study of Puppets, Masks, and Performing Objects," 4–7; all these adjectives appear in Proschan's text.

[74] Ibid., 10–11.

[75] Petr Bogatyrev, "Semiotics in the Folk Theater" (1938), in Matejka and Titunik, *Semiotics of Art*, 48.

sacharoff calls "a Superspeaker (the playwright)" whose voice fills "speaking bodies" and makes them "literally his spokesmen."[76]

I conclude this brief excursion into literary theory by considering one more semiotic approach to the performing object which recapitulates, even as it attempts to transcend, the theoretical themes surveyed throughout this chapter and this book. Roland Barthes was evidently fascinated by the tradition of Japanese puppetry known as Bunraku, which he addressed in his essay "Leçon d'écriture," first published in *Tel Quel* in the summer of 1968, and then reprinted in slightly different form in his book about Japan, *L'empire des signes*, two years later. In this text Barthes once again discovers a particular kind of performing object that surpasses mere naturalism and evades the belittling materiality of the Western bourgeois body. Bunraku consists, as Barthes describes it, of nearly life-sized puppets "worked by three men who remain in view" while musicians and narrators at the side "*express the text.*"[77] By thus clearly distinguishing among the three separate aspects (or what Barthes calls "writings") of the performance—that is, "the marionette, the manipulator, the vociferator; the effected gesture, the effective gesture, the vocal gesture"—Bunraku foregrounds "the continuity of codes" and frees the stage "from the metonymical contagion of voice and gesture, soul and body, which entangles our actors" (175, 177). This argument has obvious affinities with other modernist approaches to the theater. When, for example, Barthes asserts that the body of "the (naturalistic) Western actor" is always "subject to a kind of gymnastic drill," and therefore "it is the actor who is a marionette," he sounds remarkably like Gordon Craig, who also complains about actors enslaved by their "riotous" personalities and envisions a fantastic Oriental metapuppet. More specifically, as Barthes himself eventually declares, there is an "evident kinship" between Bunraku as thus described and "the distancing effect recommended by Brecht" (177)—an effect, by the way, which Brecht himself had similarly discovered in an alien tradition, the Chinese theater. But Barthes's emphasis is clearly rather different from Brecht's. Whereas, for the latter, theatrical "alienation" was a political act, intended "to free socially-conditioned phenomena from that stamp of familiarity which protects them against our grasp,"[78] for Barthes

<hr>

[76] Jacques Derrida, *Positions*, trans. Alan Bass (Chicago: University of Chicago Press, 1981), 19–20; Michael Issacharoff, *Discourse as Performance* (Stanford: Stanford University Press, 1989), 3, 9.

[77] Roland Barthes, "Leçon d'écriture," *Tel Quel* 34 (Summer 1968): 28–33; reprinted as "Lesson in Writing," in *Image, Music, Text*, trans. Stephen Heath (New York: Farrar, Straus & Giroux, 1974), 170. All further citations are from the latter edition and are given parenthetically in the text.

[78] Bertolt Brecht, "Alienation Effects in Chinese Acting," in *Brecht on Theatre*, ed. John Willett (New

the effect of Bunraku is preeminently metaphysical, and consists of a radical deconstruction of the ontological (and theological) assumptions which he declares to underlie Western performance.

Barthes's initial essay on Bunraku was published only months before his celebrated proclamation of "la mort de l'auteur," and his refusal, in the essay of that name, to ascribe to texts any "single 'theological' meaning."[79] Here, as against a Western theater that also locates itself in a "theological space" (173), Barthes declares that "Bunraku practices neither the dissimulation nor the emphatic disclosure of its various mechanisms, hence ridding the animation of the actor of any suggestion of the sacred and abolishing the metaphysical bond that the West cannot stop itself from setting up between soul and body, cause and effect, motor and machine, agent and actor, Fate and man, God and creature" (174). Even the Western puppet—exemplified by Punch ("le polichinelle")—Barthes declares to be a merely a fetishistic reduction of the human body: a "part," a "little thing," the very paradigm of self-division. No longer the metaphysical salvation of Western theater (as it had been for other modern theorists), the puppet, in Barthes's analysis, resumes its historical subordination as a figure of the miniature, of the material, of figurality itself. By contrast Barthes postulates a continuum extending from the Bunraku to "the modern text," with its "stressing of codes, discontinuous observations," and "anthropological gestures" (178). But such a continuum exists neither in Japanese culture nor in any "facts" of literary cause and effect, but only when Barthes declares it, in the act of cultural appropriation constituted by his essay. Barthes virtually admits as much in the preamble to *L'empire des signes*, in a striking passage that, except for its cross-cultural emphasis, might stand as the very epigraph for appropriation as I have described it in this book: "The Orient simply provides me with a stock of features whose formality and invented play allow me to 'caress' the idea of an unheard of symbolic system entirely separate from our own."[80] Japanese culture in general, and Bunraku in particular, escape from the imprisoning chain of (Western) signifiers and the theological theater, but only as a wholly

York: Hill & Wang, 1964), 91–99.

[79] Roland Barthes, "La mort de l'auteur," first published in *Mantéia* 5 (Fall 1968), is cited from *Image, Music, Text* (146).

[80] Roland Barthes, *L'empire des signes* (Geneva: Skira, 1993), 10; I am citing the translation by Steven Ungar in *Roland Barthes: The Professor of Desire* (Lincoln: University of Nebraska Press, 1983), 51. The book as a whole has been published in English as *The Empire of Signs*, trans. Richard Howard (New York: Hill & Wang, 1982).

imaginary form of cultural otherness—that is, as appropriated, "caressed," mastered, and reinscribed in Barthes's own text.

"No Strings on Me": From *Pinocchio* to the Muppets

> A boy who won't be good
> Might just as well be made of wood.
>
> —Walt Disney's *Pinocchio*

Various accounts of puppet theater from the sixteenth to the nineteenth centuries, some of them cited in this book, make clear that its audiences encompassed the full spectrum of society, in terms of both class and age. Today, however, at least in the English-speaking world, puppetry is generally considered a form of performance for children. True enough, an association of the child and the puppet has always lurked in the margins of discourse and cultural practice, for example, in the etymological link between the puppet and the doll, or in the figural momentum with which both puppets and children evoke the abstract ideas of diminution and the miniature.[81] But a broad shift has occurred in the production and reception of actual puppet performance, a shift that begins, perhaps, when the Punch-and-Judy show moved into London drawing rooms and nurseries and continues to the present day, when almost everyone except puppeteers themselves assumes that all puppet theater is children's theater. Contemporary puppeteers with whom I have spoken frequently complain that however loudly they declare the aesthetic legitimacy of a "theater of objects," however erotic or political or avant-garde their announced subject matter, and however clearly they request an adult audience, parents still bring children to any performance advertised as including puppets. One puppeteer declared to me sadly that just as children's theater seems doomed to remain a small and subordinate branch of theater, so adult puppetry seems doomed to remain an even smaller and correspondingly subordinate branch of puppetry. Not even the most relentless efforts of aesthetes and theorists to reclaim the performing object as an autonomous

---

[81] As Susan Stewart suggests, the child frequently serves as a paradigmatic image or metaphor of the miniature "not simply because the child is in some physical sense a miniature of the adult, but also because the world of childhood, limited in physical scope yet fantastic in its content, presents in some ways a miniature and fictive chapter in each life history." See Susan Stewart, *On Longing: Narratives of the Miniature, the Gigantic, the Souvenir, the Collection* (Baltimore: Johns Hopkins University Press, 1984), 44.

form of theatrical art seem likely soon to break the peculiar link between the puppet and the child that prevails in contemporary culture.

The theorists of the Prague school, whom I discussed briefly in the previous section, attempted to explain this particular cultural phenomenon as a consequence of semiotic systemization. "The signs of puppet theater predominate," writes Petr Bogatyrev, "precisely when there is an audience of children, and therefore puppet theater achieves maximum expressiveness with this audience." Conversely, "with adult audiences, the signs of theater with live actors dominate the perception of puppet theater, so that this audience is incapable of understanding all its devices."[82] Or, to put it more simply, children tend to perceive puppets as convincingly "real," while adults tend to compare the puppet to the human actor and therefore remain conscious of the former's representational inadequacy. Such an argument, however, simply reifies a culturally conditioned hierarchy of perception as a biological "fact," whereas children are evidently presented with the "codes" and "systems" of representation, and are born into a social world in which certain practices have already been designated as childish or mature, simple or sophisticated. Thus, the prevailing cultural subordination of the puppet on the basis of age (instead of class) has its own ideological charge, and it continues to reflect a master cultural hierarchy precisely in the way it links constructed social distinctions to the "natural" limitations of youthful perception. I will accordingly argue that this transformation of a low or popular practice into an institutionalized theater for children, a theater which then explodes (by means of new media such as film and television) into a truly mass culture, represents a kind of extreme version of cultural appropriation. Puppets no longer figure within social struggles merely as a rubric or metaphor of the culturally Other, but now directly participate in a process of bourgeois education that takes place in part within what Theodor Adorno and Max Horkheimer half a century ago famously called a "culture industry." In America today a child's exposure to puppet theater—which he or she may well encounter only as filmed or taped, and thus as a secondary representation of itself—becomes an early step in an expected trajectory of personal growth and cultural apprehension.

At an extreme level of this process, puppets are now commonly employed in child psychotherapy, a practice that depends on classic psychoanalytic concepts such as projection and transference but also on what one study

---

[82] Bogatyrev, "Contribution to the Study of Theatrical Signs," 63.

claims is "the intimate relation of children's mentality to folklore."[83] The latter assumption is another example of how distinctions of class tend to devolve onto the child. The psychoanalytic use of the puppet may be seen, in broad historical terms, to emerge out of what Peter Burke calls the "purism" of the nineteenth-century scholarly approach to popular culture, the notion of an "instinctive" or "irrational" *Volk* who were, as such, somehow closer to the wellsprings of human experience.[84] Thus, the same qualities of the puppet that had been cited and exalted by theorists such as Gordon Craig—its universality, its ties to shamanism, its ancient folkloric roots—appear, in psychoanalytic discourse, as indexes of the puppet's privileged access to the unconscious mind. Several researchers in the 1930s, for example, experimented with puppet shows for disturbed children featuring Casper (the German version of Punch). They observe that Casper has been, since the Middle Ages, "the ideal and the hero of the masses," and accordingly "Casper's character, his tradition, and his history gave him all the qualifications to play the role in our children's ward which he now occupies."[85] More strictly psychoanalytic interpretations of puppet therapy commonly invoke the concept of psychic "projection"—that is, the "operation whereby qualities, feelings, wishes, or even 'objects' . . . are expelled from the self and located in another person or thing."[86] Even this concept, however, seems to be conditioned (as some have observed about psychoanalysis in general) by the classical metaphor of "in-spiration" and the discursive structures of the theological theater.[87] One writer in a 1977 collection on puppet therapy remarks that "a child can completely disappear behind the guignol's (puppet's) personality, as he *enters* it completely, inhabits it, so to speak"; another writer in the same collection suggests that, while fantasizing with puppets, "the child is author, producer, stage-manager, and star actor: he is also his own and sole audience."[88] The notion that puppets provide a relatively unmediated access to the "other

---

[83] Lauretta Bender and Adolf G. Woltmann, "The Use of Puppet Shows as a Psychotherapeutic Method for Behavior Problems in Children," *American Journal of Orthopsychiatry* 6.3 (1936): 352.

[84] Peter Burke, *Popular Culture in Early Modern Europe* (New York: New York University Press, 1978), 21–22, 9.

[85] Bender and Woltman, "Use of Puppet Shows as a Psychotherapeutic Method," 342.

[86] J. Laplanche and J.-B. Pontalis, *The Language of Psycho-Analysis*, trans. Donald Nicholson Smith (New York: Norton, 1973), 349. The same writers also observe how Freud considered projection a normal psychic mechanism which also "operates in superstition, in mythology, in 'animism' " (351).

[87] On Freud's use of theatrical metaphors in general, see Philippe Lacoue-Labarthe, "Theatrum Analyticum," *Glyph* 2 (1977): 122–43.

[88] Simone Marcus, "Therapeutic Puppetry," and A. R. Philpott, "The Use of Puppets in Child Psychotherapy," both in *Puppets and Therapy*, ed. A. R. Philpott (Boston: Plays, Inc., 1977), 11, 110.

scene" of the subconscious thus reveals itself as inseparable from, or transparent with, the conceptual hierarchy of theatrical representation.

The puppets of contemporary mass culture, even more broadly, are not merely one more bourgeois appropriation of a practice whose connotations of folklore and festivity are now, in any case, little more than a scholarly memory. Today's puppets are literally tools within a complex process of cultural transmission and consumption, transacted in both literal and figural networks of intertextuality and multiple media. Puppets have always been, as I have observed, quite literally *objects*, linked by the locus of the market fair to a broad spectrum of other salable commodities. But today's puppets often exist at once as toy, performer, character, and cartoon, a crucial link in an intricate chain of consumption with which society as it were appropriates itself by endlessly constructing "proper" and "appropriate" consumers for the representations it simultaneously provides for them. In the discussion that follows, for the most part I will no longer be observing literal puppet theater at all; instead, I consider several familiar puppet characters as manifest in text, on tape, or on film, and also in their less tangible existence as cultural icons or metaphors. In figures such as Pinocchio and the Muppets, one sees both that relentless commodification which Adorno and Horkheimer describe in their critique of the culture industry, and that dialectic of ideological manipulation and utopian longing that, by extension, Fredric Jameson discovers in contemporary mass culture.[89] Even in incongruous new contexts, and even as its own literal social status turns inside out, the performing object continues to focus a range of cultural anxieties—about class, about gender, about performance itself—much as it had done for the playwrights and theorists discussed throughout this book.

In the terms of this argument it seems strikingly appropriate that the most familiar single puppet in contemporary American culture should no longer be Punch (who prevailed in both America and England throughout the nineteenth century)[90] but rather Pinocchio, the central figure in a narrative of personal maturation and a web of cross-cultural and multimedia appropriation. Carlo Collodi's famous serial novel *The Adventures of Pinocchio: Story of a Puppet* (1881–83) itself grew across the course of its composition from a simple narrative reproduction of puppet theater to what critics now agree is

[89] For these two celebrated arguments, see Theodor W. Adorno and Max Horkheimer, *Dialectic of Enlightenment*, trans. John Cumming (New York: Herder & Herder, 1972); and Fredric Jameson, "Reification and Utopia in Mass Culture," in *Signatures of the Visible* (New York: Routledge, 1992), 9–34.
[90] On Punch and Judy in America, see Paul McPharlin, *The Puppet Theatre in America: A History* (New York: Harper & Brothers, 1949), 116–55.

a quintessential nineteenth-century cautionary tale about education and the bourgeois self. The name Pinocchio evokes, as the book's recent editor and translator Nicolas J. Perella suggests, "the funny-sounding names of two of the most well-known commedia dell'arte stock characters," Arlecchino and Pulcinella—characters who are shown, in the novel, as puppets in a traveling puppet show.[91] Similarly, the novel begins by recounting how one Master Cherry and Geppetto fight over the piece of wood from which Pinocchio will shortly be made (93), a scene obviously intended to evoke the farcical combat of the *guignol* or Punch-and-Judy show. As the novel proceeds, however, it begins to evoke a series of narrative paradigms and cultural tropes, becoming at once a kind of bildungsroman, a picaresque novel, a Bunyanesque allegory, and a story of redemption about the son of a carpenter whose name is very nearly Joseph. The basic conceit of puppet-as-Everyman also recalls Plato's celebrated passage describing humanity as a "puppet made by gods," the slave of inner impulses toward good or evil, a passage that was almost certainly known to Collodi.[92] Even the novel's opening lines, in which a carpenter attempts to make a "table-leg" from a piece of wood, only to discover the wood to be mysteriously animate, seems to echo the celebrated passage in Horace in which an idol recounts, "Once I was . . . a worthless log, when the carpenter, doubtful whether to make a stool or a Priapus, chose that I be a god," a passage also cited both by the church fathers and by Renaissance Protestants in inveighing against idol worship.[93]

Collodi thus positions his book within a historically conditioned cultural hierarchy, and the novel's own cultural ascent from performance to narrative, from the popular to the bourgeois, corresponds to Pinocchio's personal journey from roguish puppet to 'ragazzino perbene' (460), meaning both "an authentic, flesh-and-blood boy" and "a well-behaved, obedient boy" (18).[94] For my argument, the particular illustrative significance of *Pinocchio* lies precisely in the way Collodi uses the "story of a puppet" (an imagined and fantastic yearning of the inanimate for the animate) as the symbolic link between a strategy of specifically *cultural* appropriation and a narrative of bourgeois self-fashioning. In the opening pages the reader first meets Gep-

[91] Nicolas J. Perella, "An Essay on *Pinocchio*," introduction to Carlo Collodi, *The Adventures of Pinocchio*, trans. Nicolas J. Perella (Berkeley: University of California Press, 1986), 480 n.24. All further citations are from this edition and are given parenthetically in the text.

[92] See Perella, "An Essay on *Pinocchio*," 4–6, 50–51.

[93] Horace, *Satires* 1.8. 1–2. The same passage is cited in Lactantius, *The Divine Institutes*, 2.4.1, and in John Calvin, *Institutes of the Christian Religion* 1.11.4.

[94] Perella cites this ambiguity ("An Essay on *Pinocchio*," 18), and translates the Italian phrase aptly as "a proper boy."

petto not even as the wood-carver he is much later said to be, but as a kind of beggar who aspires merely to the social status of itinerant puppeteer. "This morning," declares Gepetto, "an idea popped into my head. . . . I thought of making myself a fine wooden puppet; but a wonderful puppet who can dance, and fence, and make daredevil leaps. I intend to travel around the world with this puppet so as to earn my crust of bread and a glass of wine" (89). But soon, of course, Geppetto becomes Pinocchio's beloved "father," the symbolic standard to which the puppet's bad behavior is constantly referred and against which it is judged. The rest of the novel recounts Pinocchio's progress from virtual beggary to a comfortable domesticity mediated by the "magico-bourgeois" fairy, who oscillates confusingly throughout the narrative between being a potential love object, a sister, and a surrogate mother.[95]

In the beginning, Geppetto sells his coat to buy his "son" a schoolbook. Asked why he has done so, Geppetto says only that the coat "made me hot." As Collodi puts it, "Pinocchio caught the meaning of this answer at once," for "poverty . . . is understood by everyone, even by children" (135). Much later, in the long final chapter, Pinocchio goes to work as a laborer to earn the money to feed his invalid father while studying his schoolbooks in his spare time. Eventually, "by his readiness to use his wits, to work and to get ahead, [Pinocchio] was even able to put aside forty pennies to buy some nice new clothes for himself" (453–57). But even as Pinocchio, at the end, is on his way to buy the clothes that will make him look like "a wealthy gentleman" (455), he learns that the fairy has become poor and sick, and he unhesitatingly sends her the money he has saved. When his father asks him about the clothes, he replies that he "couldn't find any that fitted me well" (457). In the pointed symmetry with which Pinocchio, like Geppetto in the beginning, misrepresents his own generosity, Collodi seems to suggest the basic contradiction of the bourgeois ideology so obviously affirmed in the novel as a whole—an ideology that encompasses at once, the imperatives of community and of self, the inviolate ties of family and the impulse to social profit. Pinocchio achieves the latter by temporarily renouncing it and by learning, so to speak, both *not to* and *how to* lie. The next day Pinocchio wakes up to find

[95] For the phrase "magico-bourgeois," see ibid., 28. In the novel Pinocchio first meets someone described only as "a beautiful Little Girl with blue hair" (183) who identifies herself as a dead girl waiting for "the bier to come and take me away" (185). Then, in the beginning of the second part, Collodi now identifies the same figure as "a good Fairy who for more than a thousand years had been living near [the] forest" (191). Considerably later the fairy refers to Pinocchio as "her little brother" (257); and eventually, when she reappears in grown-up form, Pinocchio resolves to "call [her] my mother" (283).

that he was no longer a wooden puppet, but that he had turned into a boy like all other boys. He gave a look around him, and instead of the usual straw walls of the cottage, he saw a beautiful, cozy room, furnished and decorated with tasteful simplicity. Jumping out of bed, he found a fine new suit of clothes prepared for him, a new cap, and a pair of leather ankle-boots that fitted him to perfection.

As soon as he had dressed, he quite naturally put his hands in his pockets, and drew out a little ivory money-case on which these words were written: "The Fairy with blue hair returns the forty pennies to her dear Pinocchio and thanks him so much for his good heart." When he opened the money case, instead of the forty copper pennies there were forty gold pieces glittering in it, all mint new. (457–59)

The pennies transformed to gold pieces clearly recall one of Pinocchio's earlier misadventures, in which he is persuaded that if he buries his money in a "field of blessings," it will spontaneously multiply. Here at the end the "tasteful simplicity" of the room, the clothes that "fitted him to perfection," are the consequence of a social progress that echoes and underlies the more famous transformation of the wooden puppet to the "proper" boy (see Figure 9).

Since its original publication, according to Perella, "the tale has received well over a hundred complete or nearly complete translations, abridgements . . . and adaptations for the theater."[96] Today, it seems fair to claim, as did a magazine article in 1992, that "Pinocchio is the Premiere Puppet."[97] That this claim was made in terms of the puppet's value as a physical artifact for antique collectors further confirms how the famous story seems, in both its content and its reception, to describe a progress from performativity to commodification. The story does remain a staple of contemporary children's puppetry, but even there the unavoidable metadrama with which one puppet plays another, endlessly re-revealed as object or sign, curiously contradicts the story's own privileging of a "real" boyhood which is somehow other than Pinocchio's mere "life."

Among all its versions, Walt Disney's full-length cartoon *Pinocchio* (1941) is almost certainly definitive for most Americans. Thus, "Pinocchio" in its cultural totality was produced by a circular process of appropriation: moving from an observed practice (puppetry), to a text, to a so-called animation whose techniques and conventions (farcical violence, movable two-dimen-

---

[96] Ibid., 72.

[97] See *Antiques and Collecting Hobbies* 97 (August 1992).

Figure 9. Pinocchio as a "proper" bourgeois boy. From Carlo Collodi, *Le avventure di Pinocchio* (Florence, 1883). Reproduced by permission of the University of California Press from their 1986 edition, translated by Nicolas J. Perella.

sional "objects") recall the earlier forms. Disney's version also subjects Collodi's unruly and sometimes confusing narrative to a rigorous simplication and formal logic which seems to intensify its submerged ideological implications. Here a tale presented to us as a fable of infinite individual fulfillment, a utopian parable affirming that "when you wish upon a star your dreams come true," superimposes onto the child the accumulated metaphoric valence of the puppet, a figure entirely mastered by external authority. Collodi, as I have suggested, presents a Geppetto emerging from the same cultural milieu from which the book appropriates certain conventions and associations of the puppet (social trangression, farcical combat, the wooden invulnerability of the puppet-character). Pinocchio himself was always already animate, the unexpected and not entirely welcome product of an inexplicable life force latent in the wood from which he is carved. In Disney's version, by contrast, the itinerant puppeteer becomes a petit-bourgeois toymaker, his shop filled with a host of figures animated by puppet strings or clockwork machinery; and Geppetto explicitly wishes (on a star) that his newly carved marionette might be a "real boy." The Blue Fairy appears explicitly to grant this wish: "Good Geppetto," she says, "you've given so much happiness to others, you deserve to have your wish come true." One notices how the fairy stipulates that Pinocchio's animation is the consequence (and reward) of his father's personal history, even as she also pointedly effaces the social reality that presumably underlies Geppetto's fictional benevolence. For if Geppetto has made others happy, he must have done so by selling them toys; yet as far as one can see, his shop is without customers, and his craft thus seems to be a process of self-delight which the life given to Pinocchio (for his sake) merely further exemplifies. The real process of commodity exchange, inevitably suggested by Disney's transformation of the beggar to the shopkeeper, becomes an imagined and fantastic process of pure mutual gratification. Similarly, Pinocchio himself emerges from a parthenogenetic fantasy which wholly effaces the messiness of the carnal, and which also thus distantly echoes the symbolist distrust of the female body and the futurist fantasy of mechanical reproduction. "The things they can do these days!" marvels Jiminy Cricket after witnessing Pinocchio's "birth," as though the fairy's magic were simply one more of those miracles of science later to be celebrated in Disney's amusement parks.

Even before the fairy's gift of life, Geppetto had forced Pinocchio to accept his own name by manipulating his wooden head in a silent gesture of assent—a scene that seems to enact Althusser's celebrated point that when an "unborn child is expected, it is certain in advance that it will bear its Father's Name . . . [and] is therefore always-already a subject, appointed as a subject in and by the specific familial ideological configuration in which it is 'expected.' "[98] Then, in an extraordinary musical number, the "jacks" on the toy clocks in Geppetto's shop present a miniature spectacle of domination, including mechanical versions of men slaughtering animals and a woman

[98] Louis Althusser, *"Lenin and Philosophy" and Other Essays* (New York: Monthly Review Press, 1971), 176.

spanking a boy with his pants down. Richard Schickel, among others, has noted Disney's "predilection [for] jokes involving either an assault upon or the adoration of the posterior"; here, when the animate Pinocchio first attempts to walk, he immediately falls down on what Geppetto had called, in the preceding song, his "little wooden seat."[99] Such images proliferate throughout the film as if to emphasize its underlying theme of childhood discipline, providing the visual subtext for a kind of allegory depicting bourgeois subjectivity (becoming a "proper" and "appropriate" boy) as the product of parental and social domination.

Yet Disney's regularization of the story, his maintenance of a clear connection between the initial promise of "life" and its miraculous completion by way of culture, also threatens to dismantle Collodi's cautionary intentions. For in Disney's version Pinocchio must not merely be willing to work and to submit to bourgeois education, but must prove himself "brave, truthful and unselfish"—a tall moral order, one has to conclude, from a fable that also promises infinite personal fulfillment. Indeed, Pinocchio must prove himself faithful even unto death (a lesson perhaps befitting the film's appearance on the brink of America's entry into the Second World War). For Pinocchio drowns as he leads his father from the womblike belly of the whale. The fairy's final award of "real" life is not merely a transformation from puppet to boy but a veritable resurrection. In this, as in so much else, Disney seems to raise the cultural stakes of the story. Watching *Pinocchio* now, after having labored to reveal the ideological work that shapes its exquisite imagery, I find that the scene of Pinocchio's "birth" stands out with a peculiar clarity and cruelty. The Blue Fairy appears, of course, to grant Geppetto's wish that Pinocchio might be a "real boy." But when Pinocchio asks, in his first moment of consciousness, "*Am* I a real boy?" the fairy replies, "No, Pinocchio" (allowing the name to reverberate with assonant negation). "To make your father's wish come true will be entirely up to you." The Father's wish has been granted only provisionally; Pinocchio has been born to set it right. This, one must conclude, is a parable ready-made for the cold war generation who would grow up with it, as I did—a parable of infinite possibility in a world of infinite risk, a world in which bourgeois propriety in both senses of the word is always already the obstacle to the self-fulfillment it so seductively promises.

[99] Richard Schickel, *The Disney Version: The Life, Times, Art, and Commerce of Walt Disney* (New York: Simon & Schuster, 1968), 174. For other images of the posterior in *Pinocchio*, see the cancan number from the puppet show, and the scene in Stromboli's cart when Pinocchio, facing the remonstrance of the fairy, turns away from her and bends over.

I am suggesting that, precisely in giving such memorable form to the book's utopian images of bourgeois selfhood, respectability, and family, the film finds itself forced to convey the domination that underlies such values, a domination expressed in the film as an implicit system that stretches all the way from child rearing to the commodity market in which *Pinocchio* itself now figures as product. Whereas the book had affirmed a kind of "proper" capitalism rooted in the holiness of the heart's affections, the film first effaces any real perception of Geppetto (or Pinocchio) as a "real" economic agent, and then envisions capitalism itself in the form of two threatening figures who are either directly or indirectly associated with "show" business. The first of these is Stromboli, master of the grand puppet show, to whom Pinocchio is sold by J. Worthington Foulfellow (the fox) and Gideon (the cat). In the book Pinocchio merely sells his spelling book to buy a ticket to a puppet show; and the puppet master Fire-Eater, though a "huge and ugly" man with "a fearsome beard" (145), who threatens to burn the puppets to roast his mutton, nevertheless "deep down . . . wasn't a bad man" (149). In the film, by contrast, Pinocchio's first trangression stems not merely from his desire to *see* a puppet show but from his desire to *be* an "actor." In Stromboli's show Pinocchio participates in an elaborate song-and-dance act, singing, "There are no strings on me." Yet Pinocchio sings this memorable expression of freedom precisely while learning that to wander from the path of middle-class morality is scarcely to evade its imprisoning influence, and that the autonomy promised in the song is only a representation after all. After the show Stromboli counts his money and locks Pinocchio in a bird cage, saying, "To me you are belonging." Onto the itinerant "Gypsy" puppeteer, whose exaggerated Italianate accent and grotesque avarice proclaim a fantastical otherness, the film thus displaces the threat of a capitalist exploitation from which not even Pinocchio's "conscience" (Jiminy Cricket), but only the same magical intervention that brought him into the world, can rescue him.

In one more instance, the film transforms a relatively brief incident from the book into a virtual allegory of capitalism. Taking its hint from Collodi's description of a man "more wide than tall, soft and oily like a clump of butter, with a small face like a rosy apple, a little mouth that was always smiling" (359), the film invents a nameless profiteer who, in a tavern scene, offers Foulfellow and Gideon the chance to make "some real money," thus placing the mere entrepreneurial zeal of the puppet showman in its proper perspective. The profiteer's scheme, in both book and film, involves finding "lazy boys who hate books, schools, and teachers" (377) and taking them to a place called Funland ("Pleasure Island" in the film)—a sort of grand carnival with "continual amusements and games of all sorts" (369)—where they will be transformed into donkeys and sold into slavery. Both versions of the story thus repeatedly threaten to return Pinocchio to the conventional loci of puppet theater: the cart, the carnival, the fairground.[100] But the film also memorably suggests how the bland, smiling face of the anonymous profiteer conceals not only the cruelty of the fairy-tale villain but also an inexorable and mysterious institutional power. In what may be the single most frightening image of the film, he is seen supervising strange, faceless black creatures who are loading ships with crates filled with boy-donkeys, crates stamped repeatedly with the word "Sold."

That both Stromboli and the profiteer should be, in some way or other, involved with the business of entertainment seems unavoidably to direct one's attention to the film itself as cultural product and commodity. In the preceding comments I have found it impossible to avoid referring to "Disney," by a kind of metonymic shorthand, as if he were the "author" of *Pinocchio* the film. Indeed, the animated cartoon may be said to realize that dream of a virtually unmediated histrionic medium that so many of the playwrights and theorists discussed in this book have shared. "Animation is probably the ultimate 'auteurist' cinema," writes Steve Schneider, "as its directors can control every element of their films' content with a precision that extends down to the individual frame."[101] In fact, Disney's full-length cartoons were the products of an immense collaborative effort involving writers, musicians, artists, animators, and cameramen; but, as commentators have frequently noted, their packaging and marketing was designed to convey precisely the impression that Walt Disney was their sole author or artist. In the early years of his studio, Schickel remarks, "no name but Disney's ever appeared on his films," and even when he began to list the names of individual artists and animators on the later full-length features, "he carefully gave so many credits—and his name, in contrast, appeared in such very large type—that the effect was the same."[102] A little more than a year after the release of *Pinocchio*, the Screen Cartoonists Guild organized a walkout at Disney Studios. As Holly Allen and Michael Denning point out in their fascinating ac-

---

[100] Collodi pointedly includes, among the attractions of Funland, "canvas puppet theaters crowded with boys from morning to night" (367). In the book, after Pinocchio is turned into a donkey (a fate he suffers only partially in the film), he is sold "to the Manager of a circus troupe" who forces him "to jump and dance with the other animals in his company" (389).

[101] Steve Schneider, *That's All, Folks!: The Art of Warner Brothers Animation* (New York: Holt, 1988), 30.

[102] Schickel, *The Disney Version*, 190–91; on Disney's strict maintenance of ownership see ibid., 112–13.

count of the strike, "Disney's policy of crediting himself for work that was completed by a variety of artists" was the strikers' most urgent grievance.[103] Even today, however, the boxes or albums containing the restored and re-released videotape or laser disk versions of *Pinocchio* refer to it in large letters as "Walt Disney's Masterpiece"—the name, printed in simulated handwriting. suggesting not the actual corporate entity (the Walt Disney Company) but the wholly imaginary individual artist and creator.

In the most general terms, then, Disney's project is constituted by a double appropriative strategy: he produces what become familiar and virtually definitive versions of both folk and literary stories (from *Snow White* to *Pinocchio* to *Alice in Wonderland*) by means of an astonishing technique that itself involves the wholesale appropriation of numerous other artists' work. These positive forms of appropriation correspond by inversion to Disney's well-known strictness regarding the commercial rights of "his" characters and stories, a strictness the Disney organization continues to observe. As Ariel Dorfman and Armand Matterlart put it, "The man who expropriated so much from others will not countenance any kind of petty theft against himself."[104] Today, drawings and stills from films such as *Pinocchio* sell at art galleries at prices comparable to those for the work of contemporary artists, a trend that takes the process of appropriation even one step further by re-inscribing these (ephemeral and anonymous) works as certified "objects" within a bourgeois system of cultural (and market) value. In all this Disney may be considered the historical figure in whom the imperious logic of hypothetical authorship finally merges wholly with the centralizing momentum of capitalism itself, whose own logic was perhaps always visible within the former.

After the war, puppet theater reemerged as a common vehicle of children's performance in a new medium of histrionic transmission, television. By the 1950s the extraordinary success of shows such as *Howdy Doody*, Burr Tillstrom's *Kukla, Fran, and Ollie*, and many other programs featuring puppets made possible the emergence of a figure who presents the inevitable concluding example of my argument here. In 1954 the young Jim Henson was hired by a local television station in Maryland as a puppeteer on a Saturday morning program for children. Henson and Jane Nebel, later his wife,

---

[103] Holly Allen and Michael Denning, "The Cartoonists' Front," *South Atlantic Quarterly* 92.1 (Winter 1993): 93–94.

[104] Ariel Dorfman and Armand Mattelart, *How to Read Donald Duck: Imperialist Ideology in the Disney Comic*, trans. David Kunzle (New York: Internationale General, 1984), 18.

Figure 10. Jim Henson and Frank Oz manipulate Kermit and Miss Piggy while watching on TV monitors. Photograph by Murray Close and David Dagley, reproduced by permission of Jim Henson Productions.

gradually developed a stable of puppet characters they called the Muppets, who by the 1960s were well established on network television, frequently performing in commercials and on variety shows such as *Ed Sullivan, Jack Parr, The Today Show,* and many others.[105] In the late sixties Henson and the Muppets allied themselves with the Children's Television Workshop, whose innovative children's show *Sesame Street* premiered in November 1969. As commentators have noted, part of the appeal of Henson's puppets is that they were specifically designed to be seen through a camera. David Owen, writing in the *New Yorker,* explains that Henson and Nebel used soft, flexible puppets which flourished under "the intimacy of a television closeup," and they "treated the television screen itself as their theatre" by always performing with their eyes on a monitor (see Figure 10).[106] For *The Muppet Movie* (1979), the first of Henson's many successful films, he and his associates de-

---

[105] Unless otherwise noted, I base my account of Henson's career on Christopher Finch, *Jim Henson: The Works* (New York: Random House, 1993).
[106] David Owen, "Looking Out for Kermit," *New Yorker,* August 16, 1993, 31.

veloped techniques of radio and computer control which allowed what were originally glove puppet characters to appear as free-standing, independently mobile "creatures." Thus, the name Muppet might almost be translated as "media puppet." Today, after his untimely death in 1990, Jim Henson is still almost certainly the most widely known puppeteer of all time, a figure whose celebrity and cultural power invert the conventional anonymity and social subordination of puppetry in the Western tradition.

This success story, along with the extraordinary affection with which the Muppets seem to be viewed not only by the press but by nearly everyone under thirty, makes Henson a precarious subject for cultural analysis.[107] Much as Walt Disney, in the 1940s, was constructed by journals such as *Time* and the *Saturday Review* as a "hero of culture and commerce,"[108] so Jim Henson has been constructed by today's media not only as a preeminently successful artist and businessman but also in more extravagant terms. In his introduction to a retrospective volume on Henson's career, for example, Harry Belafonte writes:

> Unless you have had the experience of sitting in a village in war-ravaged Guatemala, or a humble boxlike room in the wretched South African township of Alexandra, or in a dust-covered hovel on a Native American reservation, or in the tin shacks that house the thousands who live desperate lives in East Kingston, Jamaica, or the teeming *favelas* of Rio de Janeiro, or in an overcrowded, below-poverty-level dwelling in a ghetto in New York, Chicago, or Detroit . . . unless you've seen from these places the looks on the faces of small children as they watched *Sesame Street* or the Muppets, you'll never really understand what Jim and his colleagues have done for millions of children all over the world who would never have smiled, nor dared to dream, had it not been for Jim Henson.[109]

Such discourse, of course, virtually precludes commentary, unless one were to question briefly the authoritative way in which the writer grounds the au-

---

[107] The *Chronicle of Higher Education*, November 24, 1993, records an incident at the University of Nebraska in which students held "a Barney-bashing party" to express their dislike of the titular character of *Barney and Friends*, another popular children's show on public television. Participating students reportedly commented that this show "lacks the educational quality of the show they grew up watching—'*Sesame Street*'" (A4).

[108] Eric Smoodin, *Animating Culture: Hollywood Cartoons from the Sound Era* (New Brunswick, N.J.: Rutgers University Press, 1993), 96.

[109] Harry Belafonte, introduction to Finch, *Jim Henson: The Works*, ix.

dacity and imagination of an oppressed child in the lure of an essentially passive medium, an entertainment that (as its creators commonly concede) deliberately appropriated the seductive visual techniques of the television commercial. In many other forums as well Henson continues to be portrayed as an artist effortlessly suspended between high and low culture, a triumphantly middlebrow figure who manages to unite all the hyperkinetic energy of modern multimedia entertainment with some primeval, shamanistic histrionic power. "There's something that happens with puppets which doesn't happen in any other medium," argues Jon Stone, writer and director of *Sesame Street.* "There's a magic there that Jim understood" (74). Henson himself refers to puppetry as something like "fairy tales . . . one of those pure things that somehow becomes much less interesting when it is over discussed or analyzed," something that "is talking to a deeper part of you."[110] I will presume that my arguments in this book suggest the utterly problematic qualities of these assertions, which rely on the quintessential bourgeois myth that also conditions the thematic vision of Walt Disney's films; that is, the belief in "an 'innocence' supposedly universal, beyond place, beyond time— and beyond criticism."[111]

In any case, Henson's assertion of the radical purity of the puppet is wholly contradicted by the rich histrionic texture of the Muppets' performances. From his earliest television efforts through *Sesame Street, The Muppet Show* (1976–81), the various Muppet films, and the cartoon spin-off *The Muppet Babies,* Henson's comedy has always involved parodies of and allusions to a variety of other cultural practices—films and television shows, rock music, narrative categories such as "the western," popular accounts of history, and so forth. Both *Sesame Street* and *The Muppet Show* typically feature human entertainers and celebrities from different fields. For example, on the day I wrote these lines, Hillary Rodham Clinton made an appearance on *Sesame Street,* just as the previous First Lady, Barbara Bush, had also done.[112] This characteristic technique is a self-conscious strategy of cultural reappropriation: the show is intended to "reach out to underprivileged inner-city youngsters" (53) and to "present educational material in the fast-

[110] Quoted by Cheryl Henson, in "Puppetry as Personal Expression," introductory remarks at "The Theatrical Inanimate: A Conference on Changing Perceptions," New York, September 11, 1992.

[111] David Kunzle, introduction to the English edition of Dorfman and Mattelart, *How to Read Donald Duck,* 11.

[112] See Judy Blume, "Hillary Clinton Toasts 25 Years of Sunny Days on 'Sesame Street,' " *TV Guide,* November 13–19, 1993, 8–14.

paced, accessible format of television commercials."[113] Each show announces to its viewer, in an obvious and quickly familiar parody of network commercial sponsorship, that it has been "brought to you" by whatever number or letter was featured in various pedagogic segments of that program. Similarly, the smorgasbord of cultural allusions that constitutes *Sesame Street* is specifically designed to provide a cultural framework for economically deprived children, just as the pointedly multicultural human cast is designed to open the show to the widest possible audience.

This strategy, however, also inevitably constructs the Muppets as central figures within what Marsha Kinder refers to as a "supersystem of transmedia intertextuality," a system that tends to perpetuate itself even as it also serves as a conduit for other modes of cultural consumption. In a variety of ways *Sesame Street* introduces its viewers to practices, products, and cultural categories that will eventually be available for their choosing, and thus teaches them "not only how to gain pleasure by pursuing consumerist desire, but also how to read the intertextual relations between television and cinema as compatible members of the same ever-expanding supersystem of mass entertainment."[114] On *Sesame Street* everyone is different, and everyone is the same; the careful portrayal of race and ethnicity coexists with an essentially bourgeois impulse of pedagogy and cultural acquisition. The show appropriates and repackages not merely the various media of mass culture but also high culture in the old-fashioned sense. For example, the videotape *Don't Eat the Pictures: Sesame Street at the Metropolitan Museum of Art* (1987) introduces children to the idea of cultural "highness" (Cézanne "lived a hundred years ago; he's very famous," Cookie Monster is told at one point); and even its title instantiates at the level of farce what Walter Benjamin calls the "aura" of the artistic object.

The Muppets as performers also produce and reproduce the Muppets as tangible commodities. *Sesame Street*, which airs on public television, continues to receive a majority of its funding from the licensing of dolls, toys, books, games, and software based on its popular puppet characters, and the same licensing business is also a staple of the Henson Company. The Children's Television Workshop, a tax-exempt corporation, pursues such profits with what one of its officers calls a "decorous avidity," and, as an article in *Forbes*

[113] Owen, "Looking Out for Kermit," 32.

[114] Marsha Kinder, *Playing with Power in Movies, Television, and Video Games* (Berkeley: University of California Press, 1991), 3, 40.

magazine from 1984 observes admiringly, "the soft sell pays off."[115] Thus, the whole appropriative strategy by which children are introduced to a cultural landscape within which they eventually take their own place as parents and consumers finally merges with the business strategy of the Henson organization. As David Owen writes: "The bond between the Muppets and their ever-renewing audience must be the Henson company's biggest asset. Parents young enough to have watched 'Sesame Street' as children tend to think of the show as obligatory viewing for their kids. Once you lock into the psyches of a young audience, you can leave much of the rest of your marketing to them."[116] Just so, in the beginning of the film *Follow That Bird* (1986), Big Bird announces that "*Sesame Street* is brought to you today by the letters W and B," as the named letters transform themselves into the Warner Brothers logo—pedagogy and corporate identification merging in a seamless and shameless unity.

As though in implicit recognition of its own precarious cultural position, Henson's work sometimes seems to reflect an ambivalence about show business that recalls not only *Pinocchio* but also, more distantly, the authorial struggles of canonical literary figures such as Ben Jonson and Henry Fielding. Both *The Muppet Movie* and *Follow That Bird* employ, as the nemesis of the central Muppet characters, threatening parodic figures who embody a vision of commercial entertainment as exploitation. In a major incident in the latter film, Big Bird is captured by the "Sleaze Brothers," painted blue, locked in a cage, and exhibited in their carnival. The former film similarly follows Kermit the Frog and a group of his fellow Muppets while they journey to Hollywood to become "stars"; Kermit is also pursued by an evil entrepreneur who wants him to become the commercial spokesman for his French Fried Frogs' Legs. In its early scenes the film shows Kermit happily singing a song in "the swamp," where he happens to meet a Hollywood agent on vacation. The agent tantalizes him with the possibility that, as a performer, he might "make millions of people happy," a "dream" that Kermit himself slightly rephrases, in speaking to the other Muppets, as "singing and dancing and making people happy." The presence or absence of the crucial word "millions" is, of course, an index of the film's (and Henson's) trajectory between an imagined vision of "pure" performance and the monolithic reality of the mass market. The film as a whole purports to give us, as it were, the origin of the Muppets as performers: it begins with a close-up

---

[115] Paul B. Brown and Maria Fisher, "Big Bird Cashes In," *Forbes*, November 5, 1984, 178.
[116] Owen, "Looking Out for Kermit," 42.

shot of the statue crowning the gates of a movie studio (an image of a director, like Atlas, holding up the world) and ends by returning to Hollywood for the premiere of *The Muppet Movie* itself. This metadramatic and circular structure, however, also suggests the invisible and inextricable link between the Muppets and that same vast commercial system whose more tangible representative, the violent huckster, they noisily manage to escape.

At the end of the film Kermit and the other Muppets enjoin the audience in song to:

> Keep believing
> Keep pretending
> We did just what we set out to do.

But the intentions and achievements Kermit thus proclaims in the name of the absent and invisible author seem as indefinite as the line between belief and pretense in puppetry itself. This curious assertion (whose ambiguity is reinforced by the film's self-conscious metadramatic strategy) seems to apply at once to the Muppets as literal performing objects, to the Muppets as icons, characters, or "stars" within a larger cultural system, and to the audiences of both. The words force us to question at once the subject and the object of Kermit's imperatives; to ask, that is, *who* believes and *who* pretends, and *what* is thus believed or pretended? Is an imagined audience simply being asked to believe in the "magic" by which "synthetic foam, . . . fleece, fake fur, feathers, or flocking" are invested with an astonishing pretense of life?[117] Or are we being enjoined to believe in a more stubborn and efficacious illusion that there could somehow be a cultural practice troubled by neither elite pretensions nor an impulse of popular resistance, a practice that might bring "culture" to the dominated and oppressed while producing and reproducing itself with the restless momentum of capitalist expansion?

In either case, the Muppets as puppets and performers seem conditioned by the cultural history sketched in this book even as they invert the associations and conventions which characterize that history. Just as Jim Henson himself could be both puppeteer and celebrity, a children's entertainer and a transcendent cultural hero, so the Muppets as performers and characters no longer convey even the illusion of an oppositional voice (like, say, Punch and Judy); instead, their narratives embody a utopian yearning to join with some collective whole—the harmonious, multicultural community of *Sesame*

---

[117] This list of materials used in the construction of the Muppets is from Finch, *Jim Henson*, 65.

Street, the fantastic Hollywood of *The Muppet Movie*, or the equally fantastic Broadway of *The Muppets Take Manhattan* (1984). However appropriative their general strategy, it also makes little sense to construe Henson and the Muppets as "appropriating" the performing object from some other hypothetical cultural sphere of carnivalesque festivity or social marginality. In this, however, the Muppets merely confirm what has always been true about the cultural dynamic they seem to invert. Their example suggests, one last time, that the high and the low, the elite and the popular have never been more than each other's shadow, and that appropriation, like culture itself, is always a kind of mirage, an illusion or performance not unlike those more literally histrionic practices in which it so often manifests itself.

Index